THORVALDSEN:

HIS LIFE AND WORKS.

PORTRAIT OF THORVALDSEN, BY HORACE VERNET.

THORVALDSEN:

HIS LIFE AND WORKS.

By EUGENE PLON.

TRANSLATED FROM THE FRENCH BY I. M. LUYSTER.

Illustrated

BY

TWO HELIOTYPES FROM STEEL ENGRAVINGS BY
F. GAILLARD,
AND THIRTY-FIVE OF THE MASTER'S COMPOSITIONS, DRAWN BY
F. GAILLARD AND ENGRAVED ON WOOD BY
CARBONNEAU.

SECOND AMERICAN EDITION.

BOSTON:
ROBERTS BROTHERS.
1874.

STEREOTYPED BY ALFRED MUDGE & SON,
34 School St., Boston.

PREFACE.

In publishing this work, I should deprive myself of a pleasure and fail in a duty, did I not inscribe on the first page the names of those generous strangers who have so kindly aided me in my labors: Herr Professor Thiele, whose publications are a mine of invaluable, authentic information; Herr Professor Müller, author of an excellent catalogue of the Thorvaldsen Museum; the venerable Professor Hoyen, to whom I am indebted for many useful communications; Herr Emile Wolff, a pupil of Thorvaldsen, still greatly under the influence of the master's teachings; and lastly my friends, Valdemar Hoskiœr, Captain of Engineers, and Herr Fr. Schumacher, attaché to the minister of war, who, in interesting themselves in my researches at Copenhagen, rendered my task easy and agreeable.

The Baroness von Stampe, to the great profit of my book, very kindly sent for me, and in the most touching manner communicated to me all her reminiscences of the illustrious artist whose old age had been protected and made happy by her filial affection. I beg leave respectfully to express to her here my deep gratitude.

Nor ought I to forget the kind patronage of M. Dotézac, French envoy extraordinary and minister plenipotentiary at

Copenhagen, to whom I was recommended by M. Feuillet de Conches. M. Dotézac kindly presented me to Herr Vedel, the under Secretary of foreign affairs, whose support was invaluable to me in the prosecution of my investigations.

Respecting those persons in Paris who have aided me by their encouragement and information, I fear to name them, lest I should appear to wish to make them share the responsibility of a work of so little merit. But, however slight this merit may be, it would have been still less without the counsels they have given me. This is the only acknowledgment I am permitted to make.

[The following translation has been made from a revised copy, kindly furnished by the author.]

TABLE OF CONTENTS.

PART I.

LIFE OF THORVALDSEN.

CHAPTER VI.

CHAPTER VII.

CHAPTER VIII.

CHAPTER IX.

CHAPTER X.

CHAPTER XI.

PART II.

WORKS OF THORVALDSEN.

CHAPTER I.

CHAPTER II.

CHAPTER III.

CHAPTER IV.

CHAPTER V.

CATALOGUE OF THORVALDSEN'S WORKS.

LIST OF ILLUSTRATIONS.

STEEL ENGRAVINGS.

[Reproduced by the Heliotype process.]

WOOD-CUTS.

[These wood-cuts, from the original blocks and on India paper, were printed in Paris expressly for this translation.]

AUTHORITIES.

Den danske Billedhugger *Bertel Thorvaldsen og hans Værker*, af J. M. Thiele, t. I–IV. 1831–50, in-4⁰.

Thorvaldsen og hans Værker. Ny Udgave. Texten forkortet ved F. C. Hillerup, t. I–IV. Med 205 Kobb. (III–IV ogsaa under Titel: Thorvaldsens Arbeider og Livsforhold i Tidsrummet 1828–1844.) Kbh. 1842–57, in-4⁰. Samme Værk med *tydsk Titel og Text.* ib. 1842–57, in-4⁰.

Om den danske Billedhugger *Bertel Thorvaldsen*, ved J. M. Thiele, 1837. Overs. paa Islandsk af M. Hákonarson, 1841.

Thorvaldsens Biographie. Efter den afdöde Kunstners Brevvexlinger, egenhœndige Optegnelser og andre efterladte Papirer, ved J. M. Thiele. 1.–4. Deel. I. Thorvaldsens Ungdomshistorie (1770–1804). — II–III. Thorvaldsen i Rom (1805–1839). 1.–2. D. Med Thorvaldsens Portrait. — IV. Thorvaldsen i Kjöbenhavn (1839–1844. Kbh. 1851–56).

Thorvaldsens Museum. En Fremstilling af alle Kunstnerens Arbeider, der ere samlede i Museet; ordnede efter Afdelingerne, ledsaget af et Omrids af Thorvaldsens Livsforhold og Kunstnervirksomhed, ved H. P. Holst. Kjöbenhavn, 1851.

Thorvaldsen's Jugend, 1770–1804, vom J. M. Thiele. Aus dem Dänischen von Hans Wachenhusen. Berlin, 1851, gr. in-8⁰.

Thorvaldsen's Leben nach den eigenhändigen Aufzeichnungen nachgelassenen Papieren undem dem Briefwechsel des Künstlers, von J. M. Thiele. Deutsch unter Mitwirkung des Verfassers von Henrik Helms. 1.–3. Bd. Mit dem Portrait Thorvaldsen's nach Eckersberg in Stahl-gestochen von Weger. Leipzig, 1852–1856.

The Life of Thorvaldsen. Collated from the Danish of J. M. THIELE, by R. BARNARD. London, 1865.

Description des œuvres de Thorvaldsen au Musée Thorvaldsen et description des collections d'objets d'art ayant appartenu au maître, par L. MÜLLER, inspecteur du Musée. 3 vol. in-8°. Copenhague, 1849.

Bertel Thorvaldsen, a biographical sketch by ANDERSEN. Copenhagen, 1845.

Galerie des contemporains illustres, par un homme de rien. M. Thorvaldsen, by DE LOMENIE. Paris, 1845.

Thorvaldsen the Dane, by Madame FREDERICKA BRUN. This interesting memoir, published by the MORGENBLATT in 1812, has served as the basis of all that has since been written upon the earlier portion of Thorvaldsen's life. (Nagler.)

Article THORVALDSEN, in the *Nouveau Dictionnaire universel des artistes,* by NAGLER.

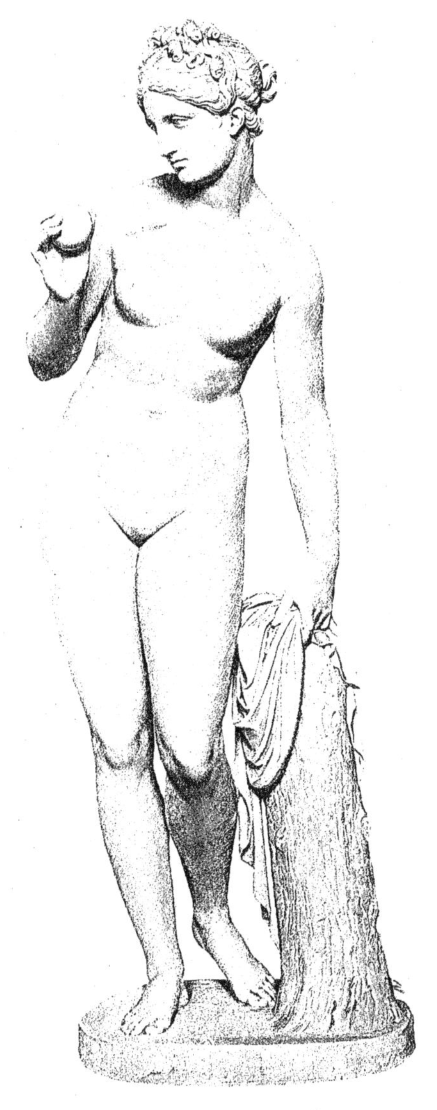

VENUS.

LIFE OF THORVALDSEN.

CHAPTER I.

Birth of Thorvaldsen. — Early Aptitude for Sculpture. — Studies at the Copenhagen Academy of Fine Arts. — His first Successes. — Departure for Italy. — Voyage. — Arrival in Rome.

HOPE.

When the tomb has closed over a great artist, and the lapse of years, exerting a softening influence, has moderated both admiration and envy, it becomes the duty of his contemporaries to gather up with prudent foresight all facts concerning the illustrious dead, while his memory is still fresh in the minds of men.

It is well known how valuable the biographies bequeathed to us by Vasari are, as materials for a history of art. We have no intention, however, of undertaking a work so extensive as that of the Italian author, which includes several generations of celebrated painters. We have limited ourselves to the study of the life and works of one artist. But, in the narrow field to which we are restricted, we have neglected no means of obtaining information, whether from persons who knew the master personally, or from others who might be acquainted with any facts respecting his habits of life or his works. We have collected everything to the minutest detail, in the hope that the materials thus brought together may, one day, be of service to some future historian of art. The life of every great man, moreover, has a character of its own, and is worthy of study, aside from the interest attached to his works.

The sculptor, whose life we propose to write and whose works we shall describe, played an important part in the great revival of art, which, beginning with Mengs and Winckelmann, was continued by David, Canova, and Bartolini, through the last of the eighteenth and the beginning of the nineteenth century.

ALBERT, OR BERTEL,[1] THORVALDSEN was born in Copenhagen, Nov. 19, 1770. His father, Gottskalk Thorvaldsen, was a poor wood-carver; his mother, Karen Grönlund, was

[1] In Danish, Bertel is the familiar equivalent for Bartholomew. Thorvaldsen was so called by his family and friends. The Italians changed Bertel into Alberto; and by this name he was known to all his acquaintances in Rome, whether Italians or foreigners. Biographers do not agree about the year of Thorvaldsen's birth. Some say 1771; others, 1772. But the artist himself always asserted that he was born in 1770; which is the date Herr Thiele has given in his Danish biography, and, following him, Nagler in the *Nouveau Dictionnaire Universel des Artistes*. It is, by a very evident typographical error, that David d'Angers, in a letter published in 1844, which attracted much attention, speaks of his birth as occurring in 1779. There have been mistakes also about the day of the month. Michaud gives the the 9th of November, and M. de Lomenie in his *Galerie des Contemporains Illustres, par un homme de rien*, the 29th. Nagler's only authority for the 19th is Herr Haste's old memorandum book. Herr Haste, a respectable magistrate, was in his youth a playmate of Thorvaldsen. As a boy he was in the habit of recording the birthdays of his companions. In reply to the questions of Herr Thiele, he stated that he believed that he got the date in his note-book from Thorvaldsen's mother. What appears a good reason for considering the 19th the correct date, is the fact that Thorvaldsen when in Denmark always celebrated his birthday on that day. But there is still another difficulty. It is not seven cities, as in Homer's case, which dispute for the honor of being Thorvaldsen's birthplace, but two islands and the open sea. While in some biographies he sees

the daughter of a Jutland peasant.[1] Gottskalk's skill was limited to carving rudely figure-heads for merchant-vessels. This employment barely sufficed to support, in a very humble way, his family, but it gave the first impulse to the mind of Bertel. While still a child, he helped his father, and began to carve in wood. There were still living, a few years ago, old carpenters who recollected perfectly the pretty child, with blue eyes and light hair, who used to come to see his father in the ship-yards of Copenhagen. All who saw the boy were attracted by him.

Bertel was gentle and timid in disposition. The following anecdote of his childhood was related to us by the poet Andersen, one of the most intimate friends of his latter years.

the light first in Iceland, David d'Angers (or M. Charles Blanc, rather, who lent him his pen), De Lomenie, and Michaud assert, on the authority of another tradition, that his mother brought him into the world during a passage from Rejkjavick to Copenhagen. No doubt this version lends more charm to the narrative, but it is incorrect, as we have been assured by the friend and biographer of the artist. Thorvaldsen was born in Copenhagen, in the house in the Store Gronnen-Gade, which is now number 7, but was formerly, when the houses were numbered by districts, number 256. Herr Thiele was kind enough to take us there.

[1] According to the learned genealogists of Iceland (John Espolin, *Annals of Iceland)*, Thorvaldsen could boast of an origin as ancient as it was illustrious. They trace his genealogy back to the eighth century; for, according to their tables, the known ancestors of the artist were descended from Harald Hildetand, king of Denmark, who, in consequence of the civil wars, was obliged to abandon his country and seek an asylum, first in Norway and afterward in Iceland, where one of his descendants, Oluf Paa (the peacock), became a powerful chief, famous in the sagas of Landöl and in the songs of the bards, who praised his generosity and taste for the arts. This chieftain, who flourished in the twelfth century, himself carved in wood. He enjoyed great celebrity in his day, and his fame still lives among the Scandinavian nations. One might say, therefore, that Oluf, after the lapse of several centuries, lived again in the person of Thorvaldsen. Such long descents are, however, much less legendary than we might suppose, for Iceland is the classic land of genealogies; and those which do not go back farther than the eighth century are not considered worthy of discussion by the *savans* of the North. At all events it is certain that in the fourteenth century there lived in Southern Iceland a wealthy man, highly respected, Odd Petersen by name, whose family and descendants almost always held honorable positions in the civil government of Iceland. One of them, Thorvald Gottskalken, pastor of Myklabye, having only a moderate fortune, sent his two sons to Copenhagen. The elder, Ari, apprenticed to a jeweller, died young. The younger, Gottskalk, who had some talent for wood-carving, found employment in the ship-yards. At twenty-seven he married, and he was the father of Bertel. See Thiele.

Bertel was playing one day, with other children of his age, in the "Kongens Nytorv," the "King's New-Market," near the equestrian statue of Christian V, who is represented as trampling under his horse's feet the monster Envy.[1] His mischievous companions, surprising him before the statue in childlike contemplation, partly with his consent and partly by force hoisted him up on the horse, and then took to flight. The poor bewildered child kept as still as the royal cavalier himself; and a comical spectacle it must have been to see him, with his red cotton cap, riding in such illustrious company. But the *gendarmes* were just passing that way, and, like true *gendarmes*, they hastened to carry off to the police-station, not the authors, but the victim, of the misdemeanor.

Little Bertel early manifested a precocious taste for sculpture. Though Gottskalk had no art-education himself, he was wise enough to cultivate carefully a talent in his son, which flattered his paternal vanity. It is not probable that the honest artisan foresaw the glorious destiny in store for his child; but he was sensible enough to see that, with some knowledge of drawing, the son might one day do better than the father. The boy was sent, therefore, when he was eleven years old, to the free school of the Royal Academy of Fine Arts; and in two years he made so much progress, that he was very soon able to render valuable assistance to Gottskalk, whose carvings, thanks to his son, were henceforward distinguished for more correct drawing and some appreciation of form.

Bertel, however, did not show equal aptitude for other branches of study which had no direct bearing on his vocation. During the six years he passed at the school of Charlottenborg he displayed so little zeal that the chaplain, Höyer, looked upon him as very deficient in elementary

[1] This statue, of the date of 1688, is in the mannered style of the sculptor Abraham Cæsar L'Amoureux.

knowledge, and when the time came for the pupils to prepare for their first communion put him in the lowest class of the catechism. The distribution of prizes at the Academy occurred at the same time, and Bertel obtained as the reward of his application the small silver medal. The Copenhagen journals mentioning the fact, the name of the successful candidate attracted the notice of the chaplain, who asked his pupil: —

"Thorvaldsen, is it a brother of yours who has just taken a prize at the Academy?"

The pupil looked up, blushing with surprise. "It is myself, Herr Chaplain."

The priest, who had come to look upon Bertel as quite a dunce, was astounded at this revelation. He changed his tone directly. "Herr Thorvaldsen," said he, "please to pass up to the first class."

At this word "Herr," the boy was electrified. Henceforward the professor always addressed him by that title, a distinction which gave Bertel a position apart in the class, and made such an impression upon him that he never forgot it. In after years, famous and loaded with more honors than ever fell to the lot of an artist, the master would frequently say to his friends, when his thoughts reverted to his youth, that glory had never been so sweet as on that day when his boy's heart thrilled with rapture.

Thorvaldsen was seventeen years old (1787) when he gained this first prize. Far from entertaining an exaggerated notion of his own merit, he only worked the harder. Calm, serious, reserved even, he said but little, and when he once had taken up his pencils and set himself to work, his companions found it difficult to divert his attention. We have said that his father intended to make him his partner in his humble toil, and the young man willingly yielded to his parent's wishes. He still carried to the shipyard Gottskalk's dinner; and, while he was resting, Bertel would take up his chisel and correct as well as finish his work.

Two years later (1789) Thorvaldsen gained another prize. A bas-relief, "Love in Repose," won for him the large silver medal. Gottskalk now came to the conclusion that his son was sufficiently instructed to devote himself entirely to the career he had chosen for him. Bertel made no objection, but the painter Abildgaard, who was his teacher at the Academy, had discovered too much talent in the boy to be willing to abandon him to a calling so unworthy of his nascent powers. He was sincerely attached to his pupil, and, while his fellow-students were trying to persuade Thorvaldsen to remain at the school, the professor went to find Gottskalk. The two had some difficulty in coming to an understanding. The father anticipated for his son, if he kept him with him, a humble condition in life to be sure, but one which would, he believed, assure to him a certain livelihood, while he looked upon a more ambitious career, in which he could no longer follow him, as an unknown path, fraught with dangers.

It was nevertheless decided that the young man should divide his time in two nearly equal portions, one to be devoted to academic studies, so that he might have a basis of solid knowledge to aid him in his profession, the other to the labor by which he was to earn his daily bread. He still continued to live with his parents, in a little house in Aabenraa, and contrived to satisfy both his father[1] and Abildgaard. Bertel now began to sketch in relief and carve detached figures in stone. His first work worthy of mention is a medallion of the Princess of Denmark, made in 1790, from

[1] A large wooden clock, bequeathed to the Thorvaldsen Museum several years ago, and placed in the room devoted to the sculptor's furniture, is a work of this period. The shield, bearing the arms of Denmark, above the door of the Royal Dispensary, was jointly carved by father and son. A more artistic work, which they also executed together, is the group of four lions around a circle in front of the entrance-way to the gardens of Fredericsberg Castle, the summer residence of the sovereign.

a poor picture; for the young artist could only have had a glimpse of the princess in passing. This portrait was, however, a great success, and the resemblance is so striking that the dealer who bought the model disposed of a considerable number of copies.

Thorvaldsen worked usually from the designs of other artists, and especially from those of his teacher Abildgaard. A woman holding a telescope, placed on the pediment of a building near the Custom House, was executed from a design of the painter Nicholas Wolff.

The slightest efforts of an artist of real merit are deserving of notice, because they are the experimental attempts of a mind seeking its true direction. It is for this reason that we mention some productions of the young sculptor which otherwise would not be worthy of a place in the enumeration of his works. "Love in Repose," for example, which, from a reverent respect, is preserved in the museum of the master,[1] is, in fact, no more than the work of a promising beginner. The Academy possesses the other bas-reliefs for which the young Thorvaldsen obtained his early prizes; the first is "The Expulsion of Heliodorus from the Temple."

Bertel prepared himself for the approaching competitive examination, in company with several of his friends, young men of his own age. With this end in view they met once a week and practised at composing subjects, taken for the most part from the Old and New Testaments. While his comrades were discussing, Thorvaldsen, ever more inclined to act than to talk, would be already busy with his clay, or perhaps his bread, and before the others had settled the questions about which they were arguing, he would have finished his model. This trait is characteristic; it shows the artist's turn of mind. Throughout his whole life he preferred to apply rather than discuss the theories of which he

[1] This bas-relief is in one of the underground galleries.

approved We shall find that he left behind him no written expression of his views upon art; and there is nothing in his few letters to show that he ever thought of attempting to expound its principles. He translated his ideas into marble; it was with the chisel, never with the pen, that he expressed the force of his convictions.

But at the time of which we are now writing, he was far from thinking he had nothing more to learn. Naturally diffident, he distrusted his own powers, and did not conceal his dread of the approaching competition from his fellow-students, who at last made his fears the subject for raillery.

Nevertheless, upon the 1st of June, 1791, he presented himself with the rest, and when the subject was given retired to his work-room. But he was scarcely installed there before he was seized with fright, and stole out by a private stairway. Just as he was escaping, he was met by one of the professors, who scolded him gently, and by a few kind words encouraged him to go back. The young man, a little ashamed of his escapade, obeyed, and set himself to work with so much earnestness that in the space of four hours he had finished the sketch of Heliodorus, which gained for him the small gold medal.

Looking at this work to-day, we can scarcely conceive how Thorvaldsen could have been the author of it. In its excellences, as well as in its defects, this bas-relief is entirely out of harmony with the other works of the master. It is frequently the case, however, that artists begin by following the traditions of the schools. They cannot, in their youthful inexperience, do otherwise. It is only when they have made themselves known by some work in conformity to the taste of their day, that, encouraged by their first success, they can cast off their fetters and strike out a new path for themselves.

In "Heliodorus," the composition is wanting in dignity, the scene is confused, and the figures have no naturalness;

but the work was in accordance with the ideas of the times, and the execution showed talent enough in the young artist to attract the attention of his contemporaries. The Minister of State, Herr Detler von Reventlow, noticed the bas-relief and had it cast. He encouraged Thorvaldsen, and headed a subscription, set on foot by the painter Wolff, to obtain for the sculptor the leisure necessary for the completion of his studies. It was the wish of his patrons that he should turn his attention to subjects drawn from pagan antiquity. Bertel accordingly composed "Priam begging Achilles for the Body of Hector."[1] Thorvaldsen treated the same subject in a later composition, but very differently. It is interesting to compare the youthful effort with the mature and masterly work. The first is commonplace: an old man is kneeling, a young man raises him with kindness. But there is nothing to indicate at first sight who the personages are, nor is there anything dramatic in the action. What grandeur, on the contrary, and what energy in the second! This old man is Priam, the unhappy father of Hector; this warrior, with steadfast gaze and frowning brow, is Achilles; we feel that his breast is swelling with that terrible wrath which the poet sings. Will he yield to pity? or will he be unmoved by a father's immeasurable grief! The companions of the hero await the end with anxiety. And, to produce so striking an effect, the artist has not had recourse to forced attitudes; the composition is simple, and all the figures are natural. Still the first work is not wholly without merit. It is said that Bishop Frederic Münter, a man of taste and judgment, was so satisfied on this point that he predicted Thorvaldsen would become one of the great sculptors of his age. Compared with the "Heliodorus," "Priam" shows a marked progress, especially in a certain degree of simplicity and

[1] This work, when he left Copenhagen for Rome, he gave as a parting gift to the engraver Lahde. It was afterwards purchased by the Danish Government and placed in the Academy's collection.

naturalness. We begin to see how the study of the antique is finally to give the talent of the artist its true direction.

At the same period, Thorvaldsen modelled a smaller bas-relief, "Hercules and Omphale"; and in 1793 he competed for an important prize, the result of which was to decide, in a great measure, his future career. If he obtained the great gold medal, he would be entitled to travel three years at the expense of the Academy. In now presenting himself as a candidate, he had no longer any apprehension, though he was not sustained by a presumptuous confidence. "Saint Peter healing the Paralytic" gained him the grand prize.[1]

Some biographers have represented Thorvaldsen as wholly uninstructed at this period. It is clear that this statement is exaggerated. The professors of the Academy were accustomed to give their pupils the best works in sculpture and design as models for study; and in the "Saint Peter" we already detect signs of an imitation, and a sort of reminiscence of the compositions of Raphael. We shall see farther on that all the religious works of the sculptor show marks of this admiration for the great painter, just as his statues and bas-reliefs from pagan subjects are imbued with the spirit of Greek antiquity. At the same time, it is only right to say that outside of the special knowledge acquired in pursuit of his art, Thorvaldsen was profoundly ignorant. Literature and history were almost sealed books to him and at no period of his life was he a man of literary culture.

The pension attached to the grand prize for sculpture, which allowed the successful competitor to travel three years, was then held by another; and, while waiting for it, Thorvaldsen remained in Copenhagen. To enable him to continue

[1] This bas-relief is in the Academy.

his studies, the Academy granted him pecuniary assistance for two years. As he was also able to get some employment, he was, therefore, in tolerably easy circumstances. He drew vignettes for the publishers,[1] taught modelling to a certain number of wealthy persons, and gave lessons in drawing. He also took some portraits, mostly drawn on parchment and slightly colored.[2]

A few medallion portraits, one of the painter Wolff, and another of the physician Herr Saxtorff, are works of this period; also two bas-reliefs, "The Seasons" and "The Hours," from designs by Abildgaard, and four original compositions, — a "Euterpe," a "Terpsichore," and two other Muses.

The painter Abildgaard, to whom belongs the honor of being the first to discover and encourage Thorvaldsen's talent, nevertheless exercised over him but little influence. This artist, who was full of mannerisms, enjoyed a popularity not at all surprising at this epoch. Without doubt, Thorvaldsen's earliest works necessarily show marks of his master's teachings. This is particularly noticeable in a small group, one of his most youthful efforts, and extremely mediocre, representing a woman seated and giving drink to two young boys, whose attitudes are very unnatural.

But while the sculptor, as soon as he had conquered his hesitation and gained confidence, boldly diverged from the style of his master, he still retained in his drawings (and this is very remarkable) Abildgaard's mode of working, for this painter drew from nature with much talent. There are in the rooms of the Academy some large anatomical studies by him which are truly fine. Though the attitudes are in gen-

[1] *Thalia*, by Haste; *Tales of the North*, by Suhm; *Prose Essays*, by Rahbeck.

[2] Some of these portraits have been found. Herr Thiele owns a little black silhouette, pleasing and delicate, of the young Bertel, drawn by himself and given to his friend the flower-painter Fritsch.

eral forced, the drawing is firm, correct, and sharp. To the end of his life Thorvaldsen drew according to the principles which Abildgaard had inculcated.

In his youth Bertel talked but little, and his clear eye was not exempt from a certain melancholy difficult to explain. Naturally timid, and unused to society, his was not an expansive nature; he was indolent too, except in matters appertaining to sculpture; and if he learned anything beyond his art, it was by observation only, or by intercourse with educated men. The last years which he passed at Copenhagen before his departure for Rome, modified somewhat the excessive reserve of which he might hitherto have been accused, and he who until then had never been known to laugh often participated in the gayety of his comrades.

Two years had now elapsed since Thorvaldsen had obtained the grand prize for sculpture, and still the pension which was to give him the means of travelling was not yet at his command. Meanwhile, the term for which the Academy had granted him pecuniary aid was drawing to a close. He petitioned that this aid might be continued for a year longer, and presented at the same time to the Academy a small bas-relief, "Numa consulting the nymph Egeria,"[1] rather a graceful work, but still marred by the forced attitude of the figures. His petition was granted, and he received also the assurance that the pension would be his the following year.

While remaining at Copenhagen, he modelled the bust of the Minister of State, Herr von Bernstoff, for Herr von Reventlow. He had never seen the minister, and was obliged to work from a painted portrait; but for the last few touches he obtained from him, with difficulty, a sitting of a few moments. He was nevertheless successful in getting a likeness. The work is also fairly executed. He undertook,

[1] In one of the basement galleries of the Thorvaldsen Museum.

under much more favorable circumstances, the bust of the Counsellor of State, Tyge Rothe. These two works are the first in order of date now in the Thorvaldsen Museum. Though the models were finished at Copenhagen, he did not put them into marble until after his arrival at Rome.

The 20th of May, 1796, Thorvaldsen embarked on the "Thetis," for Naples. The artist, who was never to see his parents[1] again, left his country recommended to the captain, Herr Fisker, by the Count von Bernstoff, and furnished with a few letters for Rome. The voyage was long and tedious. After cruising in the North Sea, the "Thetis" touched at Malaga, Algiers, and then at Malta, where she was obliged to submit to a severe quarantine. After again setting sail, she encountered on her way to Tripoli a violent storm, and had to put back to Malta for repairs.

Ever disposed to reject all study but that of sculpture, Thorvaldsen lived on board in complete idleness. His time was passed in conversation, or oftener in reverie, and his sole occupation was jotting down in a sketch-book a few notes, which illustrate the young artist's simplicity of character. From this sketch-book, preserved in the Museum with many other papers, we make a few extracts.

MALTA, 18 December, 1796.

At quarantine. — Morning as fine as one can imagine. We have just been told that we are disinfected and free. The cold is not quite so sharp as it is with us on a fine autumn morning. With the knight who brought the good news came seven boat-loads of musicians of all kinds; they took their stations under our cabin windows, and regaled us with what doubtless these people know how to do best. It is not good, and yet not altogether bad. But the beautiful morning, the novelty, the hatred and distrust of the Maltese, all at once changed into friendship and careless security; above all, the old dream of Italian music on the water, realized more or less before my

[1] His mother died in 1804, and his father in 1806.

eyes, all combined made it seem to my ears the most delicious music, although it consisted for the most part of serenade airs, which are rarely played at a fitting time or place.

MALTA, 16 January, 1797.

At five o'clock this afternoon I leave the frigate, which goes hence to Tripoli. Seated in the cutter, I am pained to see her disappear. I can scarcely hide my tears from the vice-consul, who with the pilot and another man, a stranger, is in the boat with me. I jump on shore. The pilot points out to me the captain of the "Speronara," with whom I am to sail for Palermo. He comes back immediately. He tries to console me when he notices my dejection. I sup at his house; he then shows me my lodgings, which will do very well.

17 January.

I go to bed, and at last to sleep. My host comes to wake me, me and Hector, my dog; he embraces me affectionately. I leave the house and go on board the "Speronara," for a change of linen; thence to the Danish brig to see the captain, but he is on shore. I go back to my lodgings; on the way, Hector plays his pranks, chases the goats, who jump and caper. He trips up a little girl carrying a baby, but does no harm. Then he knocks down a little boy; everybody laughs.

These notes show the natural kind-heartedness of the young Scandinavian. There is no doubt that he was deeply moved by music, statues, and pictures; but the exploits of Hector he cannot forget. Hector trips up a little girl without hurting her; he knocks down a little boy, and people laugh! Truly he is a dog worthy of his name. Like all dreamers, Thorvaldsen loves this sympathetic animal, whose discreet familiarity never interrupts the current of his ideas. A dog is always ready for play when weary with thinking we seek to be diverted. Where find a friend more patient, more accommodating, more content to be quiet, more ready for society and sport? What better friend for the poet who is composing his verses, or for the sculptor whose imagination is perfecting a masterpiece? The dogs of Thorvaldsen ought to have a place in his biography.

The captain of the "Thetis," who had promised to watch over Thorvaldsen, was as good as his word. He became fond of the young artist who, as we have already seen, was distressed at parting with him. Nevertheless the captain, who had led a hard and active life, did not approve of the idleness of his youthful charge. In a letter to his wife dated Malta, Dec. 29, 1796, he writes: —

"Thorvaldsen is still here, but looking out, at last, for an opportunity to go to Rome. He is very well: you can let his parents know. God knows what will become of him! He is so thoroughly lazy, that he has had no wish to write himself, and while on board he would not learn a word of the Italian language, though the chaplain and I both offered to teach him. I have resolved to send him to our ambassador at Naples, so that he may forward him to Rome. The young man has an annual pension of four hundred crowns, and may God help him! He has a big dog whom he has christened Hector. He sleeps late in the morning, and thinks only about his comforts and his eating. But everybody likes him because he is such a good fellow."

In another letter the captain again says: "He is an honest boy, but a lazy rascal."

It is curious to see such a judgment pronounced in good faith and with an appearance of truth upon one who subsequently became one of the most prolific and laborious sculptors of his time. Who knows, however, what germinating process, unperceived, perhaps, even by the artist himself, was going on under this seeming idleness?

Thorvaldsen, as we have seen, had decided to cross over to Palermo. We give a few more extracts from his journal: —

PALERMO, January 25, 1797.

M. Mathé and the vice-consul take me to a palace which contains some pictures by Rubens, and to a church painted by a Sicilian named Manno. He has painted the ceiling, which is pretty well done. This church has other good paintings, and a fine monument. We go afterward to call upon Manno. He is a good fellow. He shows us five pictures, among others a Saint Magdalen at prayer, which is very good. The conversation turning upon the Academy, he promises to take me there in the evening. I arrive while he is dressing. He puts on his military uniform given him by the grand master of Malta for painting a church, and takes us to the Academy, which is divided into three classes. I see the modelling class: it is weak.

January 26.

I go out this morning, and meet my interpreter at M. Mathé's. We visit the cathedral which is now building, and also an atelier of sculpture where there are several completed works. I only see one which is very poor. I go through several other churches, and in the evening to the opera. There are two or three excellent singers.

January 28.

The packet goes this morning at 7 o'clock, at the same time with the Neapolitan frigate which acts as its convoy on account of the Turks. The next day (Sunday, January 29), the crew imagine they descry Naples, which is now only about eighty miles off. I think we shall arrive there before night. I begin to feel a little better. There are several pretty women on board, and the prettiest one speaks German. There are also some ill-looking creatures with hideous faces, old women with tawny skins, and other people who are not exactly gentlemen and ladies. They say I must pay for my dog; there are so many passengers the poor beast can hardly find a place to lie down; they are packed together like smoked herrings in the bottom of the hold. At ten o'clock we cast anchor in the bay of Naples.

NAPLES, February 1.

I rise and dress at seven o'clock; go on shore. A man comes up to me and inquires if I want a *domestique de place*. I say no, but ask him to conduct me to the *piazza francese*. He consents, but on the way tells me that he is going to take me to a much better hotel; that that is detestable, and it really looked so. We pass through a great number of streets. We arrive at last at a *trattoria*, where I agree to pay four carlini, two for my lodgings and two for my board. Being very hungry, I am delighted to find something to eat. The waiter comes up to my room and asks if I wish to breakfast. I go down into the dining-hall; a great many people there, officers and priests. It is bad and dirty: in short, my dog eats more than I do, although I am very hungry. If this tavern is the best in the city, God help the bad.

February 2.

Dress to go to the resident minister's [Herr von Bourke, chamberlain to the King of Denmark]. They give me an old woman as a guide, but she does not know the way. She asks it of a glass-man who can speak German, like all the glass-men in Naples, as I believe. He is no wiser than she. The old woman is obliged to ask again, and before reaching the minister's I have with me three grown persons and a little boy to show me the way to the house. Upon reaching the minister's I have a dispute in German with a servant who tells me his Excellency cannot be seen, that he is at dinner. I do not wish to go away without accomplishing something, so I request him to take in my name. He complies in a surly way. The minister comes out, speaks to me in French; I reply in Danish, which he has almost forgotten. He then excuses himself, saying he will have the pleasure of a further talk with me if I will do him the honor of dining with him the next day. I return to my tavern through the grand promenade [*Villa reale*], where there is a superb marble group [the Farnese Bull].

February 3.

Dine at the minister's; make the acquaintance of Professor Tischbein; he begs me to come to see him to-morrow. He is to take me everywhere.

February 4.

I go to see him this morning; do not find him at home. Meet there one of his pupils, who also speaks German. See his pictures and some good drawings. When Professor Tischbein comes back, he requests one of his pupils to take me to all the studios.

We go first to a sculpture gallery, where there are a number of fine marble figures; make a drawing of one. Then to another, containing a large number of antiques, — the great Hercules and many others. But it is so cold I cannot stay long. To-morrow I will take my cloak. When all is in order, there will be nothing like it in the world.

February 5.

To day the German glass-man comes for me. We go together to see several churches, among others one enriched with a great number of marble statues. We go afterward out of town, and are lucky enough to see some of the figures found in the excavations at Portici. Two are fine.

February 7.

To-day I see *Capo di Monte:* M. Andrea has the kindness to accompany me. It is magnificent! Ah! how many beautiful things! Pictures of Raphael and other great masters; also Etruscan vases, medals, mosaics. I have to go hastily through the galleries, which I am sorry for. I must go there again another time.

February 9.

Go to Professor Tischbein's, and thence to *Capo di Monte*. See the gallery more at my leisure. Dine at M. Andrea's; after dinner return to the gallery.

But let us stop; these extracts are enough. In this confused mass of private notes the whole character of Thorvaldsen stands already revealed. His sincere admiration for the antique does not betray him into any strong or declamatory expression. He simply notes down in his memorandum-book the Farnese Bull or the Hercules, not the deep impression they make upon him. All these noble statues, so profoundly engraved on his memory, hardly draw from him the exclamation, "Ah! how many beautiful things!"

The beginning of his sojourn in Italy was not fortunate. He fell ill; and, naturally prone to melancholy, suffered greatly from the loneliness of his situation. More than once he was tempted to return to Denmark, but the thought that hereafter perhaps he might have to blush for this act of weakness restrained him. At a more hopeful moment he got into a vettura, and arrived in Rome at last, on the 8th of March, 1797. It was almost nine months after leaving Copenhagen that he set foot in the Eternal City; and, though he was entirely free to travel wherever he pleased, it is there that he lived during all the time that he was a pensioner of the Academy.

MORNING.

CHAPTER II.

Effect of the Antique Statues upon Thorvaldsen. — Zoëga. — Pecuniary Difficulties. — Ill-health. — Political Troubles. — Mr. Hope and the "Jason." — Anna Maria. — "The Abduction of Briseis."

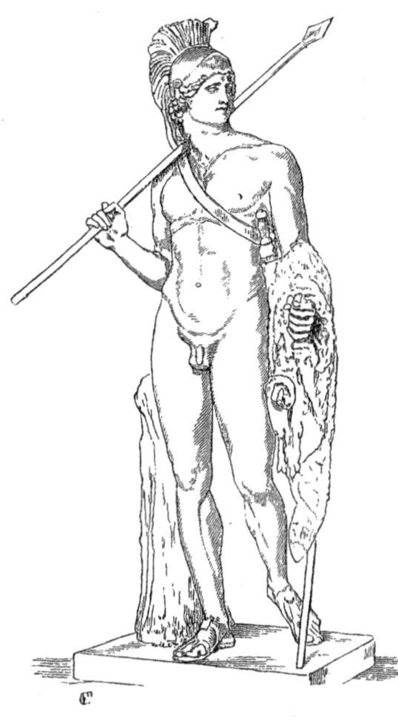

JASON.

A DEVOTED student, then a youth careless and dreamy, such had been Thorvaldsen until the moment of his arrival in Rome. But erelong a complete metamorphosis was to be wrought in him, and a new man was to appear. "I was born on the 8th of March, 1797," he used to say; "before then I did not exist." Still the transformation was not sudden: it was only after a slow period of incubation, so to speak, that he began to break his shell. Little by little he burst the fetters of servile imitation, and, once free, his creative power never deserted him.

We have already referred to the impression made upon him by the works of antique art. This admiration did not, as in southern natures, display itself outwardly. He remained in a sort of ecstasy and stupor, perceiving that he had much to learn and much to forget.

Bishop Münter, who predicted a brilliant future for the artist, had furnished him with letters to the learned archæologist Zoëga, whom the Danes looked upon as their Winckelmann. He soon became attached to the young artist, and the best proof he gave of his friendship was the severity of his criticisms. He encouraged and counselled Thorvaldsen; and, without being blind to what was wanting in him, set a proper value upon his talents. He writes thus from Genzano, Oct. 4, 1797:—

> "Our countryman, Thorvaldsen, has come to pass a week with us and see the curiosities of the neighborhood. He is an excellent artist, with a great deal of taste and sentiment, but ignorant of everything outside of art. By the bye, the Academy shows very little judgment in sending such ignorant young fellows to Italy, where they must necessarily lose a great deal of time in acquiring that knowledge, without which they are unable to profit by their stay here, and which could be acquired more easily and rapidly before coming. Without knowing a word of Italian or French, without the slightest acquaintance with history and mythology, how is it possible for an artist properly to pursue his studies here? I do not require him to be learned, that I should not even desire; but he should have some faint idea of the names and meaning of the things he sees. The rest he can pick up by association with the learned."

Zoëga's remarks are applicable, even in our day, to many young artists who go to Rome. In this case it was not so much the Academy, however, as Thorvaldsen who was in fault. He, as we have seen, had little inclination for any study which did not bear directly on his art.

It has been asserted by some persons that Thorvaldsen wasted the first years of his residence in Italy, doing nothing for a long time. We must rectify this exaggerated statement. Endowed with extreme facility of execution, the young artist had, up to that time, profited by this natural gift: as soon as a subject had been given him, he had set to work and executed a model with surprising rapidity. When he came to Rome, he began to distrust himself; and self-distrust is the beginning of progress. Studying so many masterpieces, he became more and more conscious of his own shortcomings. Henceforward, whenever he purposed producing an original work, he pondered long on his subject; and it was only after fully working out his conception in his mind, that he decided to take up the clay. But though his hands were often idle, we must not conclude that his mind was inactive.

"The snow that I had in my eyes begins to melt away," he said. He studied the antiques so thoroughly that he knew them by heart. Those which above all others impressed and attracted him were the simple and strong compositions belonging to that epoch which Winckelmann calls the period of high art in Greece. Of these he made many copies. Among others, one of half-size of the "Pollux" (one of the two colossal figures of Monte Cavallo which he greatly admired), the "Jupiter of the Capitol," the "Apollo of the Vatican," the "Venus di Medici," "Ariadne," "Sappho," "Melpomene,"[1] &c. To this list must be added copies in marble of the antique busts of "Homer," "Cicero," and "Agrippa." These last works were executed in fulfilment of his pledges to the Academy. He also copied the bust of Raphael in the Pantheon to please his teacher, Abildgaard,[2] who had begged him to do it, and put into marble the two portrait-busts modelled before he left Copenhagen, besides that of the Danish ambassador at Naples.

We know of but very few original compositions of this period. Some have disappeared, others not obtaining the

[1] These copies in 1821 were in the cabinet of Herr von Ropp, at Mietau. (Nagler.)

[2] The Baroness von Stampe has at Nysöe two heads in marble, one a Medusa, the other a Bacchus, which belong to this period.

favor of Zoëga were destroyed by the artist: such was the fate of a "Minerva," whose immodest drapery was more particularly the object of the critic's strictures. "A virtuous woman of antiquity would have blushed to appear in such a costume: how much more a goddess!" Nor do we know what has become of two groups, "Peace and Abundance," and "Venus and Mars Victor"; nor whether a statue under life-size, of "Hygeia," ordered by Dr. Lehmann, still exists. But we have seen at Herr Thiele's house "Achilles raising the conquered Penthesilea," a small group of the same size as "Bacchus and Ariadne," and of this same period.

This last work, which is in the Museum, shows the progress Thorvaldsen had made since his arrival in Rome. We see in it still the pupil of the Copenhagen Academy, but developed by intimate association with the antique. The group is a pleasing one; and the figures of Ariadne and Bacchus have a certain breadth of style, borrowed from great models. The head of the god is almost identical with the "Bacchus of the Capitol," wrongly called for a long time an Ariadne.[1] We may consider this work, therefore, as intermediate between the copies of the antique and the original works executed later under the inspiration of Greek art.

It was during the heat of the summer of 1798 that Thorvaldsen was engaged upon the "Bacchus and Ariadne," which he intended for the Academy of Copenhagen. A severe attack of fever interrupted his work; and the unfinished model (of moist clay) being in danger of destruction by the heat, the plaster-cast from it was hastily taken. The artist felt obliged to ask indulgence of the Academy for its imperfections, yet nevertheless sent it to Denmark.

Life in Rome was not altogether easy for the pensioner of

[1] It is certainly a male head; and, judging from the two little horns formed by the hair, there can be no doubt that it is the head of a god. There is a reproduction of this antique fragment in the Thorvaldsen collection. It is in the basement of the Museum, and is numbered 113.

the Academy of Copenhagen: he had his good and his bad days. The bad were due to the circumstances in which he was placed: the good he won for himself, aided by youth and hope. The Academy's pension of four hundred crowns (about twelve hundred francs) scarcely sufficed to supply the common necessaries of life. In return for this bounty, he was required to send a report of his progress every six months, and, at the end of two years, some work as proof of his application. These obligations he scrupulously fulfilled. To supply the deficiency of the pension, it was necessary to earn money; and this was not easy in those times of political agitation. In 1797 the Directory of France was seeking by every means to overthrow the Holy See and to get possession of its dominions. Bonaparte had taken Urbino, Ferrara, Bologna, Ancona; and Pius VI, in signing the treaty of Tolentino, had pledged himself not only to pay an indemnity of thirty-one millions, but to give up to France a large number of works of art. This was a real grief to Thorvaldsen: nothing in all these great political commotions touched him more nearly. General Duphot having been killed in a riot, Berthier entered Rome, Feb. 10, 1798. Pius VI, deprived of his temporal power, was taken to Florence, thence to France; the Republic was proclaimed, and it was not until 1800 that a new Pope, Pius VII, was elected. The Concordat of 1801 restored partial tranquillity to the Roman States, occupied successively by French and Neapolitan troops. That a young foreign artist through all these turbulent times should have been able to pursue his studies so regularly and persistently as Thorvaldsen did, is indeed surprising. But, though he found means to exercise and develop his talent, he could not make it lucrative. Work done as study, and sent to Copenhagen, brought him absolutely nothing. Fortunately, he fell in with an English painter named Wallis, who paid him a scudo a day for putting small figures into his landscapes. Thorvaldsen drew with great correctness; but it is a little remarkable that a young sculptor should be sufficiently well acquainted with oil painting to be able to do such work creditably. The small compensation he got for it was frequently a most valuable assistance to him in these difficult times.

But Thorvaldsen had to struggle with another enemy besides poverty. He had not fully recovered from the illness which he had contracted at Naples, when he was attacked by malarial fever soon after he was settled in Rome. He continued all his life subject to returns of this malady, which, however, did not prevent his living without infirmities to a very old age. During the first years of his residence in Rome, its periodical occurrence, and the lassitude which was its natural result, occasioned frequent interruptions in his work.

The atelier which Thorvaldsen took in the *Via Babuino* had been occupied before him by the famous English sculptor Flaxman, that other passionate admirer of the antique, whom his countrymen did not fully appreciate until after his death. Thorvaldsen, notwithstanding his early trials, was destined to be more fortunate than his predecessor. He tasted all the pleasures of fame in his lifetime; and that he did so, is perhaps owing to an Englishman, Mr. Hope, of whom we shall have occasion to speak hereafter.

At Zoëga's house, which was open to artists of every nationality, especially Germans, Danes, and Swedes, Thorvaldsen made the acquaintance of a German landscape painter, Joseph Koch. The young men became intimate, and finally hired rooms together, of an old *padrona di casa* in the *Via Felice*, Dame Ursula by name, who took charge of their housekeeping.

Thorvaldsen was six years the pensioner of the Academy, by successive renewals. When the first term of three years was drawing to a close he resolved to compose, before he should have to leave Rome, an important work. It was then that he made the first model of a "Jason," which has not been preserved. This statue, of life-size, represented the hero victorious over the dragon, and holding in his hand the golden fleece. It remained a long time in his atelier,[1] and was seen by a number of people; but it did not excite much admiration, and the discouraged sculptor finally destroyed it.

All these months of labor, however, had not been in vain. The artist had pondered long upon his subject. He had failed to embody his conception at first, it is true; but he determined to try again. In the autumn of 1802 he modelled another "Jason," and this time colossal, which would probably have met with the same fate as its predecessor, had not Madame Fredericka Brun, sister of Bishop Münter, advanced the money needed to cast it in plaster, which was done early in 1803.

The new statue of "Jason" made a great stir in Rome. The name of the artist was scarcely known; but everybody was talking of his work, and it was unanimously acknowledged by connoisseurs to be of real merit. Canova exclaimed, "Here is a work in a new and lofty style!"[2] Even the critical Zoëga did not hesitate to give his approval in flattering terms, a praise which was more precious to the artist than any coming from other sources.

The "Jason" seemed destined, however, to be but a barren success: it brought no patronage, and no one dreamt of ordering a copy in marble of this statue so highly praised. Thorvaldsen had reached the end of his means, and the Academy's bounty had already been continued to the farthest possible limit. To remain longer in Rome was impossible. After having deferred his departure from week to week and from day to day, he was forced at last to make up his mind that he must leave Italy, while his heart still

[1] He worked upon it until April, 1801. (Thiele.)

[2] "Quest' opera di quel giovane Danese è fatto in uno stile nuovo e grandioso."

yearned for the fame seeming so near, yet ever eluding his grasp. The poor artist had packed his trunks; they were piled upon the vettura, which stood waiting at the door. Plaster casts, furniture, everything had been sold, when, at the last moment, his fellow-traveller, the sculptor Hagemann, came to announce that, in consequence of some trouble about their passports, they would be obliged to wait till the next day.

This trifling incident changed the fortunes of Thorvaldsen. A few hours afterward, the rich English banker, Thomas Hope, coming into his atelier was struck by the majestic proportions of the "Jason" and asked the artist how much it would cost to put it into marble. "Six hundred sequins," replied the agitated sculptor, catching eagerly at a ray of hope. "That is not enough: you must have eight hundred," said the generous amateur.[1]

Life now assumed for Thorvaldsen a new aspect. He remained in Rome no longer a pensioner of the Academy, but an independent artist, living by his labor. From that day Fortune, who crossed his threshold with the English banker, never abandoned him. But it is only just to say that his prosperity was as much due to his own constant efforts and assiduous labor, as to the smiles of the goddess.

Mr. Hope's visit may be termed the salvation of the artist. His commission gave Thorvaldsen, for some time at least, the means of support. He was thus able to pursue his studies in Italy, retained there by his interest in the remains of ancient art. We might therefore naturally expect that the artist would now devote himself with joyful alacrity

[1] This, nevertheless, is the agreement written in French and signed by Thorvaldsen: "I, the undersigned, do promise to execute for Mr. Thomas Hope, of London, for six hundred Roman sequins, payable in four instalments, a statue, eleven hands high in Carrara marble of the finest quality, after a model now in my atelier, near the Piazza Barberini, representing Jason standing, and holding in one hand his lance, in the other the golden fleece." (Thiele.) Mr. Hope, it is true, reserved the right of making the last payment larger, in case the statue equalled his expectations.

to the task of cutting in marble the statue which had already begun to make him famous. Vain expectation! He fell, on the contrary, into a languishing and listless condition which incapacitated him for any kind of work. He scarcely took up the chisel before he laid it down again. His mind and his heart were elsewhere. The artist was absorbed in the lover.

Thorvaldsen now formed a connection which had so long and so unfortunate an influence upon his life that we feel obliged to enter into some particulars concerning it. Zoëga, the sincere friend, the severe critic, was also a charming host. He had at Genzano, near Rome, a pleasant villa, whither Thorvaldsen was frequently invited, and where after one of his attacks of fever he went to re-establish his health. Treated by the master and mistress as their own son, the house seemed a charming abode to the young man. The time passed gayly in games, rustic dances, and the society of lovely women. One of the latter made a deep impression upon the artist. She was a Roman girl with dark hair and flashing eyes, who carried her head proudly, and whose vigorous and well-developed form was statuesque in its proportions. Giorgione would have painted her with the warmest colors of his palette. Her name was Anna Maria Magnani. Her station in life was a humble one; for she seems to have been only a sort of lady's maid to the Signora Zoëga.

In the dances on the lawn where the usual *laisser-aller* of *fêtes champêtres* prevailed, and whilst all the company yielded to the exhilarating influence of the violin, the hand of the young Dane often came in contact with that of the Roman girl. His light hair, his clear complexion, his blue eyes, formed an admirable contrast to her dark beauty. Thorvaldsen's was not an inelegant figure. His features were refined, his expression intelligent, and he had that transparent and delicate beauty common to the native of the North, and which is all the more appreciated in Italy because it is there so rarely seen.

It was not difficult to foresee the result. The first to fall in love, the young girl made but little resistance. Unfortunately, this *liaison*, which should have been a mere episode of his youth, became a heavy chain for the artist. Under the first impulse of passion, he had failed to perceive the immense distance which separated him from this woman in all that concerned his tastes, and especially his character. It was not long, however, before she showed herself in her true colors. Impatient to improve her condition, the humble beauty made a new conquest, and secured a position far superior to that which her first lover could offer her, by marrying a man of higher birth and the possessor of a fortune. Madame d'Uhden, the bride, did not, however, forget the loves of plain Anna Maria, whose relations with her Bertel were scarcely interrupted. The young Dane, who had a more sensitive nature, suffered cruelly from this state of things, though the ardor of his passion would not allow him to put an end to it. He was indeed so blinded by love that when the bridegroom carried off his wife to Florence he fell seriously ill.

Nor had Anna Maria the slightest affection for her husband. Anxious above all, and at whatever price, to rise from the humble station in which her birth had placed her, she had married M. d'Uhden. But, as she was unwilling to break the tie which bound her to the artist, she was aware that she might sooner or later be abandoned by the man who was her lawful protector. Like a prudent woman, she prevailed upon her lover — whose position, thanks to Mr. Hope, had somewhat improved, and whose prospects appeared brighter — to enter into a formal engagement in writing to provide for her support in case of a rupture with her husband. Relying upon this promise, she no longer feared the storm, and was perhaps not sorry to have it burst quickly. The crisis occurred at Florence, and was at once announced to the artist by a letter dated from that city, June 12, 1803.

It was a summons in the proper form, commanding him on the part of the Signora Anna Maria d'Uhden to appear forthwith and perform the engagements entered into by him with the lady aforesaid.[1] Strange to say, this singular missive is signed *Fra Luigi Formenti, at the convent of Santa Maria della Stella.*

Thorvaldsen had no means of escape: he acquitted himself of his obligations by receiving the lady into his house. These exciting events were not of a nature to put an end to his invalid condition, still further aggravated by the excessive heat of the summer of 1803. He yielded to the entreaties of his friends, and betook himself to Albano to re-establish his health, now very much shattered.

Upon his return he made the acquaintance of the Baron von Schubart, Danish ambassador at the court of Naples. The baron and his wife had come to Rome with the intention of passing some time among the artists with whom the city was thronged. Having a sincere love for art, they showed much kindness to the sculptor, treating him as a friend and taking pleasure in introducing him to the best society, to which their rank gave them access. Through them the artist was introduced to Baron William von Humboldt, then at Rome with his family. At the baron's house were always to be met people of the highest distinction whether for rank or merit, and Thorvaldsen profited by the opportunity thus afforded him to form many acquaintances who proved useful to him in his profession. From one of these, the Countess Woronzoff, he received an order for four marble statues:[2] a "Bacchus," a "Ganymede," an "Apollo," and a "Venus"; as well as a group of "Cupid and Psyche." He was also commissioned by Count von Moltke to make two statues, companion pieces, a "Bacchus" and an "Ariadne."

In April, 1804, Thorvaldsen went to Naples in company

[1] Thiele.

[2] The price of each was four hundred Roman crowns.

with the count, and, in spite of the obstacles raised by the jealousy of Anna Maria, afterward proceeded to the villa of Baron von Schubart, at Montenero, where he passed part of the summer. His stay here was very delightful: his hosts overwhelmed him with kindness, and the pure country air and sea-bathing improved his health. As he was very soon anxious to be at work again, the baron hastened to install him in a small atelier, where he modelled the charming group of "Cupid and Psyche," one of his finest creations. Wishing, before leaving Montenero, to testify his appreciation of the kindness of his hosts, he modelled, in less than nine days, a bas-relief, the "Dance of the Muses on Parnassus," a pleasing work, well designed and executed, which he presented to the baroness on her birthday. From Montenero Thorvaldsen made a trip to Genoa, whence he returned soon after to Rome.

The success of his last works having now attracted public attention, honors began to flow in upon him. Oct. 13, 1804, he received from Florence the diploma of professor of the Royal Academy of that city. The Academy of Copenhagen had expected the artist to return home when his pension had expired, but took care not to recall him upon learning that their pupil was doing so much honor to his country in the metropolis of the arts. They sent him a gift of four hundred crowns to express their gratification at his success.[1]

Hardly had Thorvaldsen returned to Rome, when he heard that the atelier at Montenero had been struck by lightning, immediately after his departure, and that all his models, with the exception of "Cupid and Psyche," were destroyed. The amateurs declared that it was a miracle. Poets sang of it; sonnets were handed about from salon to salon; and all this

[1] Some months later (1 May, 1805) he became himself a member of the Academy of his native city, and was appointed professor in the place of Weidenhaupt. He was also chosen honorary member of the National Academy of Bologna.

excitement, which the artist did nothing to promote, contributed to the growth of his fame.

In the spring of 1805 Thorvaldsen produced his first really important bas-relief, "The Abduction of Briseis," which still remains one of the most celebrated of the master's works. In the judgment of connoisseurs, the "Jason" had placed the Danish sculptor side by side with Canova, whose glory was then at its zenith. "The Abduction of Briseis" increased his growing reputation, and some persons maintained that he had already outstripped his illustrious rival in this branch of their art, the bas-relief, in which Thorvaldsen subsequently became unquestionably the superior.

Zoëga, who did not fail to come once a month, according to agreement, to the atelier of his *protégé*, saw this bas-relief, and was so well satisfied with it that he wrote to his friend Bishop Münter, 27th April, 1805, "Thorvaldsen is now very popular, and orders flow in from all sides. There is no longer any doubt that he and Canova are the two most eminent sculptors in Rome. I am delighted to find that my predictions, which no one would believe when I made them, have been verified."

Thorvaldsen now received so many orders that the "Jason" was neglected. The "Bacchus," "Apollo," and "Ganymede" of the Countess Woronzoff were finished in 1805, whilst the "Jason" still remained in the same state. It is difficult to avoid feeling some regret at the conduct of Thorvaldsen in this matter. Mr. Hope's visit was productive of such important results that he should have considered it a positive duty to satisfy an amateur who had treated him so nobly. But artists occasionally have caprices, which we must not judge too severely. The journeys he made on account of his health frequently kept him away from Rome during a part of the year; and on his return his pecuniary embarrassments obliged him to devote himself to new works. The decree of Napoleon, 17th December, 1807, ordering the seizure of all English property on the continent, also furnished him with more or less plausible pretexts for delay. The truth is, that the work, as he had at first conceived it, no longer pleased the artist.[1] He offered to make another statue, which should be superior to the first; but here the obstinacy of the English character showed itself, and Mr. Hope could not be induced to listen to any such proposition. A long correspondence followed, and the amateur finally lost patience.[2] The matter, however, was finally settled,

[1] When Thorvaldsen at last decided to finish the statue, he said one day to Herr Thiele, who was with him in his atelier while he was working, "When I did it I thought it good, and so it is, but now I know how to do better."

[2] Sixteen years after the "Jason" was ordered, Mr. Hope wrote to Thorvaldsen from London, April 6, 1819: "It will be needless, I think, for me to have the honor of reminding you that at the beginning of 1803, in virtue of an agreement signed by you, and which I have now before me, you undertook to execute for me a statue of 'Jason,' after a model that I had the pleasure of seeing in your atelier. Over and above the sum which I engaged to remit in three separate payments, — the first when you had procured the necessary marble, the second when the statue should be rough-hewed, and the third when it should be finished, — I reserved to myself the privilege of adding to these a further sum, agreed upon between us, if the care taken in the execution of the work corresponded to my expectations and your reputation. The first two payments were scrupulously made, at your demand. I have before me the receipts. But since that time, up to the year 1816, that is to say, nearly fourteen years after the agreement made by you with me personally at Rome, I heard nothing from either you or my statue. You then alleged several reasons for having left it unfinished. Although these reasons had little weight in my eyes, since, subsequently to the obligation entered into with me, you had begun and finished an infinite number of other works; nevertheless, partly on account of the regret you expressed for treating me so ill, and your assurance that the statue should be completed without delay, and partly out of delicacy and consideration for you, I determined to forget the past and content myself with trusting to your promises for the future. Nevertheless, sir, I have just learned that not only my statue of 'Jason' has not been touched since that time, but that in the interval still other works have been undertaken and finished. Seeing, therefore, that the absent continue to be wronged, and those who are on the spot can alone hope to obtain justice, I have decided to put this business into the hands of my good friends, Messrs. Torlonia & Co. At my request, these gentlemen have kindly undertaken this commission; and I beg of you to consider henceforward the orders of their banking-house as coming from me."

M. Torlonia and his step-son, M. Chiaveri, acquitted themselves of their commission with all the courtesy of men of the world. Thorvaldsen's journey to Denmark delayed still longer the execution of the statue; and when at last it was finished the artist begged Mr. Hope to accept, as a compensation and an expression of his regret, two marble bas-reliefs, and three busts, also in marble, of Mrs. Hope and her two daughters. (Thiele.)

though it was not until 1828 that the "Jason" was ready to be sent to London.

Since the success of the "Abduction of Briseis," the distinguished people who had opened their salons to the Danish sculptor almost made it a matter of rivalry to obtain the promise of some work from his hand. The wealthy Marquis Torlonia ordered a group of "Mars and Venus," which he wished to place in the Palazzo Bracciano, as companion to Canova's famous group, "Hercules and Lycas." The United States Consul at Leghorn, Mr. Appleton, gave him a commission for a colossal statue of "Liberty," to be placed in a public square in Washington.[1] The municipality of Florence wishing to erect in the church of Santa Croce a monument to Dante, Thorvaldsen made some sketches for it; but all these works were only talked about, and were never executed. Such was the case also with a monument ordered the following year, through Baron von Schubart, to commemorate the naval victory of the Americans over the Tripoline fleet.

Thorvaldsen's health had been much benefited by his last summer's vacation at Montenero. The baron, remembering this, wrote to the artist, July 26, 1805: —

> "Tell me, for the love of God, what are you doing in Rome during this terrible heat in which you cannot possibly work? Why have you not come to our charming Montenero, which is looking even more lovely than it did last summer, when you gave us the pleasure of your company? Cannot you break away, and come here to pass five or six weeks of the hottest weather? My wife says that you owe it to your health. Say at Rome that you are ill, and are going to pass a fortnight at Montenero to finish some small works you have on hand here."

We see by this letter with what kindly feelings the baron and baroness regarded their friend. Herr von Schubart was

[1] Five thousand Roman crowns were proposed to the artist as the price for this statue.

not ignorant of the storm raised the preceding year by Anna Maria's jealousy, and now scarcely hoped to succeed. The sculptor, whose amiable disposition was ill suited to these terrible quarrels, preferred to submit quietly to the yoke than pay so dearly for throwing it off; and Mme. d'Uhden would undoubtedly have gained the day, had it not been for a happy accident. It chanced that Count von Rantzau, a nobleman of Holstein, arrived in Rome just at this time; he went daily to see Thorvaldsen in his atelier; they took a fancy to each other at once, and a friendship sprung up between them which lasted until death. The count had a letter of introduction to the baron, which he told Thorvaldsen he would like to profit by, but added that he would not go to Montenero unless he went with him. On the spur of the moment, the artist promised to accompany him. A terrible scene ensued with Mme. d'Uhden. But, his word once given, Thorvaldsen was ashamed to draw back. He was firm, and neither tears nor threats had the power to retain him. Out of all patience with Anna Maria's unjust recriminations, he departed without being reconciled; not even bidding her good-by, and leaving the care of his ateliers to an old school-fellow, his friend the architect, Charles Stanley.

Anna Maria sent word through this friend, that "the illness, vexation, and want of sleep caused by Thorvaldsen's conduct would no doubt bring her to the grave." The sculptor was little moved by this sad picture, and, that she might be aware of his feelings, he wrote Stanley a letter, intended to be seen by the poor woman, in which he made no mention of her, but asked with a great deal of solicitude about the health of his little dog Perrucca.

"What an insult!" exclaimed the abandoned Ariadne. "To show all his tenderness for that ugly brute, only to better manifest his contempt for his darling, in thus forgetting her entirely!" She gave vent to her anger in a letter full of bitter reproaches. This state of affairs continued for quite a long time; until at last, towards the end of August, Stanley wrote to his friend that Anna Maria was growing desperate at his silence. Thorvaldsen then sent her a few words which put an end to this great grief: she wrote in her turn a long letter of piteous lamentations, "ending with a very urgent request that he would bring her home from Leghorn a good pair of small English scissors." Thus ended this dramatic incident.

NIGHT.

CHAPTER III.

Baron von Humboldt.—Rauch.—The "Adonis."—The Two "Hebes." — The "Triumph of Alexander." — Grand Duchess of Tuscany. — Baroness von Schubart. — "Night and Morning." — The "Venus." Ægina Marbles. — Byron. — The "Hope." — Princess Baryatinska. — The "Mercury." — "The Three Graces."

CUPID AND PSYCHE.

"The Abduction of Briseis" and the group of "Cupid and Psyche" mark the moment when Thorvaldsen attained to the full development of his talent. Henceforward he pursued his art with ardor, confidence, and enthusiasm, sending forth from his ateliers that great multitude of works, chaste and severe in style, which have given him a place among the first sculptors of the century.

In 1805, the three statues — half-size — ordered by the Countess Woronzoff, and almost wholly sketched at Montenero, were put into marble with the greatest care.

About the same time Thorvaldsen made his first model of a "Venus." It is under life-size, and represents the goddess entirely nude. Her garments are lying on the trunk of a tree: she holds in her right hand the apple, the prize of beauty. Of the two copies in marble of this statue which still exist, one belongs to the Countess Woronzoff, the other to Mme. von Ropp. But although several amateurs were anxious to have copies of it, the artist, dissatisfied with the size he had adopted, broke up the model. He afterward executed the same Venus the size of life. In 1806, through the agency of the Countess von Schimmelmann, sister of Baron von Schubart, Thorvaldsen received a commission for two baptismal fonts for the church of Brahe-Trolleborg, in the Island of Fionia. These, so far as we have been able to ascertain, are the first religious works undertaken by him. He continued, none the less, however, to give his attention to subjects taken from the Greek mythology, which he preferred to all others; and while engaged upon the fonts, modelled a "Hebe," half-size, ordered by a Danish baron. In the right hand she holds a brimming cup, and her tunic unfastened at the shoulder leaves bare the right breast.

The zeal with which Thorvaldsen devoted himself to his art did not cause him to neglect his social relations. His atelier, always open, was constantly filled with visitors. In manner he was kind and sympathetic; and, as he conversed with ease, and told stories in an interesting way, he made the time pass pleasantly to his sitters. Not only did he receive callers with affability, but he went willingly into society. He was particularly fond of visiting at the house of Baron William von Humboldt, who was then Prussian ambassador to the court of Rome. Previous to the spring of 1807, the baron had lived in the villa *di Malta*, but was now established in a grand palace in the *Strada Gregoriana*, near *Trinità di Monti*. Here he entertained strangers and distinguished foreigners from all parts; everybody in Rome, in fact, who had any claims to distinction. Thorvaldsen met here his friend Zoëga, and the painter Camuccini; but the person who charmed him above all others was a young girl, Mademoiselle Ida Brun, afterward Countess de Bombelles, whose mother, Madame Fredericka Brun, had been a generous friend to him in the outset of his career.

Thorvaldsen had undertaken to give drawing lessons to Mademoiselle Ida, but much preferred hearing her sing, while he accompanied her on the guitar, upon which he played with much taste. A true artist, he was deeply impressed by the beauty of this young girl, who was also remarkable for her talents and cultivation. He worshipped her with a respectful admiration, and did all in his power to please her.[1]

Rauch, who came to Rome about this time, was also received at the Baron von Humboldt's. Thorvaldsen welcomed kindly the young artist, then wholly unknown, and with his usual friendliness procured him several commissions, which gave the Berlin sculptor an opportunity to show his ability. Rauch, some time afterward, received commissions to execute the mausoleum of Queen Louisa of Prussia, intended for Charlottenbourg, and a great number of important works for the city of Berlin, among which we ought to

[1] Thorvaldsen, some years later (1810), modelled the portrait bust of Mademoiselle Brun. In "L'Allemagne" Madame de Staël thus speaks of this young lady: —

"I have already said that as a general thing sculpture loses much by the neglect of the dance. The only phenomenon of that art in Germany is Ida Brun, a young girl whose social position shuts her out from a professional career. She has received from nature and her mother a wonderful talent for representing by simple attitudes charming pictures and beautiful statues. Her dancing is a succession of floating *chefs d'œuvre*, every one of which we long to fix forever. It is true that the mother of Ida has expressed in her writings all that her daughter embodies in the dance. The poems of Mme. Brun reveal in art and nature a thousand new beauties not perceived by careless eyes. I saw the young Ida, while still a child, represent Althea about to burn the brand on which the life of her son Meleager depends. She portrayed without words the grief, the inward struggle, the terrible resolve of a mother. Through her intense facial expression undoubtedly, she made us understand the conflict within; but the art of varying her gestures, and the artistic way she folded her purple mantle about her, produced at least as much effect as her countenance itself. She often remained in one position for some time, and then a painter could imagine nothing finer than the picture she improvised. Such a talent is unique."

mention particularly the monument erected to the memory of Frederick the Great.

The young Prince Louis of Bavaria, who afterward became king, and who was always an enthusiastic patron of the arts, began at that time that regular correspondence with Thorvaldsen which he ever afterward kept up. He was now collecting antique marbles for his new museum at Munich, the Glyptothek, and had in Rome very zealous agents constantly on the watch for artistic discoveries, but often puzzled to know whether the objects presented to them as antiques were true or false. Thorvaldsen, whose judgment had been formed by a long and passionate study of the works of high art, was never deceived. The agents of the prince had occasion a number of times to congratulate themselves upon having consulted him. He once prevented them from purchasing a large vase of suspicious origin, which the dealers tried to pass off for a masterpiece of antique Greek art.[1] Shortly afterward the dishonesty of these dealers was publicly exposed, and the prince hastened to thank the sculptor to whom he had already given important commissions. This interference, however, on the part of Thorvaldsen, gained him the ill-will of the men whose dishonorable traffic he had injured.

At this epoch a serious conflict was on the point of breaking out between Napoleon I and Pius VII. The first result of the contention between the Emperor and the Pope was the occupation of the Roman States, and afterward of Rome itself, by the French army. General Miollis entered the city without firing a shot, Feb. 2d, 1808, and took possession of the Castle of Saint Angelo, and all other important posts. From this time the Pope — until he was removed from Rome by his opposition to the inflexible will of the Emperor — was sovereign only in name.

[1] Thiele.

The life of artists in Rome was naturally not a little disturbed by these commotions. Nevertheless, Thorvaldsen pursued his work with a perseverance which testifies to his love of his profession. It was at this time that he executed a statue of "Mars Pacificator," eight feet in height, which the Prince of Bavaria ordered in marble.

He afterward chose in its stead an "Adonis" which he saw in the sculptor's atelier.

The "Adonis," upon which the artist worked long and steadily, was modelled in 1808, but not completely finished until 1832. It is a masterpiece of grace and antique simplicity; and is moreover the only one of the artist's works wrought out entirely by his own hands, a stipulation insisted upon by the prince, who knew that the master was accustomed to leave to his workmen the task of rough-hewing and even finishing his statues, usually reserving to himself only the last few touches. The "Adonis" is now in the Glyptothek of Munich, in the centre of the hall devoted to modern works.

Canova professed a great admiration for this statue. Meeting Mme. Fredericka Brun one day at the Villa Doria, he asked her if she had seen the "Adonis." "Not yet," she replied. "You must see it," he rejoined; "for it is an admirable statue, noble and simple, in the true antique style, and full of feeling;" and with warmth, "Your friend, madame, is a divine man." Then, after a few moments' silence, — "But it is a pity I am no longer young."

Notwithstanding these kind words, we might infer, from some remarks of Thorvaldsen, that Canova did not always act with frankness towards his young rival. "Whenever Canova had completed a new work," said Thorvaldsen, sometime afterward to an intimate friend, "he usually invited me to come and see it. He wanted my opinion. If I made any criticism, as, for instance, that perhaps it would be better to make a certain fold of drapery fall in such or such a way, he would always acknowledge the justice of my remark, embrace and thank me warmly, but never change anything. Out of politeness I used to invite him to visit me in my atelier. He would come; but always restricted himself to telling me that all my works were excellent, — *excellentissimo;* and that there was absolutely nothing to criticise."[1]

The work of restoring the palace of Christiansborg at Copenhagen, which had been devastated by the great fire, was now going on; and Thorvaldsen was charged with the execution of four circular bas-reliefs, representing "Prometheus and Minerva," "Hercules and Hebe," "Esculapius and Hygeia," "Jupiter and Nemesis."

During this same year, 1808, on the 6th of March, Thorvaldsen was made an honorary member of the Academy of Saint Luke, at Rome, and executed as his diploma work a famous bas-relief, often reproduced, and known under the title, "A genio lumen." Art is represented by the figure of a woman, prepared to draw on her tablets, and waiting for the Genius of Inspiration to pour oil into the lamp. A membership in the Academy of Saint Luke gave Thorvaldsen the right to take part in the instruction of the pupils of that school; but his influence was impaired by cabals, which have sometimes been said — and very erroneously, we think — to have been fomented by Canova. These cabals were set on foot by artists of no merit, who were jealous that "a barbarian from the remote North" should rob them of fame and occupation. Thorvaldsen's pupils were long subject to ill-treatment: attempts were made to humiliate them, and they had to complain of some acts of injustice.

In addition to these annoyances instigated by the envious, Thorvaldsen was to endure other and more bitter trials. Just before the forced departure of the Pope, he lost by

[1] Thiele.

death his old school-fellow the architect Stanley, and soon afterward his first patron in Rome, his friend Zoëga. This wise counsellor of the artist died Feb. 10, 1809. Through his illness Thorvaldsen had been devoted to him, and after his death he took a mask of his face and modelled his bust. He also made the drawing for the portrait in Welcker's biography of Zoëga. And he did not stop here; but transferring to the family of his friend part of the affection he had borne to him, he interested himself in the settlement of the estate, a matter which occasioned him much trouble and perplexity.

But in spite of political agitations and private trials, the year 1809 proved not unfruitful. The earlier and finer of the two bas-reliefs of "Hector confronting Paris and Helen" was composed at this time; also four other bas-reliefs: "Love conquering the Lion," "The Birth of Venus," "Love stung by a Bee," and "Mercury giving to Ino the infant Bacchus."

In 1810, the King of Denmark conferred upon Thorvaldsen the title of Knight of Danebrog; and hereafter, as is the custom in Italy, he was called "*Cavaliere Alberto.*" It was a convenient way of avoiding the pronunciation of his Danish name, always very difficult for the Italians.

The years 1810 and 1811 are marked by two charming compositions, "Cupid reviving the Fainting Psyche," and "Bacchus presenting the Cup to Love;" also two other bas-reliefs, "Summer" and "Autumn." The colossal statue of Mars, modelled after a sketch made some years previous, and now grouped with a statue of Love; the bust of the charming Mademoiselle Ida Brun, his own portrait as a colossal Hermes, and the lovely statue of Psyche belong to the year 1811.

The fame acquired by Thorvaldsen constantly increasing, the Danish people, justly proud of him, began to manifest an ardent desire that he should return to his native land. He had left his home young and almost unknown: he was now famous, and his country was eager to reclaim him. A quarry of marble having been discovered in Norway, the hereditary prince of Denmark, Christian Frederick, an enthusiastic patron of the arts, who had done his utmost to promote their prosperity in his native country, made this a pretext to write the following letter to Thorvaldsen: —

HERR PROFESSOR AND CHEVALIER, —

It will perhaps be agreeable to you to receive these few lines from a fellow-countryman who esteems you highly, and knows how to appreciate your merit. I take advantage, therefore, of this good opportunity to present to you my most sincere compliments.

My love for the fine arts, and my earnest efforts to propagate them in my country, naturally inspire me with a desire to see and know the greatest sculptor of his day. There is work for you here. The activity of your rich and fruitful mind will have full scope. You can, and doubtless will, be of service to the Academy, whose members watched with delight your early progress in the career of art, and who lost no time in admitting into their number a man capable of exercising so happy an influence upon young artists.

Italy is scarcely what it was: your own country is still unchanged. Perhaps you may also find that the arts have made some progress here. What an impulse would your presence give to them!

But I do not wish to employ persuasion. I rely upon your own feelings for the accomplishment of my dearest wishes as a Dane, and as President of the Academy of Fine Arts.

The Baron von Schubart, his Majesty's chamberlain, who has kindly offered to take charge of this letter, will hand you a specimen of the white marble just discovered in Norway. We expect soon a large block, and more afterward, which will be at your service; and I do not doubt that, while you stay with us, you will be able to execute works in marble. Regard this as another reason for hastening your return; and rest assured that I have no wish to confine your activity to limits too narrow for you. You will be always free to return in search of inspiration to those happy regions which are now favored by your presence. A small portion of your life for the service of your country is all I ask.

I am, Herr Professor, with esteem, your affectionate

CHRISTIAN FREDERICK,
Prince of Denmark and Norway.

COPENHAGEN, Dec. 20, 1811.

The prince's letter was not the only one received by the artist: all his friends united in soliciting him to return. Thorvaldsen would have consented gladly: he even made some preliminary preparations for the journey, when he was unavoidably detained in Rome by a commission of the utmost importance.

The French Academy in Rome had just received an order to ornament with great magnificence the Quirinal Palace. An approaching visit of the French Emperor was announced. Time pressed, and the works were begun at once. The architect Stern, who directed them, proposed to Thorvaldsen that he should compose the bas-reliefs that were to form a frieze for one of the most spacious halls, and left to him the choice of subjects. The sculptor decided to represent the "Entry of Alexander the Great into Babylon." It is one of the largest and most important of his works. There was no time to lose, as this enormous piece of sculpture had to be finished in the space of three months; and he accordingly set about it with great enthusiasm. Being especially desirous to give the composition breadth of style, he was forced to sacrifice the details to the general effect. The frieze, however, was intended for so high a position that finish of execution was of secondary importance. As soon as one piece had left his hands he took hastily from the clay a mould,[1] from which one copy only could be cast. Those who saw this work from a near point of view did not form a very

[1] Thiele.

high opinion of it. Notwithstanding all the zeal of the artist, the frieze was not finished until June, 1812. But when all the pieces were put together and placed at the proper height, the work surpassed even the expectations of Thorvaldsen's friends. The imperfections of execution disappeared, and only the harmony of the composition was seen, recalling in a happy manner the admirable friezes of antiquity.

Before the several portions of "The Triumph of Alexander" left his atelier, Thorvaldsen, by the advice of the architect Malling, took another mould of them, from which a new plaster was cast. He thought that the King of Denmark might be glad to possess a copy of this composition, for which a fitting place could be found in the "Rittersaal," or knight's hall, in the new palace. It was from this plaster that he subsequently executed the first marble copy ordered by Napoleon I, and supposed to have been intended for the Temple of Glory, now the Church of the Madeleine.[1] The price was 320,000 francs, of which the half only was paid, when reverse of fortune sent Napoleon to the Island of Elba. The Bourbon government was not eager to facilitate the completion of a work intended to glorify the new Alexander; and the artist, after offering it unsuccessfully to several European sovereigns for the sum necessary to finish it, finally disposed of it to a private individual, a rich amateur, the Count of Sommariva, for 100,000 francs.

The first hasty conception of this work met with some adverse criticisms. Thorvaldsen paid heed to those he thought just, and corrected his compositions with the greatest care. He first changed the attitude of the principal figure, Alexander in his chariot, which was too theatrical. The change was a happy one. He also modified some of the

[1] Thiele.

details of other portions. While he was putting this composition into marble, he modelled for the Danish government a new copy in plaster; for, to the deep regret of the artist, the state of the Danish finances did not allow of a greater outlay. The whole work may be said to have been remodelled; and the Romans were so delighted with it that they gave him the rather extraordinary title of "Patriarch of Bas-relief."[1] Subsequently he had the satisfaction of executing the frieze in marble for his countrymen.

Feb. 12, 1812, the sculptor was made member of the Imperial Academy of Vienna. Though "The Triumph of Alexander" occupied almost all his time, he undertook this same year several other great works. Napoleon's speech of the 26th of June, on the occasion of the general conference of Warsaw, having held out hopes for the re-establishment of the kingdom of Poland, the Polish national government wished to erect a monument in memory of the occurrence. The Emperor's words were engraved on a marble tablet, and the architrave above was to be upheld by two caryatides, for which Thorvaldsen received a commission. But these two figures met with the same fate as "The Triumph of Alexander." The artist fell ill, and could not finish the statues soon enough, and when they were ready there was no longer any Poland! They were afterward purchased by the Danish government, and placed each side of the royal throne in the palace of Christiansborg.

In June and July, 1813, Thorvaldsen suffered from another attack of that malignant fever of which he was so often the victim, and was forced to suspend work. While in this condition he received a letter from the Baron von Schubart, begging him to come to Montenero and join them in a trip to the baths of Lucca, whither they were going for the health

[1] Nagler.

of the baroness. This was a fine opportunity for the artist, and all his friends urged him to embrace it. Even the jealous Anna Maria offered no opposition, for she saw that Thorvaldsen really needed rest. He was now bound to her more closely than ever, by the birth of a daughter, to whom he was tenderly attached. He nevertheless decided to leave the mother and child in charge of an Italian family with whom Anna Maria was intimate. The father of this family was a dealer in curiosities, named Angelo Cremaschi: he had a wife and two daughters.

Having put his affairs in order,[1] and made some arrangements respecting his ateliers, Thorvaldsen left for Montenero, and thence went to Lucca with the baron and baroness. His sojourn at the baths was delightful. His reputation brought him much gratifying notice, while he was specially flattered by the attentions paid him by young and pretty women. He had now become in every respect a man of the world, and when he chose was perfectly at home in the best society. The grand-duchess of Tuscany, who was then at Lucca, received him so kindly that the report of it spread abroad. There is nothing, however, to lead us to suppose that she favored him excepting as an artist; but as the princess sent for him afterward to Florence, to confide some important works to him, this simple fact gave rise to countless rumors, some of which reaching Rome, created a great excitement in the household of Signora Cremaschi. The feminine council drew from them the most exaggerated conclusions, disquieting the jealous Anna Maria, and consequently disturbing her nursing infant.

In the month of December Thorvaldsen returned tran-

[1] His two dogs only remained to be provided for, — Perrucca and Teverino. We know how attached Thorvaldsen was to these animals. A friend in whom he had all confidence, and who afterward became a celebrated artist, the sculptor Rodolph Schadow, consented to take charge of them. (Thiele.)

quilly to Rome, his health wholly restored by this rest of several months. By letters received from Montenero, he heard the good news that the baroness was equally benefited. He was therefore much shocked when in the ensuing February (1814) he was suddenly informed, by a letter from the baron, that that excellent woman had died after a short illness. Thorvaldsen felt her death keenly. The baroness was as modest as she was accomplished. With no ostentation in her manner of bestowing favors, she liked to be of service to artists, and to Thorvaldsen in particular she had ever been a kind patron and true friend. In his heartfelt desire to testify his gratitude, he set to work immediately and modelled a bas-relief, representing her husband trying to recall his spouse, while the Genius of Death extinguishes the torch of life.

It was just at this time when Thorvaldsen had lost his best friend, that Pietro Tenerani, who was one day to become his most remarkable pupil, entered his atelier. Tenerani was nephew of a certain Pietro Marchetti, a marble-worker of Carrara, who was in the habit of furnishing the master with the marble blocks he required for his work.

A young Danish painter, Eckersberg, came to Rome at the same time, and was kindly assisted by Thorvaldsen. The two soon became friends; and Eckersberg painted the sculptor's portrait, one of the best likenesses of him that we have, — a little cold, but finely touched, it gives us a very correct idea of how Thorvaldsen looked at forty.

In 1814, the artist composed the bas-relief of "Nessus and Dejanira," and returned again to the subject of "Love Victorious," — not being satified with a previous attempt. A small statue, the "Boy Cupid," and another of the young Georgina Russell, are of the same date.

To the year 1815 belong four important bas-reliefs: "The Workshop of Vulcan," where, grouped near the god, are

Venus, Cupid, and Mars; the beautiful composition "Achilles and Priam," of which we have already spoken, — a great and masterly work, and, to our thinking, Thorvaldsen's *chef-d'œuvre;* and the two famous medallions "Morning" and "Night." The latter, it is said, was conceived during a sleepless night, and modelled in one day. It is truly a piece of inspiration. The Goddess of the Shades, launched with infinite lightness into space, slowly wings her flight, carrying in her arms her two children Sleep and Death. The "Morning" is also a very graceful work, but not so fine as the other. There is between the two all the distance which separates sudden, irresistible inspiration from ingenious and studied effort. These two medallions, prized highly by connoisseurs, soon acquired immense popularity: they were engraved on precious stones and on cameos, moulded in plaster and porcelain, — reproduced, in fact, under all forms.

While these two bas-reliefs were adding to Thorvaldsen's reputation in Rome, and the Italians themselves, in spite of their instinctive jealousy of strangers, could no longer withhold their praise, a few of his works, especially a fine series of drawings sent to the Copenhagen Exposition, attracted to him more than ever the attention of his countrymen. The Danish capital had not yet recovered from the bombardment by the English in 1807, and a large portion was still to be rebuilt. Frederick VI, the reigning sovereign, had very little knowledge of art, and being of a frank and honorable nature, declined to assume, even in appearance, a part for which he felt that he was by nature unfitted. He was glad to leave to his cousin Prince Christian Frederick its honors and its responsibilities. That prince, notwithstanding the failure of his former invitation, was so anxious to secure the assistance of Thorvaldsen, which he knew would be invaluable, that he was ready to try every means to attain his end. He therefore strongly urged the artist's friends to join their entreaties to his own; and thus the sculptor received almost at the same moment a number of pressing letters, which dwelt upon the esteem in which he was held in Copenhagen, and the need they had of his assistance. He was told at the same time that it would be unpatriotic in him to withhold it.

> "You and your works are much talked of," writes his friend Professor Bröndsted, Dec. 2, 1815, "not only by the few who have really a love and knowledge of art, but by two other classes of people, whose judgments, though not entitled to much esteem and often faulty, have weight from the influence exerted by those who hold them; and by these two classes I mean the common herd and what is usually called the *beau monde*, or aristocracy. The opinions of the latter are often neither noble nor great, as long experience has shown. But I must do them the justice to say, that latterly they have always spoken of you with an enthusiasm which has given me as well as your other friends great pleasure; though it is easy for us to see that this admiration has not its source either in just ideas of art in general, or any distinct perception of your genius and worth in particular. . . . To be brief, the conclusion of all this is, that you *ought to come* for the sake of the country as well as for art and yourself."

This was true, and Thorvaldsen recognized it. But though he had a sincere desire to devote his talents and knowledge to his country's service, he was obliged to defer this gratification to some future time. That he might execute the orders flowing in from all quarters, he had just provided himself with larger work-rooms. At the foot of the high terraces of the Palace Barberini, at the corner of the piazza and the *Vicolo delle Colonette*, he had noticed three buildings admirably suited to his purpose. They adjoined each other and had a garden. He converted them into three work-rooms, where he lived long years, composing new works and making his pupils reproduce them. He was just settled in them when these letters urging him to return came from Copenhagen. All he could do, therefore, was to send a letter of excuse to the Prince of Denmark, pleading his numerous engagements, and the necessity he was under of fulfilling them, and promising at the same time not to contract any new obligations, so as to be free to gratify the wishes of his countrymen the following spring. But many unforeseen obstacles intervened, and the project was not carried into effect until July, 1819.

This period of Thorvaldsen's life in Rome was also fruitful in great works. In 1816 he modelled a new statue of "Hebe," a variation of the one he had composed ten years before. In the first, the right breast is bare; while in the second, which is more amply draped, the bosom is entirely covered, and the whole statue is characterized by a modest grace. He made, besides, a new "Ganymede." The first holds a brimming cup, the second pours from an amphora the nectar of the gods.

The "Venus" was finished the same year, that noble and beautiful statue which the artist had so long studied, and for which he had employed successively more than thirty models. The master cast aside his first essay made in 1805, with which he was not satisfied, and devoted three years of assiduous labor to the composition of the new figure, one of his most careful works. This statue has been often reproduced: the first three copies in marble were for Lord Lucan, the Duchess of Devonshire, and — a little later — for Mr. P. C. Labouchère.[1] According to Herr Thiele, they were exposed to great risks before arriving at their places of destination in England. The left arm of the Duchess of Devonshire's was

[1] Mr. Peter Cæsar Labouchère, a native of Holland, and at that time the head of the house of Hope & Co., Amsterdam, had married a daughter of Sir Francis Baring, Baronet, and thus became brother-in-law of Mr. Alexander Baring, afterward Lord Ashburton. His son, Mr. Henry Labouchère, the present owner of the "Venus," was for several years a member of the British Cabinet, and one of her Majesty's Privy Council. He was raised to the Peerage under the title of Lord Taunton. It is he who figures with Thorvaldsen in the bas-relief of Homer. The resemblance is said to be perfect.

broken when the vessel was unloading, and the break was concealed by means of a gold bracelet.[1] This copy is at Chatsworth. The vessel which carried Lord Lucan's was wrecked on the coast of England. But "Venus Astarte, daughter of the salt sea," rose again from the bosom of the waters, thanks to the efforts made to save her. She was uninjured! Finally, the statue impatiently expected by Mr. Labouchère safely arrived in port. The powerful arm of the crane was just lifting it from the vessel, when the rope broke, and the weighty box slid through the hatchways and fell heavily to the bottom of the hold. The cargo, fortunately, was wheat, and the goddess was once more preserved. Ceres had saved Venus.

While engaged upon his "Venus," Thorvaldsen made at the same time the famous restoration of the Ægina marbles, which in the eyes of connoisseurs brought him as much well-earned honor as his own fine original compositions. A work of this nature was, in fact, no common undertaking, and to grapple with its difficulties required a very extensive acquaintance with Greek art. But, as we have already seen, Thorvaldsen thoroughly understood the subject; and he now gave the best possible proof that he did so, for it is doubtful whether any other artist could have been found capable of solving the problem so satisfactorily.

The Ægina marbles were discovered in 1811, in the Island of Ægina, by Baron von Haller, Cockerell, Foster, and Linkh. They formerly ornamented the pediment of a temple consecrated to Jupiter Panhellenius. In 1812 they were bought by the Prince of Bavaria, for 150,000 francs. He had them transported to Rome, and Thorvaldsen was charged with their restoration. A great number of fragments, some-

[1] The same statue was also broken at both ankles; and, to conceal the breaks, anklets have been placed upon them.

times whole limbs, were wanting. The artist was fully aware of the magnitude of the task proposed, and it was not without considerable reluctance, therefore, that he assumed so great a responsibility; but, after once undertaking the work, it very soon absorbed him and became a favorite occupation. To prosecute it with more facility, he hired premises in the Corso, where he had room enough to bring all the fragments together, recompose the pediment, and study every part in reference to the whole; supplying carefully all the missing pieces, and preserving in its purity the semi-hieratic style of the work. Thorvaldsen was not more than a year in making this restoration. The statues were in Parian marble, and he used so much care in matching the tints of the new pieces as almost to deceive a practised eye. He was frequently asked by visitors to the atelier, which were the restored parts. "I cannot say," he would reply, laughing. "I neglected to mark them, and I no longer remember. Find them out for yourself, if you can." Unfortunately the restored parts of this magnificent pediment, in the Glyptothek of Munich, can now be distinguished from the others, at a first glance, by the difference of color; the hue of the new marble so carefully matched having changed, as might have been expected, by exposure to the air, whilst the old remains the same.

The following year, 1817, Thorvaldsen produced, besides a marble of "Love Victorious," modelled in 1814, a Bacchante known as "The Dancing-girl," the bust of Lord Byron, a "Young Shepherd with his Dog," a group of "Ganymede and the Eagle," and a statue of "Hope." In the poet Andersen's autobiography, we find this account of the sculptor's interview with the author of "Childe Harold." "It was in Rome," said Thorvaldsen, "that I made the bust of Lord Byron. When this nobleman came to sit to me in my atelier, he took a seat opposite me, and put on directly a strange expression entirely different from his natural one. 'My Lord,' I said to him, 'please keep perfectly still; and I beg of you do not look so disconsolate.' 'It is my natural expression,' replied Byron. 'Really!' I said; and without paying attention to this affectation I began to work in my own way. When the bust was finished, everybody thought it a striking likeness, but my lord was dissatisfied. 'This face is not mine,' he said; 'I look far more unhappy than that,' — for he was obstinately bent upon looking miserable!"

Thorvaldsen's simple nature, it is clear, could scarcely comprehend so extraordinary a degree of imaginary wretchedness. The character of the two men was as opposite as their careers in art were divergent.

The group of "Ganymede and the Eagle," "The Young Shepherd and Dog," and the statue of "Hope," show, by their severity of style, the results of Thorvaldsen's assiduous study of the Ægina marbles. One day when he was working upon "The Ganymede," his model, who had a very fine figure, sat himself down in a corner of the atelier and unconsciously assumed a very charming attitude. Thorvaldsen was struck with it, and it suggested to him the composition of "The Young Shepherd." The dog was modelled from his favorite "Teverino." As to the statue of "Hope," it is wholly an archaic work. A reduced copy was subsequently erected over the tomb of the Baroness von Humboldt.

Several academies had already conferred upon the Danish sculptor the honor of membership: in the September of 1817 he received from the Perugia Academy of Fine Arts a diploma of *Accademico di merito*. Carrara conferred a membership upon him, February, 1818; and the restoration of the Ægina marbles earned for him a similar honor from the Academy of Archæology at Rome.

Walking one day in the Corso, the artist saw, seated on a curb-stone, a porter, whose attitude was both so natural and uncommon that he was directly impressed by it. As usual, he made a rapid sketch of the figure in his note-book; and it furnished him with the action for his "Mercury," one of his finest creations, which was finished the following year, 1819. There exist several copies in marble of this beautiful and severe work.

The elegant statue of the Princess Baryatinska, in which the artist, without sacrificing any of the severity or purity of the antique style, has succeeded in preserving the aristocratic air and characteristic British type of his subject, is of the same year. Among Thorvaldsen's portrait-statues, modelled from life, this is, in our opinion, his finest work. Owing to various causes, the marble, which was finely cut, remained in Thorvaldsen's possession, and passed, finally, into his museum.[1]

"Our Lord giving to St. Peter the Keys of Paradise," in the chapel of the Pitti Palace at Florence, is a work of the same period. The group of "The Three Graces" was also completed at this time. The first sketch was made in 1817; and the master intrusted to his pupil, Tenerani, the task of separately studying each figure. This preparatory work done, Thorvaldsen took the statues in hand himself, and finished them entirely. Subsequently he again took up the same subject, but treated it very differently. Though both of these groups have received the appro-

[1] The statue was ordered by Prince Baryatinski: its price was fixed at 3,000 Roman crowns, a third of which was paid in advance. The prince died, and Thorvaldsen neglected to get the address of the princess, who also died several years afterward, and in the mean while had entirely forgotten her statue. After the death of his mother, her son reclaimed it, offering to pay the rest of the stipulated price; but the trustees of the Museum of Copenhagen, already in possession of the treasures bequeathed by the artist, did not feel it their duty to give up so precious a work. The sum that had already been paid was given back to the young prince, for whom Herr Bissen made a marble copy of the statue.

bation of eminent judges, we find much to criticise in them, neither really satisfying us. A little Love, which figures in both, is justly much admired; and there are in existence, it is said, more than a dozen separate copies of it in marble.

THE NEST OF LOVES.

CHAPTER IV.

Miss Mackenzie Seaforth.— Illness of Thorvaldsen.— Stay at Albano. — Convalescence. — Excursion to Naples. — *Liaison* with a Viennese Lady. — Departure for Denmark.

LOVE VICTORIOUS.

THE last two years of Thorvaldsen's life in Italy, previous to his departure for Copenhagen, were kept in a state of agitation by affairs of the heart. Poor Anna Maria was to encounter formidable rivals: it was her lot to contend both with an Englishwoman, virtuous and well-born, and a seductive Viennese.

To women of much intelligence, there is a powerful charm in a man's celebrity. While others of lower aims are won by the attractions of rank or fortune, they, first captivated by the fame of the artist, become easily enamoured of the man himself. This was the case with Thorvaldsen. Absorbed in his work, and in the love of art, he undoubtedly would have resisted allurements of this sort, had they not been so unceasing. We beg pardon for thus entering into details respecting the artist's private affairs, but our disclosures help to reveal his character; and surely the feelings of the man can never be indifferent to those who admire the works of the artist.

Thorvaldsen was intimate with several English families, who took a warm interest in his welfare. Nothing, they thought, was more desirable for the master, whose health at that time required great care, than a regular and peaceable life. Letters which have since come to light put us upon the track of a sort of conspiracy[1] long and discreetly carried on. In a letter to the artist from Mr. Arthur Carignan, that gentleman paints a glowing picture of the domestic felicity enjoyed by one of his friends, and shortly afterward in the postscript of another letter he incidentally introduces the person destined to play the principal part in this romantic drama. "It is possible," he writes, "that Miss Mackenzie Seaforth, accompanied by an older lady, will come to visit your atelier. In this case I recommend her particularly to you, and all the more because the young lady has a very happy talent, not only for the fine arts in general, but especially for the art of modelling."

Miss Frances Mackenzie, who was of an honorable Scotch family, did indeed come to the atelier with her aunt Mrs. Proby. She was not remarkable for her beauty, but she pleased by more solid qualities. She had a fine and cultivated mind, was especially well-informed with regard to art, and was possessed of a true taste and real talent for sculpture. She paid frequent visits to the artist, feeling for him at first a great admiration, and soon a profound sympathy.

In the spring of 1818, Thorvaldsen, in an excursion to Tivoli with some gay friends, caught a violent cold, accompanied by fever, from viewing the falls at night. He was so ill that he was obliged to remain at Tivoli, and keep his bed. Growing worse, he was taken to Albano, as the air of Tivoli

[1] Thiele.

is hurtful to invalids. It was now expected that he would quickly rally; but the artist had not the requisite patience to remain quiet, and insisted, in spite of all advice, upon returning to Rome in so weak a condition that he had a return of one of his old attacks of depression. His friends now began to be seriously alarmed, and insisted upon his returning to the pure and bracing air of Albano; but he obstinately refused to go there alone, away from all society.

Miss Mackenzie, deeply concerned at the dangerous condition of the great artist, her friend, promised him that, if he went to Albano, she would go with her aunt to Genzano, which is in the neighborhood. She did so; and Thorvaldsen followed the two ladies, who visited him frequently and even came to live at Albano, that they might be at hand to give him the care which his state of health required. Such affectionate kindness and delicate attention, together with the pure air, produced a happy change; and Miss Mackenzie had the pleasure of seeing Thorvaldsen gradually restored to life and health. Her joy in such a result, and his tender gratitude, together with the influences of the spring in beautiful Italy, — to which an artist especially is so susceptible, — created a close bond between them.

It frequently happens that men of active minds, who apply themselves closely to work, continue young much longer than those whose existence has been frittered away in trivial pursuits. When these thinkers, these indefatigable workers, are turned aside from their usual course by any fortuitous circumstance, they surrender their hearts with the *naïveté* of children, and resume their youth just at the point where they seem to have left it behind forever.

Thorvaldsen was forty-eight years old. Nothing was more natural than that he should have yielded to a tender passion, but that he should have given himself up to it so unreservedly is indeed strange. He behaved like a youth of twenty. Instead of returning to Rome, though he was entirely convalescent, he planned a pleasure trip to Naples, and induced his friends to accompany him. Throughout all the journey he was not himself, but a young lover. In their charming excursions to Sorrento, to Capri, to Ischia, he cared so little to conceal his affection that Miss Mackenzie, seeing her British reserve in peril, was sometimes obliged to be cold in order to keep him within proper bounds. The artist would then appear to suffer all the torments of love. Rumors of this trip and the approaching marriage of Thorvaldsen were not slow in reaching Rome, and he even received letters of congratulation.

"Miss Mackenzie is a charming person," writes Baron von Schubart from Rome to Naples, where the artist still was. "She is well-born, and remarkably well-educated and intellectual. All the English hold her in high esteem; and the popularity you now enjoy with them must increase, if you marry their countrywoman. She has too good a heart not to make you perfectly happy, and everybody will applaud the union of two such excellent persons. I am even persuaded that, if it should be necessary, Miss Mackenzie would willingly adopt the little Eliza as her own child."

Thorvaldsen did not reply. He returned to Rome in the month of October, and his first interview with Anna Maria was terrible. The eyes of the jealous Italian flashed fire, her anger broke out in curses, and she finally threatened in her desperation that, if he dared to marry the Englishwoman, she would kill him, kill her child, and then put an end to her own wretched life. It was not in the artist's nature to hold out against such dreadful threats. Although he did nothing to appease the anger of his offended mistress, he feared to push her to the last extremity. He temporized, and when she saw that he was making no preparations for an approaching marriage her fears were gradually dispelled.

The return to Rome had also modified the situation. The young Scotch girl had been in the pleasant habit of seeing Thorvaldsen ever at her side, paying her assiduous court. When she saw him returning to his work, and busy in writing up a voluminous and delayed correspondence, she felt neglected, and committed the imprudence of showing herself a little piqued. Thorvaldsen perceived it, and thought this pretension almost ridiculous.

It is very certain that, enfeebled by illness, his imagination excited by the somewhat romantic circumstances attending his restoration to health, the artist had experienced a momentary intoxication. During the journey, the charm of a new life and the beauty of the scenery had contributed to prolong the illusion. Returning to Rome, and finding again in his atelier the true object of his worship, Art, the truth broke upon him; and he realized that his feelings were those of friendship only. From that time the rôles were reversed. He continued his visits, and was simply affectionate: the English girl became more and more demonstrative, and it soon became evident that there was no longer any love except in the heart of Miss Mackenzie.

While Thorvaldsen hesitated between his mistress, whose jealousy he still feared to exasperate, and her whom the world obstinately persisted in calling his betrothed, he began to detect between Miss Mackenzie and himself an incompatibility whether in character or habits of life, which seemed to him to be an obstacle to their living together in perfect harmony. The young girl was probably not quite beautiful enough to excite in an artist a veritable passion. Owing to her excellent British education, she had moreover very rigid ideas of propriety and social decorum, to which Thorvaldsen, who, though well-bred, was very unconventional, could scarcely accommodate himself. In the free and easy life they had led while travelling, this incompatibility was scarcely noticed; but in society at Rome it was felt in its full extent.

Time wore on, bringing no relief from this embarrassing situation. To put an end to it, a crisis was needed; and it was another woman who occasioned it. The artist's hour of fate was at hand. It was on the stroke of midnight, so it is related, on the last night of the old year (1818), that his heart was suddenly taken captive. When the worthy Herr Thiele records this event, upon which he does not love to dwell, he veils his face, and without hesitation pronounces a censure that may seem, perhaps, a little severe. "Henceforth," he says, "our artist appears willing to set at defiance all duty and the opinion of the world: he takes the wreath with which a host of admirers had encircled his brows, and sets it upon the abundant tresses of his adored goddess,—the sight of whose dazzling beauty transports him with joy,—whilst his Good Genius turns away his face and weeps."

There had just arrived in Rome, in company with a German family, a lady who also bore the name of Frances,—a woman in all the warm splendor of thirty-five, ardent and impassioned, whom her contemporaries describe as "a radiant setting sun, flushing with its golden rays a beautiful autumn evening." Is not that the artist's favorite hour? And shall we be as severe as Herr Thiele?

The sculptor and the lady became speedily enamoured. How far their *liaison* was close and complete, it is not for us to decide. Frequent visits, a very brisk correspondence,—that is all we know.

"Write in a letter *burn this* is the sure way to have it preserved," says somewhere the author of "Les Causeries d'un Curieux"; and this is precisely what happened to the tender Frances.

"Burn my letters," she does not fail to say again and again, "for no one must ever know that I write to you. The world judges in its own way. My heart declares me innocent, and yours must recognize me as such."

Now these notes are preserved with Thorvaldsen's other papers in one of the cabinets of the Museum. It is true that the gentlemen who are their custodians consider them as a sacred deposit, and never permit any indiscreet eye to rest upon them. However ardent the expressions in these letters, they offer no evidence of a nature to compromise their author, further than they prove the existence of one of those passionate attachments which find vent in words that evidently come from the heart, in soul-felt raptures, such as it would be vain to look for in a mere commonplace *liaison.* "With what joy I live over again in memory those delicious hours, when my heart was wholly my dear Alberto's, and his equally mine." Again: "Our love is all my happiness: I crave none other upon earth." . . . "My last thought, the last act of my life, will be a prayer for you." And when they must part: "Could you quit me like an indifferent acquaintance? That would be impossible!"

Thorvaldsen was equally enamoured, and according to Herr Thiele "was for some time only the satellite of this radiant star of love."

Letters in the mean while arrived for him from Scotland, where they were expecting soon to see the sculptor and his betrothed. Poor Miss Mackenzie, how she was then neglected! The artist gave bad reasons for his rare and irregular visits. These excuses were at first accepted. It is so hard to renounce a dream of happiness, it is so easy to deceive ourselves and cling to a dear illusion.

Unfortunately Thorvaldsen did not take much pains to conceal his behavior. The object of his passion lived directly opposite Miss Mackenzie; and the poor, forsaken girl could see him going day after day to visit her rival, could count the hours of their *tête-à-tête*, and compare them with those she passed neglected and alone!

She bore her grief in silence; she drank the cup presented to her without complaint, and was an object of compassion even to those who did not wish to see her the wife of the artist. Finally an English lady of rank, the common friend of both, thought it her duty to interfere, and to demand from Thorvaldsen a formal declaration of his intentions. In consequence of this explanation, Miss Mackenzie left Rome, May 5, 1819. She wrote to the sculptor from Florence some very dignified and truly touching letters, wherein she both reproaches and pardons him for his inconstancy in a truly Christian spirit. "If you enjoy all the blessings that I crave for you, you will be happier than I could have made you, even in the happiest days of our union. Adieu."

Directly upon writing these lines, she repaired to Switzerland, unwilling to appear in England, where her marriage had been announced in the papers.

A few years afterward (1826), Thorvaldsen was at a party, turning over the leaves of an album and talking gayly, when two ladies entered the same drawing-room. One of the two was Miss Mackenzie. The artist became pale and silent, and suddenly disappeared. In 1837, however, when Miss Mackenzie again returned to Rome, and years had softened the bitterness of this memory, they were reconciled through the kind offices of friends, though in future their relations were only those of friendship. Miss Mackenzie died in Rome, Feb. 24, 1840.

In conclusion, it is only just to add that Thorvaldsen was greatly distressed by the wrong he had done to the poor girl, whose letters deeply touched him. These regrets brought his *liaison* with the beautiful Viennese to a quicker termination, for in order to free himself from the difficulties of a false position he hastened to carry out his plan of a voyage to Denmark. He left Rome, July 14, 1819.

From this time Thorvaldsen seems to have been free from

all entanglements. Anna Maria herself no longer appears in his life; and, though we have no precise information on this point, we are inclined to believe that he separated from her before leaving Rome. He secured to her, however, a maintenance, and did not lose sight of his child.

THE AGES OF LOVE.

CHAPTER V.

The Lion of Lucerne. — Reception by the Academy of Copenhagen. — The Frue Kirke, or "Church of Our Lady." — "Journey through Germany." — The Emperor Alexander. — Monuments of Copernicus, Prince Poniatowski, Prince Potocki. — Return to Rome.

THE LION OF LUCERNE.

THORVALDSEN had been twenty-three years absent from his country, when his engagements finally permitted him to return. On leaving Rome, he went first to Florence, then to Parma, and to Milan, where he remained only a short time. He then crossed by the Simplon to Lucerne, whither he was called to make arrangements for the monument which Switzerland wished to raise to the memory of her children who died in defence of the Tuileries, Aug. 10, 1792.

The events of that fatal day which hastened the fall of the monarchy are well known. While Louis XVI, to "spare the nation a great crime," allowed himself to be dragged to the Assembly which a few hours later was to declare the abolition of royalty, the mob rushed to attack the Tuileries, which were guarded only by a handful of faithful defenders, consisting of noblemen, national and Swiss guards. These repulsed the assailants, and might perhaps have entirely put down the riot for that day, had not an order arrived from the king, commanding them not to fire upon the people, and to retire. A few, however, of the unfortunate Swiss remained in the palace, to whom it had not been possible to make known the royal will. Exposed to all the fury of the populace, they were massacred without mercy, heroic but unavailing victims of their devotion to a lost cause.

An officer of this loyal Swiss guard, who had escaped the rage of the mob, General Pfyffer von Altishofen, had retired to Lucerne. He conceived the idea of erecting in his garden a monument to the memory of his unfortunate comrades-in-arms. All Switzerland responded to the call, and numerous subscribers hastened to put down their names. Several sovereign princes also desired to contribute; and through Herr Vincenz Rüttiman, the Swiss ambassador at Rome, Thorvaldsen was solicited to execute the monument.

Though he was far from well at this time (1818), and little disposed to undertake any new works, he was induced to accept the commission, and modelled a sketch, representing a lion mortally wounded lying with his head resting upon the royal escutcheon of France, upon which he still maintains his hold. The conception is in keeping with the loftiness of the subject; while the grand simplicity of the composition is worthy of the chivalric devotion it was designed to perpetuate.

Bienaimé, one of Thorvaldsen's pupils, was employed to begin the work after the sketch of the master, and when this was done Thorvaldsen finished it himself. Never having seen a live lion, he went to antique statues for inspiration. The plaster was sent to Lucerne in the beginning of 1819. The monument was intended to be in bronze, but by Thorvaldsen's advice that idea was abandoned. An immense niche, thirty-two feet nine inches in height, was hollowed out of the solid rock, and there the sculptor Lucas Ahorn, copying the plaster model, carved out of the native granite the colossal lion. He began the work in March, 1820, and finished it in August, 1821.

Upon quitting Lucerne, Thorvaldsen continued his route through Schaffhausen, Stuttgart (where he visited the sculptor Dannecker, then engaged on a colossal statue of Christ), Heidelberg, Frankfort, Coblentz, Cologne, Munster, Hambourg, Sleswig, and arrived in Copenhagen the 3d of October.

He proceeded directly to the Charlottenborg Palace (the Academy of Fine Arts), where apartments had long been prepared for him. The first person he saw there was the old janitor, who had served as a model for the pupils when Thorvaldsen was one of the students. This meeting, bringing back as it did all the memories of his youth, filled him with deep emotion. He threw himself upon the neck of the old man, and embraced him affectionately.

The news of Thorvaldsen's arrival soon spread throughout the city. The friends of his childhood, and others who had been in Italy and had seen him in Rome, hastened to greet him. He gave them all a cordial welcome. Then followed a throng of people who knew him only by reputation. The artist, who still retained his simple manners, was a little bewildered by such an ovation. People crowded around him, he said, as though he were the great Kraken of the

North,[1] that marine monster celebrated in Scandinavian legends.[2]

Among the few friends of his boyhood was a counsellor of justice, Herr Haste,[3] who had accompanied him twenty-three years before on board the "Thetis." This magistrate thus relates his interview with the sculptor: —

> "When we were alone at last, — for he had had a court about him, like a foreign prince of illustrious lineage, — he went to his desk to get his album, and showed me some verses I had written in it as a souvenir twenty four or five years before. He pressed my hand silently, and returned to his desk from which he took a medal. 'See here, my dear friend,' said he, 'some friends in Rome who hold me in esteem have had this medal struck off in my honor. I have brought four with me, and I am going to give you one of them. It is only in bronze: I have a gold one, but I shall not give that to you. The man must not be forgotten in the metal.'"

Whilst all the journals vied with one another in giving Thorvaldsen a cordial welcome, the Academy of Copenhagen organized a grand reception, which took place on the 15th of October, in the great hall of the arquebusiers, and was attended by the whole city. The students went to meet the sculptor to the sound of drums and trumpets, and lined the street through which he passed. Cannon were fired, a cantata composed for the occasion was sung by the choral society, and the poet Oehlenschlaeger made a formal address. "If our ancestors," he remarked, "were once guilty of throwing down in Rome the old masterpieces of art, they are to-day, thanks to the genius of a son of the North, raised up again in all their pristine beauty."

The reception ended with a grand banquet, Thorvaldsen

[1] Nagler.

[2] The Norwegian sailors used often to relate stories about this extraordinary animal, which Bishop Pontoppidan has described in his Natural History of Norway. It is probable that it resembled in more than one respect the sea-serpent famous in our day.

[3] See note 1, page 4.

occupying the place of honor between Oehlenschlaeger and Count von Schimmelmann. The health of the students was proposed by the sculptor, a toast which was received with loud applause by all the assembly; but the enthusiasm became tremendous when Count von Schimmelmann rose and gave, "Here's to the fair daughters of Denmark, or, in other words, here's to the Graces of our Thorvaldsen." [1]

Finally the artist was received at court, and met with the most flattering reception from the king and all the royal family. To enable him to sit at the table of the sovereign without violating the strict etiquette of the period, the dignity of Counsellor of State was conferred upon him.

All these attentions were a little fatiguing to Thorvaldsen. He could not at first escape them even by retreating into his atelier; for to see the artist at work became the fashion of the day, and visit followed visit without cessation. A great lady, seeing him one day take some clay into his hands and begin to model, said to him, "I suppose, Herr Professor, you do not do such work yourself when you are in Rome!" "I assure you, madam," the artist replied good-naturedly, "that this is the most essential thing."

Advantage was taken, moreover, of Thorvaldsen's presence in Copenhagen, to consult him upon all questions relating to art: he was called upon to suggest the most suitable means for developing a taste for it in the country, and to make reports.[2]

Works for public buildings also occupied his attention. Not only the royal palace and the city hall were to be enriched with sculpture, but likewise the palace chapel and the Metropolitan Church of Our Lady, — the *Frue Kirke.*

This church had just been rebuilt, and Thorvaldsen was allowed free scope to follow the bent of his own fancy in the

[1] Thiele.

[2] He was also commissioned to make busts of Frederick VI, his queen, the two princesses royal, and the young Prince Frederick Charles Christian.

planning of its entire embellishment. And it was now that he first conceived the plan of that series of sculptural embellishments which was finally to embrace every part of the edifice inside and out, and in which are comprised almost all his works on religious subjects. For the pediment, "The Preaching of St. John the Baptist"; for the doorway, "Christ's Entry into Jerusalem"; for the inside of the church, the colossal "Christ and the Twelve Apostles"; behind the altar, the grand frieze of "Christ on the road to Calvary"; and for the side walls, "The Baptism of Christ" and "The Lord's Supper."

Though he received only the order for "The Preaching of St. John" and the "Christ and Twelve Apostles," at this time, his brief stay in Denmark was nevertheless profitable to himself as well as to his country. He left Copenhagen Aug. 12, 1820,[1] and travelling by easy stages returned to Italy by way of Germany. At Dresden and Berlin he was warmly welcomed by his friends. At Warsaw, whither he was called by negotiations long pending for important works, he arrived Sept. 19. Here he was presented to the Emperor Alexander.

The course pursued by the Sovereign of all the Russias at the time of the invasion of France by the allied troops, had made him very popular in Europe, nor was it forgotten in France that he had strenuously opposed Blucher's vindictive proposals to dismember the country.

Hearing that the sculptor wished to make his bust, he willingly consented, though he had refused a similar request of Canova, — perhaps because that sculptor's name had been so closely associated with Napoleon's family. Thorvaldsen, on the contrary, though a Dane, was the adopted sculptor of Germany. The emperor treated him with great kindness: he gave him several sittings, and when he found that the

[1] The government gave him 2,300 Danish crowns — about $1,400 — to pay his expenses.

military coat he wore was a hindrance to the artist he not only immediately bared his throat, but also his chest. It was, however, a point of etiquette that the sculptor should remain at a respectful distance from the Sovereign of all the Russias. Upon Thorvaldsen's falling ill, the emperor directly sent his own physician to him; and when the artist came to take leave of him, the monarch, who had previously presented him with a ring set in diamonds, threw aside all stiffness of etiquette, and embraced him cordially.

Before quitting Warsaw, Thorvaldsen had a few copies of the czar's bust hastily cast in plaster, and presented them to several grand personages; and after he returned to Rome he received so many orders that he kept for years skilled workmen continually employed in reproducing the bust in marble.

While Thorvaldsen was at Warsaw, the President of the Royal Society of the Friends of Science and Belles-Lettres of that city made an agreement with him for a monument in honor of Copernicus,[1] to be placed in the square of the University. The statue was finished three years later; but various circumstances prevented its being sent home, and the inauguration did not take place until May 11, 1830.

But the especial object of Thorvaldsen's journey to Poland was the equestrian statue of Prince Poniatowski. The first proposition in regard to it was made in a letter written in 1817, by Count Mokronowski, in the name of the committee formed for the purpose of erecting a monument to the Polish hero. Thorvaldsen now arranged the matter in person with

[1] The Poles have always shown themselves very proud of the works of Copernicus, who in 1504 was made member of the Academy of Cracow, a very high distinction, and much sought after at that period. In 1801, the Society of the Friends of Science at Warsaw proposed a prize for the best paper on the discoveries of this learned man. The statue to which we refer was erected at the cost of the Polish nation by means of a subscription; 40.000 florins, however, were still wanting to complete the required sum, and a learned minister of state, Abbé Staszic, paid the deficit out of his private purse.

the committee. But when he returned to Rome the work was so long neglected, that the delay led to a correspondence in which the Poles expressed their impatience, very urgently at first, and finally in very angry terms.[1]

The first idea of the sculptor was to represent the hero in the national dress, urging his horse to leap into the river where he met his death, while the animal hesitates and struggles with his rider. Water was to flow from a fountain in front of the pedestal. The first model, which was approved of by the committee, carried out this idea; but whether they changed their minds, or whether the family objected to the immediate cause of the hero's death being so plainly recalled, this model was thrown aside, and a thoroughly Roman statue substituted, representing the prince in antique costume. The work as it was finished has some resemblance to the equestrian statue of Marcus Aurelius on the Capitoline Hill. Finally completed in 1827, it was sent by way of Dantzic in 1828, and reached Warsaw in 1829. Owing to the time required to cast it in bronze, it was not ready to be put in its place before the 11th of May, 1830.

Then followed political complications; and the Russian government, not caring to allow the inauguration of a statue calculated to excite national sentiment in Poland, it was kept out of sight. What has become of it? It is difficult to say positively. Some assert that it was melted down and the bronze used for cannon; others, that it was only taken apart and placed in the arsenal of Modlin, where it was

[1] They wrote to him in 1825: "In choosing a sculptor to perpetuate the glory of Copernicus and Poniatowski, the whole nation has unanimously selected you, as the artist the most famous and most worthy of rescuing from oblivion some memories at least of our past glory. Can so noble and lofty a heart be insensible to such a choice? It often happens that artists are forced to celebrate pride without merit; but you, sir, in working for Poland, have undertaken a more honorable task, that of immortalizing the sublimest virtues, creative genius, valor, and patriotic devotion. Let these motives speak to your heart, warm your genius, quicken your creative chisel. Send us as soon as possible your masterpieces, that Poland, in contemplating her heroes may bless the artist who has restored them to life."

still to be found in 1842. According to a journal, the "Kunstblatt,"[1] the Russian government thought of transporting it to Russia, and the family protesting against this attempt it was melted down. But we are more inclined to credit the version of the "Athenæum."[2] According to the English journal, the pieces of this statue were given to the Prince of Warsaw,[3] who, in putting them together, changed Poniatowski into a Saint George. Under this title the statue was removed to his country-seat in Mohilew. If this be so, it was the fate of the unfortunate prince to be deprived of his national garb that he might enjoy an apotheosis as a Roman general, only to be finally transformed into a canonized saint.

While at Warsaw, Thorvaldsen decided to comply with the wishes of the Princess Potocka. This lady was anxious that the artist should design a mausoleum in memory of her husband, Prince Potocki, killed at the battle of Leipsic. She had written to him upon the subject as far back as 1816. It was the wish of the princess that the monument should be placed in one of the chapels of the cathedral of Cracow. It was to consist of a group of two figures, one personifying the hero prematurely cut down at twenty-two, the other Poland, under the form of a beautiful woman, stately and Juno-like.

Thorvaldsen repaired to Cracow, in October, 1820, and persuaded the princess to consent to a change of plan; and subsequently merely represented the young prince leaning on his sword. This figure recalls to mind that of the Apollo Belvedere, to which the artist had been requested to go for inspiration.

From Cracow, Thorvaldsen proceeded to Troppau, where

[1] No. 40, p. 160, 1842.

[2] No. 1162, p. 139, 1850.

[3] The "Athenæum" must mean General Paskewitsch, who, having forced the capital of Poland to capitulate, Sept. 8, 1831, and placed the country again under the Russian yoke, was made Prince of Warsaw by Alexander.

the Congress was assembled. He was honorably received by these illustrious personages, especially by the Emperor of Austria, to whom he had been recommended by the czar. The Emperor Francis gave him a commission for a monument in memory of Prince of Schwarzenberg, for which the artist made a sketch; but for some cause, unknown to us, the order was not fulfilled.

Thorvaldsen was at Vienna, where he had passed three pleasant weeks, when he heard, while at the house of the Prince Esterhazy, of a serious accident to his Roman ateliers. The news was reported in the "Diario di Roma." A letter from his pupil Freund, received nearly at the same time, gave him the particulars. The floor of one of the ateliers in the Palace Barberini had given way, and two marble statues, "The Young Shepherd" and "Love," had fallen with it. The head of the shepherd, the arm which held the crook, and the ears of the dog, were broken off. "Love" had lost its wings and right leg The plaster of "Ganymede with the Eagle" was broken in pieces. Thanks to the efforts of Tenerani and Freund, the other statues were rescued from the ruins almost uninjured. By a very lucky chance, the statue of "Adonis," placed that very morning near the wall, escaped unhurt.

Thorvaldsen had intended to go to Munich; but this bad news decided him to return immediately to Rome, where he arrived Dec. 16, 1820.

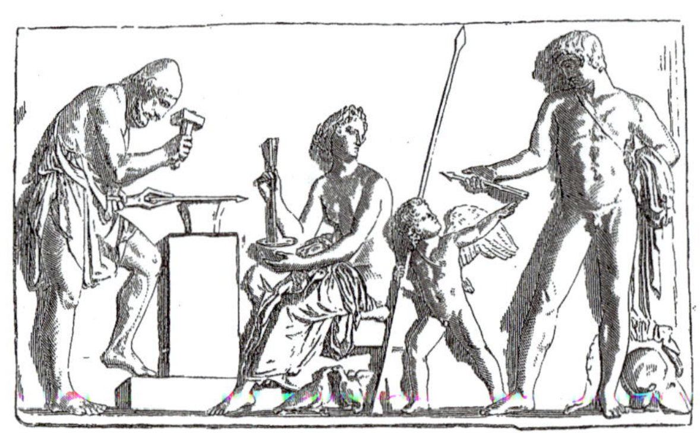

VULCAN FORGING ARROWS FOR CUPID.

CHAPTER VI.

The Prince Royal of Denmark. — Prince Louis of Bavaria. — "Christ and the Apostles." — The "Preaching of St. John the Baptist." — Consalvi. — Pius VII. — Cabals against Thorvaldsen. — Leo XII. — Thorvaldsen President of the Academy of St. Luke.

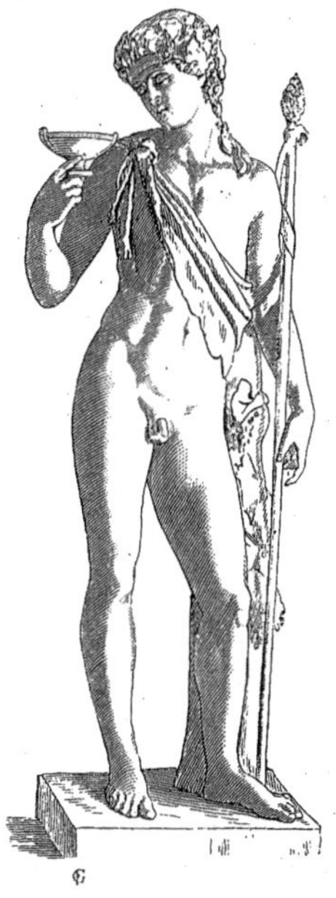

BACCHUS.

A FEW days after Thorvaldsen's return to Rome, a grand banquet was given in his honor at the *Trattoria Fiano*, Dec. 28, 1820. More than one hundred and fifty artists were present. The gayety was at its height, when Christian, prince royal of Denmark, presented himself and asked permission to join the party. He took a seat next to the sculptor, and his presence far from being a restraint upon the assembly only increased the hilarity; while his toast to cisalpine and trans-alpine art excited to the highest point the enthusiasm of the guests, who were chiefly Germans.

Subsequently the Prince and Princess of Denmark visited the ateliers of the artist, who constituted himself their cicerone, and introduced them to the antiquities of Rome. He also modelled their busts.

For a long time Thorvaldsen had been in constant correspondence with Prince Louis of Bavaria; but from the year

1821, when the prince and the artist met in Rome, relations of the strictest intimacy, notwithstanding the difference of rank, were established between them. The Prince of Bavaria who, in 1825, succeeded to the throne, is one of the most original and interesting characters of this century. When still young, he was enamoured, like all Europe at that time, with military glory, and took part in the campaign of 1809 against Austria. But the pupil of the universities of Landshut and Göttingen soon abandoned the career of arms to give himself wholly to an irresistible love of the arts. Hereafter he kept aloof from public affairs, and devoted himself with all the enthusiasm of his nature to pursuits no less worthy of a fine intellect. To enrich Bavaria with splendid museums, and to make Munich one of the great artistic cities of the world, was the one earnest desire of his heart. Compared with the magnitude of his projects, his means, unfortunately, were limited. He was not, however, discouraged by this difficulty. Imposing upon himself a strict economy, with the money thus saved he bought up the choicest works he could find either in painting or sculpture. The Greek and Roman antiquities which zealous explorers were then actively engaged in excavating from the soil of Greece and Italy were the special objects of his passion, and his agents did their best to secure them for him.

Thus little by little was formed that magnificent museum of sculpture called the Glyptothek. When he became king, he enriched his capital with fine monuments, mostly in the Greek style. We also owe to him a picture gallery, the new Pinacothek, at Munich; also the Walhalla, a sort of temple and museum, at Ratisbon. The prince, moreover, cultivated the Muses: his writings in prose and verse indicate, in a very marked degree, the peculiarities of his character.[1]

[1] Though very popular at first, the King of Bavaria lost favor with the nation on account of the undue influence which from 1830 he allowed the clergy to exert. His *liaison* with the beautiful Lola Montes is well known. Though this favorite of the

In 1821, Thorvaldsen modelled the bust of the prince, who promised him his portrait in exchange. On the eve of his royal friend's departure, the sculptor gave a grand banquet in his honor at the Signora Buti's, to which all the artists in Rome were invited. How much the prince enjoyed the fête is seen by the letter he wrote immediately after his return to Munich.

NYMPHENBOURG, near Munich, May 15, 1821.

HERR COUNSELLOR OF STATE, —

No, not that. Dear, good, and great Thorvaldsen! Kings are indeed powerless to bestow what is signified by that name. Long after military glory — glory stained with blood — has ceased its din, the name of the great artist still lives, pure, sublime, blessed of Heaven, and his immortal works forever engender others. My last hours in Rome were made pleasant by the banquet kindly given me by my excellent Thorvaldsen. But to say good-by was all the more painful.

Say many kind things from me to the worthy family Buti and to Nano. Do not forget to remember me to the Signora Girometti, a true, very true Roman woman; nor to the amiable Moretta.[1]

I made the journey in ten days, so Rome does not seem so far off. I am at home again, and you, beloved and excellent men, are still near my heart. I leave to-morrow for Wurzbourg. My portrait, therefore, may not reach Rome before next winter. I prefer that you should get it later, rather than in a bad condition, you who have represented me in living marble. Adieu, till we meet again.

LOUIS, Prince Royal, who sets great store by his Thorvaldsen.

old king professed liberal principles, her interference in affairs of state was the cause of fresh complications, and she was obliged to leave Bavaria, in February, 1848. The month following (March 20), the king was forced to abdicate in favor of his eldest son, Maximilian II.

King Louis, who lived to be an octogenarian, continued to the last to interest himself in the fine arts, and to patronize artists. He also regained all his old popularity, the nation remembering only the wise administration of the finances during his reign; nor was it forgotten that Bavaria owed to him the fine canal that unites the Danube to the Maine, and bears his name "Ludwigskanal" The first railroad in Germany — from Nuremburg to Furth — is also one of his enterprises.

[1] The letter of the prince is in German, excepting this sentence: "Dite della mia parte molte belle cose alla brava famiglia Buti ed ad Nano, e non dimenticatemi presso la vera, la verissima Romana, la Signora Girometti, neppure presso l'amabile Moretta." Even in German, King Louis had a style peculiarly his own, which is often as odd as it is original.

On the 16th of October, 1822, the prince writes again: —

Dear, well-beloved, and great Thorvaldsen, — I am very happy to hear that my painted portrait pleases you. When you look at it, remember that it represents a man who, separated from you by the Alps and the Apennines, is still always near you in thought.

In conclusion, he says: —

I am very anxious that the "Ilioneus Niobides" should be restored by you, and that the "Adonis" (the marble) should be finished by your master-hand. Be kind enough, also, not to forget the gospel bas-reliefs;[1] and you will infinitely oblige him who has for you the greatest esteem and deepest affection.

These intimacies with royal personages made no change in the character of Thorvaldsen. Since his return to Rome he had been constantly occupied; for he had not only to execute important works for his own country, but others of no less importance to Germany. The monuments to Poniatowski, Prince Potocki, Field-Marshal Schwarzenberg (a sketch only was made of the latter), and to Copernicus, required an immense deal of room, and obliged him to provide himself with new ateliers. He had, however, a perfect phalanx of pupils and workmen, who in their several capacities rendered him important services.[2] It is not surprising that he needed so many auxiliaries, when we consider that the master was working at the same time on the "Christ," the "Twelve Apostles," the "Preaching of St. John the Baptist,"

[1] These bas-reliefs must be those which the artist undertook to model in 1817, and which represent the "Annunciation of the Virgin," and the "Holy Women at the Sepulchre." The prince wanted the marbles for a church he proposed to erect in Munich.

[2] Herr Thiele gives the list of those who assisted him at this time, some of whom became themselves famous artists: Amadeo, Babone, Bardi, the brothers Bienaimé, Bogazzi, Cali, Carlesi, De Angelis, Ercole the Hungarian, Ferenczy, Freund, Gaëti, Galli, Hermann (Joseph), Hofer, Kauffmann, Kessels, Landini, Launitz, Leeb, Livi, Marchetti, Mareschalchi, Michelangelo, Moglia, Moïse, Monti, Orlowski, Paccetti, Pettrich, Raggi, Restaldi, Santi, Schneider, Stephan the Hungarian, Tacca, Tanzi, the brothers Tenerani, Vacca, Wolff. Here we have already a respectable phalanx, though some names may be forgotten in the list.

and all those grand compositions which ornament to-day the *Frue Kirke* at Copenhagen.

Each day brought also a new order, sometimes it was a bust, sometimes the reproduction of a former work. Nor must we forget his spontaneous efforts, his artistic fantasies, the fruit of a fertile imagination.

One day he received a note from the Baroness Reden, wife of the Hanoverian minister at Rome. "The little Albanese," she writes, "whom I spoke to you about at the Prince of Denmark's, has just come: she will be here with me until four o'clock. If you would like to see her, I shall be delighted to introduce her to you."

This little Albanese was a remarkably beautiful child about thirteen years old, whom the Secretary of the Hanoverian Legation had seen while passing on horseback through one of the streets of Albano. The young girl, who belonged to a poor family and was named Vittoria Cardoni, became famous among the artists. All the painters and sculptors endeavored to reproduce a beauty at once so pure, so perfect, and so strange; but, as all confessed, none of them fully succeeded, and Thorvaldsen no better than the rest. He, however, made use of the pretty bust he modelled from her for one of the female figures in the "Preaching of St. John." It is the woman seated and holding a child.

After leaving Copenhagen, Thorvaldsen seems to have devoted much thought to his grand religious works. In an old pocket-book which he had with him on his journey, a number of sketches have been found of the apostles or other biblical figures, which were either passing fancies of his own, or hints gathered from works he had seen in his travels. On reaching Rome, he went seriously to work and made a large number of drawings. As early as 1821 he began his sketches in clay. As soon as a few of these were ready, he called in his pupils to his aid. His custom was to give the clay sketch to a pupil, with precise directions respecting the living model who was to sit for it, and the casting of the drapery; the master, while the work was in progress, correcting and modifying and sometimes beginning it again. It was only by this means that he was enabled to carry on with such rapidity and simultaneously so large a number of works.

The "Saint Paul" was intrusted to a young artist who did not prove equal to the task, and the master himself modelled it anew. To Bienaimé, the elder, was given the study of "Saint Peter," and he succeeded better in bringing his sketch to the desired point. These two apostles are incontestably very superior to the other ten.

When after many trials Thorvaldsen had fully decided upon the attitude he would give his "Christ," he admitted Tenerani to a certain participation in the work, but only to study the details of the figure. Subsequently, when engaged himself upon the large clay model, he was attacked with lumbago caused by the dampness of the atelier, and he therefore again put the figure temporarily into the hands of Tenerani. Though forced to give up a work which required the free use of his limbs, he could not remain inactive; and he employed his leisure in fulfilling a commission of the Milan Academy of Fine Arts for a monument to Appiani, representing the Genius of Art singing the praises of the painter, while the Graces deplore his death.

As soon as Thorvaldsen had recovered from his attack, he again took into his own hands the statute of "Christ," finishing the clay with care. Meanwhile the "Apostles" and the "Preaching of St. John" were slowly advancing under the hands of his pupils,[1] so that in 1822 this complex work had

[1] Bienaimé, the younger, Tenerani, the younger, and Marchetti, were intrusted with "Saint Matthew," "Saint Thomas," and "Saint James." The other apostles were studied, "Saint Philip," by Pettrich; "Saint James," by Bienaimé, the younger; "Saint Simon," by Emile Wolff; "Saint Bartholomew," by Carlesi; "Saint Andrew," by Joseph Hermann. As to the "Saint John," executed by Paccetti, it was put aside, and begun again in 1824 by Marchetti. Paccetti's was modified subse-

already made great progress, and a large portion of it been put into plaster.

It had soon to undergo the bitter criticism of jealousy. This did not seem, however to disturb the artist who, encouraged by the approbation of competent judges, wrote to a friend: "My recent works of large dimensions, especially the models of the colossal statues of 'Christ,' and the apostles 'Saint Peter' and 'Saint Paul,' have been fortunate in securing the approbation of all the connoisseurs in this city."

Passing from one composition to another with remarkable versatility, Thorvaldsen carried on at the same time his works intended for Germany; going from his "Christ" to the monument of Poniatowski, and from the "St. John" to the statue of Prince Potocki, or the monument of Copernicus.

In the summer of 1822 he found near his atelier a large building extremely well lighted which had served as a stable for the Palace Barberini. He quickly converted it into what he called his "grand atelier," because he immediately collected and placed in it his models of large size. All the figures in the "Preaching of St. John the Baptist" were here set up, so that the effect of the composition as a whole could now be estimated. In 1823, he composed his first "Angel of Baptism."[1]

Thorvaldsen was now at the zenith of his fame: he had not even a rival in Rome since Canova's death, in October, 1822 Six months afterward the arts were threatened with another loss: an accident happened to the Danish sculptor

quently and used for "Saint Thaddeus," in order to finish in haste the twelve apostles when the artist was urged to send without delay all the plasters to Copenhagen, because they wished to consecrate the new church. These plasters were sent from Leghorn, January, 1828.

[1] This work, which was not included in the contract, he intended to present to the *Frue Kirke*; but Lord Lucan, having bespoken it in marble, Thorvaldsen soon after made a new composition in which the angel is kneeling, and it is this which is now in the church.

which might have cost him his life. Thorvaldsen, after having supped as usual at the Signora Buti's, had returned to his rooms accompanied by the son of this lady. The child was very anxious to join with other boys of his age in the noisy demonstrations with which Easter is celebrated in Rome, and Thorvaldsen had promised to lend him his pistols. While the artist pulled the trigger of one to make sure it was not loaded, the young Buti possessed himself of the other. It went off and Thorvaldsen fell, wounded. The shock was violent, but fortunately the wound was not serious. Two fingers of the left hand were struck; but the ball had spent its force in passing through his clothing, and after encountering a rib, from which it glanced off, finally flattened itself against a button. Thorvaldsen was obliged to nurse himself a little, and wear his arm in a sling for a few days. His friends could do no less than celebrate such a providential escape. A grand fête was given upon the occasion, and numerous felicitations in prose and verse were addressed to the artist.

Thorvaldsen, whose intercourse with the great dignitaries of the Roman Church had hitherto been very slight, had now an opportunity to be presented by the Prince of Denmark to the illustrious Cardinal Ercole Consalvi, the able adversary of Napoleon I., the negotiator of the Concordat, and upon whom fell the chief burden of the quarrel between the Papacy and the Empire.

The Romans professed a great veneration for Pius VII., and had almost as much for Consalvi, who deserved it no less. As to the cardinal, he gave to the Holy Father the respect and affection of a son; and from the year 1822 had proposed to himself the erection of a monument to his memory, though the Pontiff at that time was still living. In the will of Consalvi[1] is this clause: —

[1] See the "Memoirs of Cardinal Consalvi," by J. Crétineau, Joly, vol. i., 2d ed., 1866. H. Plon.

Deeming it unbecoming that so famous a pontiff as Pius VII. and one who has deserved so well of church and state, should not have after his death (may God prolong his days) a tomb in the basilica of St. Peter, which seems likely on account of the small inheritance he will leave to his nephews, I, moved by my devotion and attachment to his sacred person, inspired by the gratitude I owe to him, as the first cardinal of his creation, and loaded with benefits through his sovereign goodness, have resolved to erect to him at my own expense a mausoleum in the aforesaid basilica. To this end I have endeavored, by retrenching my annual expenses, to set aside the sum of twenty thousand Roman crowns. If I die before his Holiness, as I hope to do, upon my heir and trustee will devolve the duty of applying the above sum to the erection of this tomb; the execution of which shall be confided to the chisel of the celebrated Marquis Canova, and failing him to the celebrated Chevalier Thorvaldsen, and, if he cannot execute it, to one of the best sculptors in Rome. The following inscription shall be engraved on this tomb: —

PIO VII., CHARAMONTIO, CÆSENATI, PONTIFICI MAXIMO.
HERCULES, CARDINALIS CONSALVI ROMANUS.
AB ILLO CREATUS.

The tomb shall have three statues: one on the urn, that of the Pope himself; on the two sides, the virtues, Strength and Wisdom.

Signed, E. CARDINAL CONSALVI.

ROME, Aug. 1, 1822.

Pius VII. preceded his faithful friend to the tomb, to the profound grief of Consalvi, who now took steps to put into execution the project recorded in his will; but, as Canova was dead, he sent for Thorvaldsen. This was in the month of November, 1824. When the messenger came to notify the artist, he was engaged upon one of his religious works, the "Angel of Baptism." Surprised at the message, he repaired to the palace inhabited by the cardinal, and upon giving his name was received with respect and conducted to His Eminence.

Thorvaldsen, who had the highest veneration for the prelate, so highly appreciated the honor done him by the offer of the commission, that with his usual rashness he accepted it in spite of the immense amount of work with which he was already overwhelmed. In returning to his studio, he, so habitually discreet and reserved, related with exultation to the friends he met the extraordinary instance of good fortune, as he regarded it, which had befallen him.

In confiding to him, a Protestant, the erection of a monument in St. Peter's to the head of the Catholic Church, the cardinal undoubtedly gave him a high proof of esteem. But in default of Canova, the Catholic sculptor, Consalvi could find no artist who could be preferred to Thorvaldsen. Such is the interpretation we put on the terms of the will, which assigns only a secondary place to the Danish sculptor.

This commission caused great surprise in Rome. Thorvaldsen's enemies made it the occasion for new and violent attacks. All went on well, however, while the cardinal lived, and the artist had no reason to be disturbed by the cabal. He accordingly set to work, following the precise instructions given him, and from which it would have been difficult to deviate. It was then the established rule, founded on precedents, that a monument in honor of a deceased pope should be composed of the portrait of the pontiff and two allegorical figures. The form was of necessity to be pyramidal, so that it might be placed in one of those great niches designed for such works, in the interior of St. Peter's.

The first sketch, in clay, was made in January, 1824.[1] The Pope is seated: he has a palm-branch in his hand, while two angels hold above his head a starry crown. This composition was not accepted, because these two attributes, the

[1] The first two sketches found of this monument are hastily pencilled, the one on the back of a letter dated Nov. 12, 1823, the second on another letter of 10th December. (Thiele.) In the Museum of Copenhagen a great number of similar sketches are preserved.

palm and crown, belong to saints; and of course Pius VII., who had just died, was not canonized.

On the 24th of January, 1824, at the age of sixty-seven, Cardinal Consalvi died, universally mourned. He had long before placed in the *Monte di Pietà*,[1] in Rome, the twenty thousand crowns for the erection of the monument; and, thanks to this deposit, no difficulty could be made with the artist concerning payment. But he was subjected to many annoyances through envy and intolerance, and was far from seeing the end of the vexations this affair was to cause him.

Thorvaldsen made another sketch, in which the Pope is represented as resigning all his pomp as sovereign and pontiff. He has laid aside the tiara, and is seated, bowed down under his sufferings. Though there was much pathos in the composition, it did not agree with the received ideas of the church,—it was not thus the Father of the Faithful should be represented at the moment of his earthly deliverance. He had therefore to compose still another model.

While the artist was thus occupied, he also gave his attention to the bust of the Holy Father, having already studied the face. He had several good pictures to refer to, and a mask above all was very useful to him. Hardly had he begun this part of his work, when the cardinal died.

The numerous friends of Consalvi desired to have a medal struck in honor of the illustrious statesman. A committee was formed, headed by the Duchess of Devonshire and the Hanoverian ambassador, Baron von Reden. The subscription-list, filling rapidly up, reached so large an amount, that after two medals had been struck off, one by Girometti, the

[1] This deposit was made a few days after his first interview with the sculptor. In the official declaration made at the time, Consalvi states that the sum is deposited by a person who is not named, doubtless because he was averse to publicly parading himself as the donor. But the recent publication of his will, the last clause of which we have given, affords positive information on this point.

other by Cerbara, there remained a surplus of seven hundred and sixty-four crowns.[1] It was therefore decided to erect a monument in honor of the cardinal, and Thorvaldsen was sent for. The artist, glad of the opportunity to show his respect, immediately accepted the commission.

The monument was to be placed in the Pantheon, where the heart of the cardinal was deposited. With the aid of a bust belonging to Signor Torlonia, of a portrait painted by Lawrence, and the medal of Girometti, Thorvaldsen modelled the bust; and, being assisted by the suggestions of a person who had lived long and familiarly with the cardinal, he produced a faithful portrait as well as a fine work of art.[2]

The erection of the monument was delayed by unforeseen obstacles: to remove them, Baron von Reden had recourse to the new Pope, and it was not without difficulty that the mausoleum was inaugurated the 17th September, 1824.

As the sarcophagus bore only a simple inscription, the artist thought the monument incomplete, and took upon himself the expense of a supplementary bas-relief. One of the most important services rendered by the cardinal to the Papacy was beyond dispute the recovery, by his able negotiations at the Vienna Congress, of the provinces lost to the Holy See by the treaty of Tolentino in 1799. In Thorvaldsen's composition these provinces are symbolized by six female figures who, presented to Pius VII. by Consalvi, kneel to the Holy Father while he gives them his benediction.[3]

[1] Thiele.

[2] The committee gave Thorvaldsen for his marble the sum of four hundred and forty crowns, and the remaining three hundred and twenty-four crowns were employed in the purchase of the sarcophagus.

[3] Shortly after Thorvaldsen had made the committee a present of this bas-relief, he in turn received, through Baron von Reden its president, a silver cup. ornamented with medallions. It bore the effigy of the cardinal, with the following inscription encircled by vine-leaves: "Gli Amici del Defunto Card. Consalvi all' Amico A. Thorvaldsen. Roma. MDCCCXXV." The artist subsequently gave this cup to his daughter. (Thiele.)

The monument to Consalvi was completed long before that of Pius VII., which required a great deal more labor and study. The latter was not, however, neglected; and a third sketch, which satisfied both the artist and the persons appointed to carry out the wishes of the deceased cardinal, was finished by the end of the year 1824. It represented the Pope clothed in his sacerdotal robes and seated in his pontifical chair; his heavy cope falls over his left arm, his right hand is raised in the act of benediction.

The sketch having been accepted, Thorvaldsen set to work to finish the monument, taking care meanwhile to maintain a prudent reserve with regard to it.[1] The statue of the Pope himself was completed in 1825; and, becoming directly the subject of discussion in Rome, occasion was given to the envious to attack it as the work of a heretic. This hostility, however, had no other effect upon Thorvaldsen than to make him devote himself with all the more ardor to the completion of his task. The other two statues, "Strength" and "Wisdom," were already designed: Thorvaldsen put them at once into the hands of the pupils who were to model from them the first sketches in relief. "Little do I care for these cabals," he used to say to his friends: "I have got the commission for the monument, and I shall finish it, I promise you."

At the very time while the spirit of intolerance was busy exciting these miserable jealousies, the artist, by a singular coincidence, was solicited, in behalf of the Convent of the Capuchins, to make an ornamented cross with inscriptions, intended for the *Piazza dei Cappuccini* adjoining the *Piazza Barberini*. It was scarcely a work worthy of Thorvaldsen;

[1] Bienaimé was the pupil selected to make from it a colossal model. The bust had already been finished by Thorvaldsen, who had been long at work upon it. The head was to be covered with the tiara, and that the drapery might be easier modelled the pontifical robes were intrusted to the artist. In consequence, no visitors were, during that time, admitted to the atelier.

but, comprehending the advantage that might accrue to him from having such a commission, he accepted it willingly, and tried so hard to satisfy the monks that the cross was soon erected (April 20, 1825). He would receive no compensation for it, a piece of generosity which very much impressed the Capuchins. We may, however, be permitted to suspect that they had shrewdly anticipated such a result, when applying to a heretic artist. However this may be, the sculptor's liberality is recorded on the paper containing the estimate of the cost, where we read: "Tutto è conchiuso! S. Francesco é un gran Santo! Saremo quattro benefattori. Il Cavaliere Thorvaldsen, benefattore, s' incarica dell' esecuzione," etc.

Thus the artist was enabled to refute with a new fact[1] the argument which had been used against him, that a Protestant could not properly be intrusted with the execution of a work having a Catholic destination. To reply in this manner was better than any argument.

Meanwhile the mausoleum of Pius VII. was not finished, and even those who defended Thorvaldsen though he did not pay sufficient attention to it. The truth was that the artist, overwhelmed with the vast amount of work he had on hand, could not devote himself exclusively to any one subject. His enemies took advantage of this delay, to accuse him of a want of respect to the memory of the Holy Father. They wrote shameful anonymous letters,[2] and the cabal became so powerful, that it was for a moment doubtful whether the monument would be erected in St. Peter's. Two unexpected circumstances, however, foiled these hostile attempts.

Canova, who was President of the Academy of St. Luke at the time of his death, was succeeded in this honorable post by the historical painter Camuccini. But after three years, according to the regulations of the Academy, the painter was

[1] The monument of Consalvi had been inaugurated the preceding year.

[2] See Thiele, vol. ii. chap. xii.

to be replaced by a sculptor. Thorvaldsen's superiority made him the proper person to fill the presidential chair; and his enemies, who had no strong candidate to oppose to him, were in a complete quandary. His friends loudly declared that it would be a disgrace to the Academy to nominate any one but him, while his opponents replied that it would be a positive scandal to invest with such functions an artist who was not a Catholic. But, whatever the result, the controversy could only redound to the honor of the sculptor; for, if he were rejected, it would only be for reasons which had nothing to do with art: his merit was not called in question. Thorvaldsen made merry with his friends over the embarrassment of the party in opposition. That the majority was in his favor was not doubtful, but there was another difficulty in the case, which even his partisans looked upon as serious. The President of the Academy in the discharge of his duties was, on certain solemn occasions, obliged to be present in his official character at the ceremonies of the Church; and the question now arose, whether the pontifical government would be pleased that a Protestant artist should, in such cases, be called upon to represent the Academy. It was thought prudent to submit the matter to the Holy Father. "Is there any doubt that he is the greatest sculptor we have now in Rome?" asked Leo XII. "The fact is incontestable," was the reply. "Then there can be no hesitation, and he must be made president. Only there are times when he will see the propriety of being indisposed." The words of the Sovereign Pontiff removed all scruples. Dec. 16, 1825, Thorvaldsen was elected President of the Academy of St. Luke by a majority of votes, for the usual term of three years. The decoration *pro merito* belonging to this title was sent to him.

The liberal decision of Leo XII. argued well for the erection of the monument of Pius VII.; but the Sovereign Pontiff went still further. Expressing a desire to see the mausoleum of his predecessor, he signified his intention of going in person to the atelier of the president of the Academy. In one way this was a token of official approbation. The Holy Father came, and pausing, so it is said, by accident before the bas-relief of the "Ages of Love," highly appreciated the ingenious delicacy of that profane composition.

This bas-relief was modelled during the Holy Week of 1824. For several days, according to custom, the ateliers were all closed; and the artist profited by the seclusion to compose this charming creation, as a rest to his mind after his great works. He had first intended the composition to decorate a vase for which he had long been keeping a large block of Carrara marble. The subject was suggested to him by the famous picture found at Stabiæ, — "The Sale of Loves." In Thorvaldsen's bas-relief, Psyche plays the part of saleswoman. She distributes the loves according to the ages of the customers. This graceful composition had an immense success, and was reproduced so many times that the sculptor had not always the leisure to superintend carefully enough the different copies.[1]

Notwithstanding the visit of Leo XII., the monument of Pius VII. remained still a long time in hand before it was finished. Difficulties of another kind also retarded its erection. In November, 1830, the artist was sent for to make a careful examination of the place designed for it in St. Peter's; when, not having been aware that the Pontiff was to be buried in the mausoleum, he found he had made a wrong estimate of the length required,[2] — a mistake which greatly affected the general aspect of the monument. Nor was this all. The height of the recess having been incorrectly measured, the

[1] Later, he was himself astonished at the great difference he found between one of the copies and the original. The first marble, which is a simple bas-relief, was executed for Mr. Labouchère. This Englishman was then at Rome urging Thorvaldsen to finish the statue of "Venus" which he had ordered.

[2] It was necessary to make the length correspond to that of the coffin.

whole system of proportions, which was made dependent upon the principal figure, was found to be wrong. In the endeavor to restore the general equilibrium of the monument, two new figures were added, — two angels placed at the right and left of the Pontiff.[1]

It required all the skill of the artist to surmount these difficulties; but at last, after many vexatious delays and impediments, the monument of Pius VII. was finally erected in the Church of St. Peter at Rome, in 1831, seven years after the commission for it had been given by Cardinal Consalvi.

[1] Thorvaldsen, who was determined not to leave the monument incomplete, modelled these angels with incredible rapidity, putting the plasters for the time being in place of the marbles, which were finished subsequently. (Thiele.)

HORSEMAN, FROM THE FRIEZE, "THE TRIUMPH OF ALEXANDER.

CHAPTER VII.

The Monument to Appiani. — Criticisms upon it. — The Monuments to Prince Schwarzenberg and to the Duke of Leuchtenberg. — The King of Bavaria in Rome. — The Grand Duchess Helena. — Maria Louisa. — Bust of Napoleon. — Medals stolen from Thorvaldsen. — Journey to Munich. — Bartolini.

GANYMEDE.

THE history of the mausoleum of Pius VII. has obliged us to anticipate a little: we now return, therefore, to the period at which Thorvaldsen was zealously working upon his grand sacred compositions for Copenhagen and the large sepulchral monuments for Germany.

We have already referred to a monument in memory of Appiani, inaugurated at Milan. In August, 1826, the committee sent a letter of warm thanks to the sculptor, accompanied by two copies of the commemorative medal struck off at the time. Notwithstanding this official approbation, the work was very soon subjected to severe criticisms; and so ill-natured an article appeared in the "Estensore di Milano" of the 3d of September, that the artist's friends hastened to write complimentary letters to him on the subject. Among the expression of sympathy called forth by this occasion, one highly appreciated by Thorvaldsen himself deserves special mention. It was from the bootmaker Anselmo Ronghetti. This man, who was a very skilful workman, had a great passion for the art of sculpture. Thorvaldsen had known him since the year 1819, and held him in high esteem, as he did every artisan who excelled in his trade: he often spoke of him and looked upon him as a friend. He had left casts of his feet with him, and the bootmaker was in the habit of sending him from time to time some new masterpiece of his workmanship. He also wrote to him twice or thrice a year; and did not fail to do so on the occasion of the Appiani monument, forwarding at the same time a pair of boots, of a new style called *ronghettines*, which the artist received with great pleasure. His acknowledgment of the present Ronghetti had framed, and hung it up in his shop, where he had also placed the bust of Lord Byron given to him by the sculptor. Opposite was a work by Marchetti.[1]

Among the enthusiastic admirers of Thorvaldsen in Rome was a very celebrated improvisatrice named Rosa Taddei. It is well known how fond the Italians are of these *Academie*

[1] Ronghetti, as his letters show, was very tenacious of his personal dignity. Like most Italians, he was also very sharp and quick-witted. One day a dandy from Paris, who was under the necessity of getting a pair of boots in Milan, came to the shop and was imprudent enough to express openly his regret at being reduced to such an extremity. The bootmaker flushed up to the roots of his hair with anger, but, concealing his rage at this blow to his vanity, said meekly, that, lest he might not succeed upon a first trial, he would only make one boot, which would serve as a guide for any alterations that might be required. It proved to be a marvel of its kind, and so delighted the dandy that he hastened to the shop to express his satisfaction. "Monsieur can have the mate made in Paris," was the disdainful rejoinder of the bootmaker, who thus had his revenge. Thorvaldsen was fond of telling this anecdote so characteristic of Ronghetti.

di poesia, in which are exercised the talents of fluent professional orators, *de omni re scibili et quibusdam aliis.* Thorvaldsen also had a taste for these improvisations; and Rosa Taddei, having one evening begged him to be present at the performance, drew with much formality from the urn, as a subject for improvisation, "The Progress of Sculpture." The artist became, as it were, a mark for the eloquence of this woman. All went well until the moment she gave him, through inadvertence, the name of Son of God (*un figlio di Dio*); when the uproar was great among the scandalized audience. The feminine orator had need of all her presence of mind to retrieve this false step. She, however, succeeded and to the general satisfaction finished her grandiloquent discourse with these words: "If it is in Denmark that Thorvaldsen was born into life, it is in Italy that he was born to art!" — a platitude which had immense success.

While Thorvaldsen was occupied with his great sacred compositions, his German works required also constant attention.

The monument in honor of Prince von Schwarzenberg was never executed, nevertheless the studies it occasioned produced an interesting work; viz., a great lion intended to be placed in front of the pedestal of the statue. When he made the "Lion of Lucerne," the artist had not a living model: for this new composition he was more fortunate, as there was in Rome at this time in a menagerie a large and very beautiful lion, which the artist went often to study.[1]

As to the monument of the Duke of Leuchtenberg (Prince Eugène de Beauharnais), difficulties of every kind long delayed its completion. The duchess,[2] his window, had deputed

[1] The plaster model was finished in 1825. Later it was cut in marble. This marble, the only one in existence, is in the Museum of Copenhagen,

[2] The duchess was sister of King Louis, of Bavaria.

Herr Leon von Klenze, the architect-in-chief of the King of Bavaria, to design the mausoleum she proposed to erect to the memory of her husband in the Church of St. Michael, at Munich. The architect not only made a general plan of the monument, but also a drawing for the group of statuary, and with the approbation of the duchess sent it to Thorvaldsen, April 24, 1824.

Though it was not very agreeable to the artist to accept a plan so precisely traced out, he willingly undertook to execute a monument to the memory of a prince who, by the nobility and integrity of his character, is one of the finest types of honor history has bequeathed to us.

The sculptor agreed to execute the principal figure, while the rest of the work was intrusted to Tenerani; but he requested at the same time some modification of the plans of Herr von Klenze.[1] After a tedious correspondence, the two seemed at last to come to an understanding; but as a long time elapsed without the artist's giving any information about his work, or answering the most urgent letters, it was concluded that he was wholly neglecting it.

Prince Louis, now King of Bavaria, had occasion to write at this epoch to Thorvaldsen. He recommended to him a young artist of Munich, named Schwanthaler, who has since acquired a high reputation.[2] In a postscript he added: "I beg as a favor that you will pay attention to the monument of my late brother-in-law. Kind regard to the good Buti. Mille saluti a loro, anche al bravo Tenerani belle cose della parte mia."

These entreaties could not induce Thorvaldsen to put

[1] There is reason to think that everything would have been easily arranged between the architect and sculptor, had not a third person been ordered by the duchess to see Thorvaldsen in Rome. Neither Herr von Klenze nor the artist was pleased with this interference, preferring to settle their affairs without intervention. Hence resulted misunderstandings and delays. See Thiele.

[2] The prince greatly desired that Schwanthaler should study under the master, and, "in order that he might really be his pupil," that he should enter his atelier in that capacity. The colossal statue of Bavaria is by this artist.

aside the statue of Poniatowski upon which he was then engaged. Nevertheless, while waiting for the master to take in hand the principal figure, for which a mask of the Duke of Leuchtenberg had been sent to him, Tenerani was busy upon the other parts of the work. But the duchess, who had received no information concerning it, at last wrote herself the 26th December, 1826: "At the end of nearly three years, during which you have wholly neglected the mausoleum, I am convinced that it is impossible for you to fulfil the stipulations of the contract. I therefore renounce, with deep regret, the idea of seeing the monument erected by your hand."

In spite, however, of the silence he had maintained, the artist himself had at this very time begun to work upon the principal figure, and proceeded so rapidly with it that the completion of the work now only depended upon Tenerani. This favorite pupil had gone away upon a journey.[1] Thorvaldsen, though he had the greatest regard for him, became impatient at his absence and invaded his atelier. Once there, he could not refrain from putting his hand to the work, which he soon finished.

Tenerani was then an independent artist, working in his own atelier. Upon his return, he manifested much dissatisfaction at this infringement of his rights; and, some evil-disposed people encouraging this feeling, Thorvaldsen received[2] a summons to choose a referee. A law-suit soon followed, which lasted almost two years, and was finally settled before the Roman tribunals by a judicial ver-

[1] In September, 1827, the artist sent word that he would be glad to receive the second of the stipulated payments. The duchess's agent in Rome wrote at once to Munich, where the good news excited great surprise, and at the same time considerable anxiety; for Thorvaldsen had kept so quiet while at work upon it that there was reason to fear he had deviated from the plan agreed upon. The duchess wrote once more; but it is doubtful whether it were not now too late to follow her instructions. (Thiele.)

[2] Nov. 18, 1827.

dict.[1] By this time the monument of the Duke of Leuchtenberg had arrived in Munich, whither the sculptor went shortly afterward to superintend its erection.

Works executed to order, which restrict the artist to a plan traced out beforehand, are rarely undertaken with much enthusiasm, whatever interest may be attached to the subjects. Whenever Thorvaldsen felt himself less hampered by his engagements, he hastened to return to works of his own choosing, finding in them a relaxation for his mind. Thus in 1828 he began a series of bas-reliefs, known as the "Triumphs of Love," which represent the god conquering the four elements, earth, air, fire, and water. These compositions, which have been often repeated in marble, form a very charming series.

The violent attacks called forth by the Appiani monument did not prevent the City of Pisa from applying to Thorvaldsen to erect a mausoleum in the Campo Santo to the memory of Andrea Vacca Berlinghieri, a celebrated oculist of that city, who had recently died.

As soon as the news got abroad, and even before Thorvaldsen had received the commission, the jealousy of the Italian sculptors broke out afresh, and with greater violence. Positive threats were now resorted to, and he was summarily commanded to renounce the work in favor of some native artist. But he was not to be intimidated by such means; and when the commission was officially offered to him, he made all the more haste to accept it. A letter from one of his friends, the Chevalier Antonio Piccolomini Bellarti, of Sienna, dated March 6, 1826, had already informed him of the success of the subscription set on foot to defray the cost of the monument. It was agreed that the artist should take for the subject of his bas-relief "Tobit restoring

[1] The adjustment is dated Oct. 29, 1829. Thorvaldsen paid the same day four thousand crowns to Tenerani as a discharge in full of all claims. (Thiele.)

his Father's Sight."[1] This was rapidly modelled,[2] while the medallion was copied from a portrait painted by the oculist's widow.

The erection of this mausoleum gave rise to a very bitter controversy in the petty journals of Tuscany, but Thorvaldsen cared little for their ill-natured criticisms. His greatest annoyances arose from his position as President of the Academy of St. Luke. Every day the jealousy of which he was the object brought upon him some new vexation; and it was with joy that he hailed the approach of the year 1828, when, according to the rules, he was to lay aside an office in the performance of whose duties he had never, it must be confessed, taken a zealous pride.

It was therefore with unmixed satisfaction that he delivered his farewell address at the annual meeting on the 26th of December. He was on the same day unanimously elected vice-president of the department of sculpture; but he made small account of this new honor, and now that he was freed from the burden of the presidency never again attended the sittings of the Academy. Formal admonitions on the subject were sent to him, in which it was declared that his prolonged absence was not sufficiently canonical (*non bastantemente canonica*); but they produced no effect, for the artist was determined to free himself entirely from obligations which had become unendurable. He even endeavored to resign his professorship, but was induced to yield to the earnest desire of the Academy, expressed in an official letter,[3]

[1] Thorvaldsen had asked two thousand crowns for a bas-relief and a medallion. The president of the committee replied, July 6, 1826, "that they would be greatly obliged if the artist would be kind enough to reduce the price, not that they thought it excessive, considering his great reputation, but because their resources were insufficient to meet it." Thorvaldsen entered readily into the views of the committee, and with his usual disinterestedness reduced the price one-half.

[2] About the month of August, 1828, the plasters were sent to Pisa, and the marbles were finished a year later.

[3] Sept. 11, 1831.

that he would retain the title at least for a short time longer.

The King of Bavaria, desiring to enjoy again the society of friends and artists in Rome, had purchased the Villa di Malta, where he took up his residence at the beginning of the year 1829. He thus became Thorvaldsen's near neighbor, and the royal dignity did not hinder him from resuming his old habits of friendly familiarity.

A day or two after his arrival in Rome, his majesty repairs to the famous *Osteria Ripa di Grande*, in company with Joseph Koch, Catel, Thorvaldsen, and several other artists, and sits down at his old place, marked by a bad penny nailed on the table. The repast is a gay one: they talk, they discuss every thing, even politics are not excluded; for we hear that, in a moment of extreme good humor, all the guests get upon the table, clinking their glasses, and shouting with all their might, "Down with Don Miguel!"[1]

Some days after, the king surprised Thorvaldsen in his atelier, and, before the sculptor was aware of his purpose, hung round his neck the cross of commander of the crown of Bavaria, saying, "It is on the field of battle that the soldier is honored; and so the artist, too, ought to receive his reward of merit on the very spot where he has done so many great things."

The prince came often thus to visit the sculptor. More than once Thorvaldsen, working near his open window, heard himself called by a passer-by, inviting him to come and dine. It was the King of Bavaria.[2]

There was another personage of high rank at this time in Rome, who kept up an infinitely greater state than the

[1] The Duke of Leuchtenberg, son of Eugène Beauharnais and nephew of King Louis, espoused Donna Maria, daughter of Don Pedro. This princess became Queen of Portugal, when her uncle, Don Miguel, lost the throne he had usurped.

[2] Thiele.

Bavarian monarch, — the Grand Duchess Helena of Russia. Every night there was a fête at her palace, whither flocked all the best society, eager to swell the train of the princess, who dazzled all eyes by her beauty. Thorvaldsen was commissioned to model her bust. She came to sit to him, and he produced a work which won him universal praise.

It is a fact without precedent in the sculptor's life, that he this year declined a commission. The Archduchess Maria Louisa, widow of the Emperor Napoleon I., had lost her second husband, the Count von Neipperg, and wished to erect a mausoleum to his memory in the Church of Saint Louis, at Parma. She sent to beg Thorvaldsen to undertake the work, but he refused the honor.

By a somewhat singular coincidence, he, almost at the same time, accepted a commission from a Scotch gentleman, Mr. Alexander Murray, for a colossal bust of Napoleon I. Thorvaldsen, who had never had an opportunity of seeing the emperor, got together all that he needed for his guidance, statues, medals, engravings, and succeeded in producing a work grave in character, which has the air of an apotheosis rather than a portrait. The bust is supported by an eagle with outspread wings; an arrangement which may be seen in several of the busts of Roman emperors.

A fervent admirer of antiquity, Thorvaldsen was also an enthusiastic collector of works of ancient art, — vases, engraved stones, statuettes, cameos, medals. These collections are now in the Museum in Copenhagen, where they fill several rooms on the first floor. At the time of which we are now writing, the house where he lived was undergoing repairs, and he thought it prudent to close all access to his apartments, so that no one could enter his rooms except through the lodgings of Signora Buti. Meanwhile, he one day noticed that he had been robbed of a large number of medals. Great was the grief of the collector, and in the first outburst of his anger he was rash enough to suspect the honest people with whom he lived. A legal examination became necessary, when it was found that the thief was a miserable fellow whom the artist had employed to keep his accounts. As soon as there was a hope of recovering his medals, Thorvaldsen's anger cooled. The benevolent feelings so natural to him resumed their sway, and he himself took steps to stop the prosecution, not wishing to ruin the culprit. A short time afterward, a small bag was thrown into his room through the window, which contained a part of the stolen property. The author of the theft disappeared from Rome. Every possible search was made among the dealers for the articles which had not been restored, but without success. Thorvaldsen felt the more regret, as a number of the pieces thus lost belonged to his friend, Professor Bröndsted, who had left them in his care.

This incident, unimportant in itself, had an unfortunate effect on the mind of the artist, inspiring him, as we shall hereafter see, with an exaggerated distrust of his fellow-men.

Called to Munich by a desire to superintend in person the final arrangements for the erection of the monument of the Duke of Leuchtenberg, previous to its inauguration, Thorvaldsen left Rome, Jan. 22, 1830, in company with Count Vash, Prussian ambassador at the court of Naples, and arrived on the 14th of February following in the Bavarian capital. Notwithstanding the changes of detail which the artist had ventured to make in the original design, the duchess was so well satisfied with the work that she had already had it lithographed, with the intention of giving a copy to each member of her family.

Scarcely had he arrived, when the artist presented himself at the palace. Although the king was ill and had kept his bed for several days, Thorvaldsen was conducted without delay to the royal bed-chamber, with the intention of giving his majesty a surprise. "Am I not dreaming!" he cried, on seeing him. "Am I really awake! Thorvaldsen in Munich!" Great was the rejoicing; and for several weeks, both at court and in the town, there were constant festivities in honor of the unexpected guest.

The inauguration of the mausoleum of the Duke of Leuchtenberg was to have taken place on the 20th of February, the eve of the anniversary of the prince's death.[1] But the sculptor, having found it necessary to make some changes in the architectual part of the work, in order that the monument might be seen to better advantage in its place in the Church of St. Michael, begged that the ceremony might be delayed. It was accordingly postponed to the 12th of March.

As soon as the mausoleum was exposed to view, it became the mark for some unfriendly criticisms: upon the whole, however, it was far more admired than censured. No impartial critic can deny the beauty of the statue, nor the remarkable execution of the marble group of the two genii which Thorvaldsen had finished with his own hand.

Shortly after the revolution of 1830, the author of the "Triumph of Alexander," and the monument of Prince Eugène Beauharnais, received an honor more flattering than any which it has been our pleasant duty to record. The French ambassador at Rome announced to him (May 1, 1831) that he had been made an officer of the Legion of Honor. "This mark of distinction," he writes to the sculptor, "is no more than justly due to the genius whose chisel has reproduced for us, among so many master-pieces, the triumph of the greatest conqueror of whom history makes mention, and the features of a famous soldier whom France, in the day of her adversity, had no sooner adopted as her son, than she was called upon to mourn his loss. This statue of the hero will serve as a palladium to the city, of which it is the most

[1] Michaud says that Prince Eugène died on the 26th of February. It is a mistake. See in the Catalogue the inscription on the mausoleum.

noble ornament; and your name, emerging from the sphere to which you vainly seek to confine it, will be associated with those noble deeds which thrill all hearts to-day, and keep the whole world suspended between admiration and fear."

It must have been about the time of his journey to Bavaria that Thorvaldsen had, at Florence, a singular interview with Bartolini. He had long been personally acquainted with the famous Italian sculptor, whose life was a constant and terrible struggle, first with poverty until his fine talent was at last recognized, and a struggle not less obstinate with incessant persecutions instigated by envy after he had gained for himself a high position in art. Lorenzo Bartolini was, moreover, not of a temper to shun the combat: his independent spirit refused to stoop to the arts of pleasing, and his character took a coloring from the almost belligerent habits into which he seemed to be forced by circumstances.

He had heard that Thorvaldsen was in Florence, and he expected to receive one of his earliest visits. The Danish artist, however, having for several days neglected to present himself at the atelier of Bartolini, the Italian regarded the delay as a mark of indifference, and a failing in the courtesy one great artist owes to another. He was so much hurt by it that he enjoined upon his pupils, in case Thorvaldsen should finally make his appearance, to tell him that he was not at home. He did come at last, and was told that the master was absent. He insisted, and gave his name: the reply was the same. "But it is impossible for Signor Bartolini not to be at home to me! Be kind enough to tell him that it is the Chevalier Thorvaldsen who wishes to see him."

Bartolini was keeping aloof in a small atelier at the end of the large room in which his pupils were working, and overheard the colloquy. Irritated by the persistence of one with whom he thought he had reason to be offended, he half opened the door, and, thrusting out his head, "No, sir, I am not at home to you!" he cried out, and shut the door.

Thorvaldsen, who was used to being everywhere received with the greatest respect and attention, retired, stupefied at this strange behavior, which seemed to him a piece of inexplicable eccentricity, the cause of which he probably never knew.

CUPID REVIVING THE FAINTING PSYCHE.

CHAPTER VIII.

Horace Vernet. — Mendelssohn. — Troubles in Rome. — Atelier and Garden of Thorvaldsen. — Roman Society. — The History of the God of Love. — Byron's Monument. — Walter Scott. — "The Adonis." — Statue of Maximilian I. — Monuments of Gutenberg and Schiller. — Departure of Vernet. — Cholera. — Thorvaldsen's Return to Denmark.

THE LITTLE DANCING-GIRL.

On the 25th of March, 1830, Thorvaldsen arrived in Rome on his return from Bavaria. Events which took place shortly afterward in France caused great excitement in Italy, and especially in Rome. Scarcely had the news of the revolution in Paris reached the papal dominions, when the French ambassador quitted the city and repaired to Naples. During the first few months following his departure, Horace Vernet, director of the French Academy in Rome, and now sole official representative of France at the Holy See, found himself invested by circumstances with diplomatic functions. He acquitted himself of his delicate duties with his well-known intelligence and energy, and through him the French interests, which might have been seriously compromised, were protected.

Horace Vernet and Thorvaldsen were great friends: the one set a high value upon the talent of the Danish artist, the other professed a passionate admiration for the painter; and we do not doubt that the conduct of Vernet at this time contributed to increase still more the enthusiasm of the sculptor. Notwithstanding that they were very unlike in temperament, these two great artists maintained a lifelong friendship, based upon reciprocal esteem.

The situation was a very difficult one for Horace Vernet.[1] The new ideas had penetrated into the pontifical States, and there were found people prejudiced enough to wish to make the French residents in Rome responsible for their diffusion. Pamphlets the most hostile were freely circulated, and anonymous letters poured in upon the director of the Academy. He was not the man to be intimidated by such threats: in the name of France, he called upon Cardinal Albani to put a stop to these annoyances.

The composer, Felix Mendelssohn, to whose charming genius we owe so many sweet melodies, was then in Rome. One of his letters, dated March 1st, 1831, shows that this state of agitation continued for a considerable time.

"The most to be pitied in the present state of affairs," he says, "are the ladies Vernet, who are in a very unpleasant position. Singularly enough, the hatred of the whole population is directed toward the students of the French school of art: it is pretended that they alone could easily bring about a revolution. Horace Vernet has received a number of threatening anonymous letters. Lately he even found, stationed in front of his atelier, an armed Transteverino, who took to flight on seeing him go after his gun; and, as these

[1] See the interesting publication of M. A. Durande upon Joseph, Charles, and Horace Vernet. Paris, Hetzel.

ladies are now entirely alone at the villa, the situation is the more painful for the family."

Though the French were more specially threatened, all strangers in Rome were uneasy; and the most alarming reports were circulated.[1] Thorvaldsen, whose success had raised up for him many enemies, naturally had, more than any one else, serious reasons for alarm: so thought the young Danish artists, who proposed to form a guard to protect his works and his collections. He at first welcomed this mark of devotion on the part of his countrymen; but, when the troubles seemed to grow more serious, he would no longer accept it. "It would be paying too dear," he said, "for my own protection or that of my statues, to expose one of you to being killed. If they want only my money, well and good, — I will try to earn more; if it is my life, let them take that too. Must I not give it up some time or other?"

In spite of the firmness of this language, Thorvaldsen was of too pacific a temper to relish such a life of excitement. He no longer felt at home in Rome, and thought seriously of changing his place of residence: so it would appear, at least, from some letters found among his papers, in which his friends endeavor to persuade him to leave Rome and go to

[1] Thorvaldsen had his share of trouble in these agitations. One day he was surprised by a call from the executor of Cardinal Consalvi's will, who begged him to receive directly the 12,000 crowns still due to him for the monument of Pius VII. The sculptor replied that, the work not being wholly finished, the time for payment had not come; but the gentleman insisted, and urged him to get without any more delay into the carriage waiting for him at the door. The city was in a turmoil, and the directors of the *Monte di Pietà* feared an attack upon the bank, known to hold the deposit of Cardinal Consalvi: they wanted the artist either to draw out the 12,000 crowns immediately, or leave them there at his own risk. He chose the first alternative, but felt afterward very uneasy with his bags of money in the carriage. At Torlonia's, where he wanted to get them to receive the money on deposit, the greatest agitation prevailed: the court was filled with *gendarmes*, an attack was expected at any moment, and he was dismissed without ceremony by the clerks. Thanks, however, to the obliging interference of Madame Torlonia, he was relieved of his inconvenient burden. (Thiele.)

Marseilles, and thence by way of Paris to London, where they would join him.

Some intimation of this project seems to have reached Bavaria; for King Louis tried to persuade him to come to Munich, offering to make him professor in the Academy of that city, and Counsellor of State on extraordinary service.

These entreaties did not, however, induce the artist to take any decided step. The political excitement having subsided, the round of social entertainments was resumed with more ardor than ever. Thorvaldsen had always been fond of going to evening parties, where the chief attraction for him was the pleasure of meeting pretty and elegant women, of whom it seems there were many in Rome at that time.

Roman society was wholly captivated by Horace Vernet, whose directorship is still remembered as a marked epoch in the annals of the French Academy. Mendelssohn, too, the young and ardent musician, intimate with both the illustrious masters, was at every entertainment; and it was at one of these parties that he met them both for the first time.

"At my first ball at Torlonia's," he writes, "not knowing any lady, I stood looking on, watching the crowd, and not dancing. Suddenly I felt some one clap me on the shoulder, and at the same time a strange voice said to me: 'So you too are admiring the beautiful English girl?' What was my astonishment, upon turning round, to find myself face to face with the Counsellor of State, Thorvaldsen, who, standing at the door of the *salon*, was never tired of admiring this lovely creature. Scarcely had he asked me the question, when I heard loud talking behind us: 'But where is she, this little English girl? My wife has sent me to look at her, *per Bacco!*' The speaker was a wiry little Frenchman, with gray, bristling hair: he had in his button-hole the ribbon of the Legion of Honor. I recognized directly Horace Vernet. Thorvaldsen and he immediately began a very serious and learned conversation upon the subject of this beauty; and what charmed me above all was to see the young girl, so much admired by these two old masters,[1] who were never tired of looking at her, go on dancing with the most adorable innocence and unconsciousness. Thorvaldsen and Vernet requested an introduction to her parents, and troubled themselves no more about me, so I could have no further talk with them that evening. Several days afterward, however, I was invited to the house of the kind English people I met in Venice, who wished, they said, to present me to some of their friends. Now these friends were no other than Vernet and Thorvaldsen. I was enchanted."

The two masters, who met every evening in society, often visited each other also in their ateliers. Mendelssohn saw them constantly. He thus describes the painter's studio: "Among alleys of evergreens, now in blossom, exhaling a delicious perfume, in the midst of the shrubbery of the Medici garden, is a small house, from which invariably issues some noise which is heard from afar, — shouting, or quarreling, or maybe an air played on the trumpet, or the barking of dogs, — that is the studio. The most admirable disorder reigns throughout. Guns, a hunting horn, a monkey, palettes, a brace of dead hares or rabbits; everywhere pictures finished or half finished; the 'Investiture of the Tri-colored Cockade'; portraits begun of Thorvaldsen, Eynard, Latour-Maubourg; studies of horses, the first sketch and studies for the Judith, the portrait of the Pope, heads of Moors, pifferari, papal soldiers, my unworthy self, Cain and Abel, and last of all the interior of the studio itself, — all hanging on the walls."

[1] Mendelssohn speaks as a young man when he calls Vernet and Thorvaldsen "these two old masters." The painter, in fact, was hardly forty years old; and the sculptor, not yet sixty, was in his prime.

At the foot of the terraces of the Palace Barberini, we breathe a quieter atmosphere. How many visitors from all countries have wandered in turn through these ateliers of the sculptor, have strolled through that little garden, fragrant with the sweet scent of oleanders, under that green arbor, contrasting with the dark tint of the great flower-pots; while tame tortoises crawled peacefully along the paths and flower-beds!

"Thorvaldsen," writes a visitor, "lives in Rome in the Palazzo Tomati, Via Sistina, on the Pincian Hill. The first story is devoted to his private apartments. The atelier is higher: you reach it by a narrow staircase. When you knock at the door, the great sculptor, like Poussin, opens it himself. The furniture of the apartment is simple and primitive, but a multitude of fine paintings ornament the walls. Here are bookcases filled with books, rare vases, collections of medals, and gems. All around are fine engravings, sketches, portraits of princes and artists. In front of the house is a garden, which can be reached from the atelier, and where aloes, wild roses, and other flowers straggle over blocks of marble. Thorvaldsen is remarkable for his great activity, for the close attention he gives to everything upon which he is engaged. You follow the idea in his work with extreme ease. His conversation, when he is only executing, not planning, is easy, sprightly, and at the same time full of thought and shrewdness. No one among the artists takes a more devoted interest in zealous young beginners. Of the men who have earned their right of citizenship in the artistic world, he is one of the greatest. Art has given him the highest rank, a rank which no one can ignore, even in Germany, that country of hereditary titles. His is incontestably a mind of the first order. To a remarkable energy, he joins that easy facility which seems only to belong to graceful talent. He ends his life, commenced in hardships among peasants, in the first ranks of society, where he inspires as much interest as veneration." [1]

The sculptor was often seen in his garden, walking with a slow step and dreamy air, and moulding in his hands a bit of clay: at the first glance, he might be taken for an idle man. But what activity under this apparent calm! and how finely organized that brain which could, without effort, carry on at the same time so many and such various works, profane or sacred, light or severe!

The hardest task for the artist was his correspondence: it was a great effort for him to write; and he finally fell into a phlegmatic habit in regard to it, from which he seldom, if ever, departed. When he suspected a letter of containing a disagreeable request, he would refrain from opening it, and allow his correspondence to accumulate for months, until some friend kindly undertook to look it over and reply for him.[2]

[1] M. Fayot, in the journal "L'Artiste."

[2] Generally Thorvaldsen did no more than sign his letters. Excepting his Danish correspondence, most of the letters in other languages, French, German, Italian, have but little interest except as autographs: we shall limit ourselves therefore to giving two of these signatures.

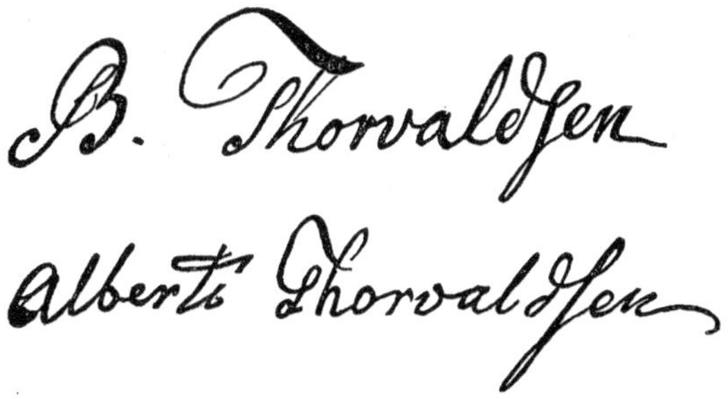

These autographs have a firmness, especially the first, which is sculptural in character. In one, he retains the familiar name of Bertel; in the other, he translates it into Italian. Thorvaldsen never destroyed the letters he received, writing on the backs of them the rough draft of his reply, when, as a rare thing, he answered them

Thorvaldsen was passionately fond of music, and played the guitar like a true *virtuoso*. "My character as a pianist," writes Mendelssohn, "procures me here a peculiar pleasure. You know how much Thorvaldsen loves music. He has in his atelier an excellent instrument, and in the morning I play something to him from time to time while he works. When I see the old artist mould his brown clay, give with a hand firm and delicate the last touch to an arm or a drapery, when I see him creating these imperishable works which will command the admiration of posterity, I feel myself happy in being able to give him pleasure."

At this period he had much to do with the god of Love. After having represented him as the conqueror of the universe in the four bas-reliefs of which we have already spoken, he undertook a series of compositions illustrating the history of the son of Venus, a history rich in incident and more varied than any of the ancient fables. It was to him, however, only a recreation. "I am going to busy myself about Cupid's little affairs," he used to say. "The mischievous boy pulls me by the sleeve: I must give it a shake to get rid of him."

He was not, however, erudite enough to find for himself all the subjects that he represented, of which the greater part are taken from the less known portions of the Greek anthology. He was aided in this undertaking by a friend, a learned poet (more scholar than poet) named Ricci, who lived at Rieti, near Rome. Ricci having had the misfortune to lose his wife, the artist volunteered to compose a monument for her tomb in the church at Rieti. The poet was extremely grateful, and the kindly relations between the two friends became still closer. Devoting himself to studies which were quite to his taste, Ricci furnished the sculptor with the

himself. He also covered the blank portions with sketches and plans. Herr Thiele found all these scraps, such precious material to the biographer, in a cellar of the Palace Tomati in Rome, buried under a heap of rubbish.

subjects of his bas-reliefs in Italian verse. He even proposed having Thorvaldsen's compositions engraved, to illustrate a history of Love, to be written by himself in imitation of the old poets.

The artist took much pleasure in this pastime, and the suggestions of Ricci were carried out with such astonishing rapidity that these illustrations of the exploits of the son of Venus soon grew into a sort of poem in bas-relief.[1]

The bust of Lord Byron, modelled by Thorvaldsen in 1817, had been well received in England. Several years after the poet's death at Missolonghi, his fellow-countrymen proposed to erect a monument to his memory, and the committee formed for the purpose determined to apply to the same artist. Like all liberal thinkers of the day, Thorvaldsen was a philhellenist, and therefore willingly engaged to execute the work. Byron, for whom personally he had had but little sympathy, he now thought of only as one of the heroes of Greek independence.

Sir John Hobhouse, chairman of the committee, wrote, on the 22d of May, 1829, to beg the artist to undertake the work, offering him, at the same time, the sum of one thousand pounds sterling. The English are very generous when they have a monument to erect to one of their distinguished men. But Thorvaldsen on his part always cared more for the honor than for the profit he might derive from his works. Though he earned a great deal of money, he lived frugally because his habits were simple, while at the same time he was very liberal in matters of business. Of this it would be easy to give numerous proofs.

[1] All these little subjects were moulded and cast in September, 1831. Thorvaldsen continued the series the following year; and Ricci published a volume called "Anacreonte Novissimo del Commendatore Alberto Thorvaldsen in XXX. Bassorilievi Anacreontici, tradotti dal Angelo Maria Ricci, Roma, 1832, 8°." This work, dedicated to the sculptor, and containing thirty plates engraved in outline after the bas-reliefs, seems to have had some success. Ricci had already published in 1828 a collection of poems under the title "L'Anacreonte di Thorvaldsen."

The sculptor accordingly replied that the price proposed would suffice not only for a statue, but also for a bas-relief, to be placed upon the pedestal. The committee left the design of the monument entirely to him, asking only for a drawing, to be submitted to the subscribers, and suggesting that it would be easier to conceal the lameness of the illustrious deceased if he were represented in a sitting posture.

The sketch was finished in 1830, and the next year the first model in plaster; but quite important changes have been made in the marble, which represents Byron seated on a broken Greek column, holding in one hand a pen, in the other the poem of "Childe Harold."

The bas-relief, representing the Genius of Poesy, was finished at the same time, though the marbles were not ready to be sent to London until April, 1835. Before it was put up, the monument was subjected to many vicissitudes. The committee first proposed to place it in Westminster Abbey, or St. Paul's; then in the British Museum; in the National Gallery; and finally in Kensal Green Cemetery. But the Anglican clergy, who are not remarkable for their tolerance, were more hostile than the Romish clergy had been in regard to the mausoleum of Pius VII. They were displeased that a poet who was in their eyes immoral and impious should be thus honored. Ten years passed away and the monument had not yet found a place, when in 1845 Trinity College, Cambridge, Byron's Alma Mater, offered to receive it. The marbles, not without difficulty, were discovered in one of the vaults of the London custom-house; and the monument was finally placed where it now stands, in the college library.

In 1831, Thorvaldsen received a visit from another representative of English literature, Sir Walter Scott. It is reported of this celebrated historical novelist, that he did not manifest much interest while at Rome in works of art, since he did not even go to see the Vatican: we mention this with reservation, as an assertion to which we can scarcely give credit. At all events the author desired to be presented to the sculptor. Walter Scott, well versed as he was in the tongues of the North, could only speak his own; and as to Thorvaldsen, it was impossible for him to follow a conversation in English. A person present at their interview has recorded the particulars.[1] These two illustrious men accosted each other with touching cordiality; but their conversation, as may be suspected, was strangely fragmentary, consisting only of interjections and monosyllables. Meanwhile one could hear coming from each the words: *conoscenza — charmé*, *plaisir — happy — connaissance — piacere — delighted — heureux*. Very concise language; but the two new friends were so pleased, that they seemed to understand each other wonderfully. They shook hands with the greatest friendliness, they clapped each other on the shoulder, and when they parted followed each other with their eyes, making all the while the most demonstrative gestures.

Whatever was frank, open, and natural delighted Thorvaldsen. The simplicity of his nature could not accommodate itself to the strangeness of Byron's: he could make nothing of his exaggerated melancholy. Walter Scott, on the contrary, pleased him at first sight: he understood him at once. During the great novelist's stay in Rome he modelled his bust.

While welcoming with the greatest cordiality his favorite artist in Munich, the King of Bavaria nevertheless had not failed to reproach Thorvaldsen for the little zeal he had shown in the finishing of the "Adonis." On his return to Rome, Thorvaldsen, mindful of the complaints of the sovereign, resumed the work with considerable ardor. Connoisseurs who were regarding the marble as almost finished, and admiring its careful execution, were therefore much sur-

[1] M. Kestner, Etudes Romaines.

prised to see the sculptor subjecting it suddenly to a radical change; for, in spite of the praises lavished upon this statue, he was only half satisfied, and considered it not yet fit to leave his hands. He therefore retouched it with a boldness which alarmed those who saw him busy with it. The troubles in Rome interrupted the work for a time; and it was not until October, 1831, that the artist announced to his royal friend that it was completely finished. King Louis was loud in his rejoicings over the good news, and again urged Thorvaldsen to accept the position of professor in the Academy of Munich. He also inquired how far the statue of Maximilian I, of Bavaria, which he had more recently ordered, had progressed.[1]

The model of this equestrian statue, twice the natural size, was not finished until 1836: it was sent to Bavaria the same year, and was exhibited at the royal foundery. The statue and the horse were cast in one piece the following year by Stiglmaier[2] so successfully that it was scarcely necessary to finish it with the chisel. In 1839, the monument of the ancestor of King Louis was solemnly inaugurated in Wittelsbachplatz, at Munich. It is one of the most beautiful equestrian statues of modern times. The elector is represented armed *cap-à-pie* in the costume he wore at the time of the Thirty Years' War. Thorvaldsen, who did not consider a monument complete without bas-reliefs on the pedestal, had modelled two compositions for the two sides; but, as soon as the king learned what he had done, he wrote to

[1] King Louis gave him this order, Feb. 15, 1830, the day after the artist arrived in Munich, as a testimony of the satisfaction his visit afforded him.

[2] Stiglmaier was the son of a blacksmith. King Louis, discovering his natural talent, sent him to Italy to study the science of casting: he afterward intrusted him with a number of works. Stiglmaier cast the colossal statue of Bavaria, erected on a hill near Munich. This statue, which is more than sixty feet high, was cast from a model made by the sculptor Schwanthaler, the same artist who was recommended by King Louis to Thorvaldsen. Stiglmaier also cast the statue of the King Maximilian I, a work by the sculptor Rauch, also at Munich, and which must not be confounded with the equestrian statue of the elector of which we have just spoken.

the sculptor that political considerations would not permit him to make use of them.[1]

It was at this period that Thorvaldsen began the monument to the memory of Gutenberg, and a little later that of Schiller. He did nothing further, however, than make miniature models of the two works. The first had been ordered by the City of Mayence, in 1832; and the statue was made from his drawings and small models by his pupil Herr Bissen, a Danish sculptor of true talent, who has since executed some fine works for his country. The inventor of printing is represented in the dress of an old German craftsman of the Middle Ages, holding in his right hand movable types, and in his left the Latin Bible, the first printed book. One of the bas-reliefs illustrates the invention of the printing-press; the other, that of movable types: Gutenberg figures in it in company with his collaborator, Faust.

All the work was cast in bronze at Paris, by M. Crozatier, in 1836; and the monument was inaugurated at Mayence the 14th of August, 1837. This city, to thank Thorvaldsen, who would not accept any remuneration for his models, made him an honorary citizen.

The artist took also a collaborator in the execution of the Schiller[2] mounment, intended for Stuttgart, where it was inaugurated with great ceremony the 8th of May, 1839.

Though Thorvaldsen had several times manifested a desire to leave Rome, where political agitations disturbed his peace of mind, he had not had the leisure to arrange his plans. All his time was taken up by important works. He

[1] The two models were put aside, and are now in the Museum at Copenhagen. See description in Catalogue.

[2] He engaged to compose the sketches, and only asked for this work the repayment of his expenses. One of his pupils, M. Matthiae, executed the monument. The sketches, sent to Stuttgart in 1835, were approved; and the plasters were then cast according to agreement. The models were forwarded from Rome to Munich, to be cast in bronze by Stiglmaier: they were left for some time on view at the Royal Foundery, and were visited by a great number of amateurs, while the bronzes were sent to Stuttgart.

was also retained in Rome by the attraction of a most choice society, of which Horace Vernet was the life. Unfortunately for the sculptor, the director of the French Academy was soon to leave Rome. Before his departure, Vernet, whose bust Thorvaldsen had modelled in 1833, finished his friend's portrait. This portrait, painted with a vigorous and discerning pencil, renders the features and character of the master with great truthfulness.[1]

Vernet was too popular in Rome for his departure not to be regarded as an important event, and an occasion for sincere regret. As he was to sail in the month of February, the artists of every nationality among whom he had lived for several years gave a farewell banquet in his honor at the Palace Ruspoli, of which we find some interesting particulars in a letter dated from Rome and published by Herr Thiele: —

> "It is very singular that, no matter at what assembly Thorvaldsen may be, or who the person is for whom the fête is given, there always comes a time when the festivities seem to be in honor of him. So it happened again on this occasion. The company having proposed a toast to Horace Vernet, Thorvaldsen, who was at his right, presented him with the crown of laurel, left until this moment on the bust of the painter. But Vernet would not allow him to put it on his head. He rose, seized it, and placed it on Thorvaldsen's brow, saying, 'It belongs here!' At the same time he threw himself on the sculptor's neck and embraced him. This scene called forth indescribable enthusiasm, and the old Ruspoli Palace shook to its foundations with acclamations and applause."

The same writer tells us that this fête had its "to-morrow." The festivities took place on a fast day; and, as it was difficult to scrupulously respect religious laws on such an occasion,

[1] This portrait is in the Copenhagen Museum, in one of the rooms of the first floor. The engraving facing the title-page of this work is taken from it. The artist is represented in his working-dress: the bust upon which he is engaged is that of Horace Vernet. The painter thought at first of representing his friend leaning upon the "Lion of Lucerne." M. Philippe Delaroche Vernet has a sketch of this first composition.

the organizers of the banquet took the precaution to solicit beforehand the indulgence of the ecclesiastical authorities. Notwithstanding this, the *gendarmes* came the next day to arrest the landlord of the Palace Ruspoli for having permitted his guests to eat flesh on the eve of the Purification of the Holy Virgin. The culprit took refuge for a time at the Villa Medici, which enjoys the right of asylum: the affair was afterwards arranged and he escaped imprisonment, but only by the managers of the fête paying for him a fine of a hundred Roman crowns.

The departure of Horace Vernet left a void in Roman society. No one felt it more than the sculptor, who from that time thought more seriously of quitting Rome. Notwithstanding their separation, the two artists always remained the best of friends.

"Dear and illustrious colleague," wrote Horace Vernot some months afterward, "I cannot allow a friend of mine to start for Rome without taking one word of remembrance to you. I do not know whether M. ——, to whom I gave a similar commission, has fulfilled it. . . .

"I am certain that you have never for a moment imputed negligence to me. The sentiments of respect and friendship which I have for your genius, as well as for you personally, are a sure guaranty of the inviolability of my attachment and of my veneration for both one and the other, — to say nothing of my gratitude for your kindnesses to me. It was mentioned in our newspapers that you thought of making a journey to Paris.[1] Imagine my joy at such news! I wrote you then, as I have told you above; but the time has passed, and I very much fear I must renounce the hope of seeing you here. Adieu, dear and illustrious friend! If I can be of any use, command me. You will know how pleased I should be to be able to give you fresh proof of my friendship.[2]

"Faithfully and affectionately yours,

"HORACE VERNET.

"PARIS, Jan. 8, 1836."

[1] Thorvaldsen never went to Paris.

[2] After Thorvaldsen's death, the Baroness von Stampe carried to Paris the ring he had bequeathed to Horace Vernet. The painter received it from her with deep and

Vernet, as we here perceive, felt for Thorvaldsen a friendship mingled with respect: the sculptor was more than twenty years older than he, and already his long white hair gave him a venerable aspect.

We are indebted to M. Philippe Delaroche Vernet for the following letter, of a later date, however, from Thorvaldsen to his grandfather.

The sculptor wrote French with great difficulty. We give the letter, — ill-expressed as it is, and written apparently from his dictation, — because it shows that, when he had the cause of an unfortunate artist to plead, he could overcome his usual indolence with regard to his correspondence.

ROME, June 9, 1838.

(*In the hand of Vernet,*
"*Answered July* 3.")

MY VERY ESTEEMED FRIEND, —

I have been intending to write you for a long time. It was always my hearty desire; but if I have not been able to do so sooner, pray pardon me, because I have been so overwhelmed with work I have had no leisure to write. I ought also to tell you that I have always been flattering myself with the hope of soon being able to see and embrace you. Unfortunately, my affairs forbid it, and deprive me of a pleasure which would have been to me, of all others, the most delightful.

How great my satisfaction would be, were I able, upon leaving Rome, to make my journey by way of Paris! The admiration I should feel at the sight of the many *chefs-d'œuvre* you have executed since your departure hence would give to my soul the greatest happiness; for you know, most dear and tender friend, that for me you are and always will be the first painter of the century. I shall, I think, soon set out for my native country in a Danish frigate which the government has put at my disposal; and, deprived as I am of the happiness of visiting you, I must tell you that I shall not fail to perform that duty at another time.

reverent emotion. "He took the ring," says the baroness, "and put it on his finger. He then held it to his forehead, and bowed his head upon it for a while, as though buried in memories of the past."

It remains to me now to ask of you a great favor: of which the particulars are already explained to you in a letter from our friend Rienhart [and by a postscript by M. Ingres] that you will receive at the same time with this.

A letter from M. Bartholdi, received day before yesterday by M. Ingres, informs us that he thinks of giving up M. Sievert, his relative. M. Ingres has despatched another to-day to M. Bartholdi, urging him, in spite of the reasons he has given us, by no means to abandon thus a young man in the midst of his career, with a prospect before him of a fine success and happy future.

All who know M. Sievert take a lively interest in him from his sad position. Then you know what it is to be a stranger in Rome, and obliged to live for six months on credit.

We heartily wish him all possible success. Your good judgment and grand imagination will be in this grave matter of the best service to this young man, and I shall be eternally grateful to you for any kindness you may show to him.

Be so kind as to favor me with a word of reply, that I may know if you enjoy perfect health, and to acquaint me with the result of the application made to M. Bartholdi in behalf of M. Sievert, his relative.

In this hope, please accept my compliments and assurances of respectful attachment. I embrace you with all my heart.

Your very devoted friend,

ALBERT THORVALDSEN.

P. S. I am also looking forward with the liveliest interest for good news of your very dear family; for I have heard with great pleasure that you have already acquired the title of grandpapa.

At the close of the year 1836, on the 31st of December, the Academy of St. Luke, in Rome, unanimously resolved that, to render homage to the talent of the illustrious Danish artist, a gold medal should be struck in his honor. On this occasion the president of the Academy wrote him a most flattering letter.[1]

[1] This letter is as follows:—

Insigne e Pontificia Accademia Romana delle belle arti,
denominata di S. Luca. Li 31 Dicembre, 1836.

ILLUSTRISSIMO SIGNORE,—

Gli insigni meriti di V. S. Illustrissima ed il favore che da tanto tempo compiacesi rendere alla Pontificia Accademia rilasciando a pieno suo uso l' intero onorario che

Thorvaldsen had already fully decided upon quitting Rome (1837), when the cholera broke out in that city with great violence. He held no public office, and consequently there were no claims of honor to keep him there in presence of so serious a danger, at a time, too, when his own country called eagerly for his return. Therefore, while the Academy of St. Luke was summoning the artists to take part in a religious procession, on the 14th of August, to the Church of the Jesuits, where there was a miraculous image of the Virgin, he yielded to the persuasions of several of his fellow-countrymen, and left with them.

Meanwhile, the travellers had not been informed that the inhabitants of the small towns in the vicinity had thought it prudent, in fear of the plague, to establish a sort of sanitary cordon around Rome; repulsing, with arms in hand, all who attempted to approach. In consequence of this measure,

le compete di cattedratico di scultura, hanno mosso la Congregazione generale adunata jeri appresso la proposizione fattane dal Consiglio dei 12 del cadente, ad esternarlene con alcun atto straordinario la comune riconoscenza.

E stato quindi con unanime ripetita acclamazione determinato, che sia coniata in onore di V. S. Illma una medaglia d' oro, la quale nel dritto abbia l' emblema accademico di San Luca, secondo lo stesso di Lei disegno, e nel rovescio la seguente epigrafe: —

ALBERTO THORVALDSEN
SCULPTORI. CELEBERRIMO SODALI.
BENE MERENTI. EX DECR. ACADEMIÆ.
ANN. MDCCCXXXVI.

Lietissimo di potere coll' annunzio di quest' atto accademico, cosi vivamente grato al mio cuore, par complimento al quadriennio della mia Presidenza, altro non mi rimane se non di pregare V. S. Illma a gradire questa si spontanea e solenne dimostrazione dell' ossequio ed amore de' suoi affettuosi colleghi, e di far voti sincerissimi al Cielo perchè ci servi per lunghi anni nel Sig. Commendatore Thorvaldsen uno de' più grandi ornamenti dell' Accademia e di Roma, uno de più insigni e celebrati maestri di che si onorino le arti europee.

Con questi sentimenti dell' animo desidero, che V. S. Illma mi abbia costantemente per suo con tutta la venerazione

Di V. S. Illma
Dev^mo^ obl^mo^ Servitore,
G. CAV^E^ SALVI, *Presidente.*

Prof. SALVATORE BETTI,
Segr. perp.

when Thorvaldsen and his friends had reached the first village on their route they were warned off by a sort of improvised militia, who ordered them to turn back immediately, threatening to fire upon them if they did not obey.

It was necessary, therefore, to return to Rome, where the epidemic was raging fearfully. The artist thought it likely he should never see his country again, and judged it prudent to make his will. In this document, dated Aug. 24, 1837, he bequeaths to his native city of Copenhagen his works, and his collections of objects of art and antiquities, on condition that a suitable building, exclusively devoted to them, should be provided by the city. He had already, by a deed of prior date, assured a sufficient income to his daughter, whom he had acknowledged in 1835, and for whom he had arranged an honorable marriage.[1]

It was a sad time, the summer of 1837 in Rome. Constant work was Thorvaldsen's refuge from painful thoughts, excited by the presence of an epidemic which every day carried off numerous victims. The master now undertook a statue representing a young girl dancing the *saltarello*. This figure was intended to ornament one of the halls of the Palace Torlonia, which already contained the first "Dancing Girl" of the artist, and a similar work by Canova.

Having first blocked out the subject in clay to his satisfaction, the sculptor sent for a model. A beautiful Roman girl, accompanied by her mother, sat for it for a short time, when she began to feel ill. In a few moments she grew worse; and the symptoms leaving no doubt as to the nature of her illness, — an attack of cholera, — the artist had her

[1] Thorvaldsen's daughter, Eliza-Sophia-Charlotte Magnani, married a Danish colonel, Herr von Paulsen, by whom she had two children, a son and a daughter. The daughter died when scarcely eighteen years of age. The son is still living in Rome, where he married, and, we think, has children. Becoming a widow, Madame von Paulsen married an Italian, Signor Giorni, by whom she had two other children. She died several years since. The deed referred to (dated 1832) assured to Madame von Paulsen the income of a capital of 40,000 crowns (about $22,000), deposited with the National Bank of Copenhagen.

directly taken to her home. She recovered, nevertheless. Some time afterward her mother brought her back, but Thorvaldsen would not consent to let her sit again: he finished the figure without a model.

From that time he thought only of getting away from Rome: he made every arrangement to carry out this long-deferred project, and wrote to inform his friends in Copenhagen. The news spread rapidly in Denmark, where it was received with general joy. The king immediately notified Prince Christian, President of the Academy, that he had given orders for a government frigate to be sent to Leghorn, during the summer of 1838, to bring home Thorvaldsen and all his works. The artist was not only officially apprised of this, but received a private letter from the prince, expressing the satisfaction he felt at the prospect of his return.

The sculptor had his boxes packed in advance, and sent them off one after the other to Leghorn, to the number of sixty-two: they contained his statues, pictures, antiquities, and his books. When, in July, Herr Dahlerup, captain in the royal navy of Denmark, informed him that the frigate "Rota" was at anchor, before Leghorn, waiting to take him, his suite, and effects on board, he was all ready to start. He left Rome, with the hope, however, of returning once more, and embarked for Copenhagen the 13th of August, 1838.

CUPID AND ANACREON.

CHAPTER IX.

Arrival of Thorvaldsen in Copenhagen. — Enthusiastic Welcome. — Apartments in the Charlottenborg Palace. — The *Frue Kirke.* — His Parsimony and Generosity. — Herr Thiele.

THE THREE GRACES.

AFTER a month's voyage, Thorvaldsen again, for the second time, beheld his native land: he came no longer as a visitor, as twenty years before he had come, but to take up his abode there for the rest of his life. How describe the enthusiasm of his countrymen? how picture the ovation he received? His progress may be likened to that of an illustrious prince, a beloved sovereign returning to his kingdom after the conquest of a province. Such a triumph is rare, even in the annals of conquerors.

The nation was proud of the great artist, who, sprung from the lowest ranks, had raised himself by his merit: she celebrated his return with a joy almost delirious. And we must do the Danes the justice to remark, that they know how to appreciate the work of their compatriots, and that they do not willingly sacrifice them to strangers, as is too often the case in other lands.

It was known that Thorvaldsen had set sail in the "Rota," and the ship was expected with impatience. The 15th of September, at a quarter past six in the evening, she entered the Sound, and a courier arrived in all haste to announce in Copenhagen the great news. The wind being very light and the current against her, it was calculated that she could hardly reach the roadstead of Helsingöer that evening, or be expected in Copenhagen before the following morning. The next day was Sunday. The whole population was on foot at an early hour, but the day passed in vain and anxious expectation.

The frigate, retarded by the current, cast anchor near Helsingöer, where the Sound is but little wider than a broad river. An invitation was immediately sent by the Danes to the Swedish city of Helsingborg, and the next day, a steamer, the "Queen Maria," having on board a company composed of the inhabitants of both cities, and carrying the flags of the two nations, came to salute the "Rota." The steamer passed around the frigate, while the band played national airs, which were taken up alternately by choirs. The "Queen Maria" coming alongside the frigate, Thorvaldsen went on board of her, where he was greeted with a patriotic hymn: the pastor of Helsingöer, Herr Boye, made an address, and the festivities lasted a good portion of the day.

The artist afterward returned on board the "Rota," where he walked the quarter-deck to a late hour of the evening. At nightfall a superb aurora borealis enveloped the frigate. This phenomenon is not rare in the northern seas, but the national enthusiasm willingly regarded it as a sort of miracle in honor of Thorvaldsen. It was the god Thor, binding with a radiant aureole the brow of one of his most glorious sons.

The steamer tried to tow the frigate, but did not get her beyond Kronborg before Monday morning. The fog was thick, and it was therefore impossible to enjoy the beautiful view which the Sound presents of the Island of Zeeland and of the Swedish coast; a charming spectacle, recalling in some of its features the Bosphorus or the Bay of Naples, on fine summer evenings. The "Rota" advanced slowly through the fog, escorted by two boats, one Danish, the other Swedish, from which rose national songs, keeping time with the regular stroke of the oars.

Though the citizens of Copenhagen had been kept on the *qui vive* all day Sunday, they nevertheless had lost none of their enthusiasm, and on Monday all eyes were still fixed upon the steeple of the Church of St. Nicholas, where a flag was to be run up as soon as the ship should heave in sight. But the man who kept watch at the Sextus battery could see nothing for the fog, and the impatience waxed greater.

A few moments before noon, the sky suddenly cleared. Then, far off in the distance, was seen the "Rota," with all her canvas spread, sailing toward the harbor. The flag was quickly waving from the top of the spire: at the same moment rose from the city below a prolonged shout, and all the population hurried to the port.

In spite of the rain, which fell copiously, preparations were directly made to receive Thorvaldsen according to the programme of the committee presiding over the festivities.[1] Boats with flags and streamers flying, and containing members of various civic associations, were very soon seen leaving the military port, and proceeding down the harbor to meet the frigate. On one flag, the artists', was emblazoned the Three Graces of Thorvaldsen; the poets were ranged under the banner of Pegasus; the students, under Minerva; the physicians, Æsculapius; the mechanics, Vulcan; while the

[1] Herr Thiele has preserved the minutest details of this fête.

boat of the naval officer who had command of the flotilla bore the device of Neptune. When beyond the battery of "The Three Crowns," the boats divided into two ranks, each forming the half of a circle, in the centre of which moved the frigate. At this moment a brilliant rainbow spanned the heavens, making a triumphal arch above the "Rota." Again the sky of the North seemed anxious to celebrate the return of its son.

Presently all the boats approached the ship, and one decorated in Pompeian style came alongside. It held Herr Freund and Herr Thiele, who passed on board the "Rota."

Thorvaldsen was standing on the quarter-deck, perfectly calm, smiling good-naturedly, and regarding with a sort of *naïve* astonishment all these solemn demonstrations, as though he did not exactly understand that they were in his honor. As soon as he saw his two friends, he ran to them, and embraced them cordially, hardly leaving them time to pay him the compliments they had been charged with presenting. Meanwhile from all the barks arose an immense concert of voices, chanting in chorus a hymn composed in honor of the artist by the poet Heiberg, and which was long echoed back from the shore by the enthusiastic hurrahs of the crowds lining the wharves. At the same time the "Rota" was boarded, so to speak, by the crews of the whole flotilla. Everybody wanted to get a good look at the illustrious old man. In a few moments the ship became dangerously crowded, and Thorvaldsen was hurried into the long-boat and taken ashore by Capt. Dahlerup.

As soon as his departure was known, the Danes, who had boarded the "Rota," rushed precipitately to their boats, and the deck was cleared in an instant. Now took place an impromptu rowing match between the boats, trying to catch up with the one carrying Thorvaldsen. Meanwhile, the sailors of the frigate had manned the yards, and were saluting with their acclamations the great artist whom they had had the honor of bringing back to his country.

The old man was received, on landing, by the members of the Academy of Fine Arts, together with some of his early friends. Thorvaldsen's eye was clear, his expression mild and intelligent. The long, white hair which fell on his shoulders was a fitting framework for his regular features. His form was tall and erect, and his step firm. His fine figure and the simplicity of his bearing excited a profound interest and sympathy in the crowd, and it was with difficulty that a passage was cleared to the carriage waiting for him on the quay. The pressure was so great that he was carried through Amalia Street and Amalienborg Square to the palace of Charlottenborg, without perceiving that the horses had been taken out, and that his carriage was drawn by the people. When he was told of this, he refused to believe it. So excessive a demonstration was not of a nature to please one of his simple manners and character.

The carriage entered the courtyard of Charlottenborg, and soon the place was besieged. The crowd, assembled in the square, tried to enter by the great gate, which had been prudently closed. The porter not replying to the reiterated ringing of the bell, a man who had contrived to effect an entrance through the janitor's window constituted himself the mouth-piece of the crowd and declared that they would not disperse without seeing Thorvaldsen. As soon as the artist heard of this desire, he allowed Herr Thiele to lead him to the balcony of the great hall overlooking the Royal Square.

"Would not any one think," he said, smiling, "that we were in Rome, and I were the Pope, about to give the benediction *urbi et orbi*, from the balcony of St. Peter's?"

He uncovered to salute his countrymen, and was greeted with prolonged hurrahs. The crowd was so great in the square, that the equestrian statue of Christian V seemed to swim in an agitated sea; while children hung in clusters on the street lamp-posts. Charlottenborg was decked with flowers to welcome its new guest; and in the evening there was a torchlight procession organized by the young artists.

After such a day, Thorvaldsen doubtless flattered himself that he should return to a tranquil life; but he was mistaken. This was only the prelude to other solemnities, other ovations, and it was long before the artist enjoyed a moment's repose. Like a sovereign, he must bear the weight of his grandeur without appearing to be fatigued by it.[1]

We shall not enter into a detailed account of all these festivities, which would detain us too long. Few men have been to such a degree the object of the persistent attentions of their fellow-citizens. The newspapers, which had celebrated the sculptor's return, continued to inform the public of his slightest actions; every post brought him an incredible number of letters, congratulations, requests for assistance, petitions which he was asked to sign. Nor was poetry wanting, for the Muses are cultivated with enthusiasm in Denmark. Among the letters which had long been awaiting his arrival in Copenhagen, we must mention one, remarkable for its singularity. The Secretary of the His-

[1] The next day it was an excursion to Sans-Souci, the pleasure palace of Christian Frederick, where were assembled all the members of the Academy of Fine Arts, of which the prince was president. They held a meeting in the forest; after which they went to dine at the Hotel Bellevue finely situated on the borders of the Sound, a favorite retreat of the citizens of Copenhagen on Sundays in summer. The following day a more formal meeting took place, at which the Vice-President announced that the Academy had decided to have a medal struck in honor of Thorvaldsen, and bearing his name, which should be given as a prize to the pupils in sculpture. The execution of the medal was entrusted to Professor Christensen.

As to the city government, it bestowed upon the veteran sculptor the diploma of honorary citizenship.

The artists who had been in Italy, and who had formed themselves into an association under the name of the *Roman Society*, got up a private dinner in honor of the sculptor, who made his appearance decorated with the Order of the Baiocco, having the small copper coin of that name hung round his neck by a green ribbon. At dessert, they did not fail to crown him with laurels.

Another grand fête took place at Roeskilde, then the seat of the Danish Parliament.

torical Society of Rhode Island, in North America, wrote to inform the sculptor that the said Society had elected him an honorary member, on account of his being the living representative of the first native American of European blood; recent researches in American antiquities having established the fact that a certain Thorfinne Karlsefne had, in 1007, commanded an expedition to Rhode Island, and passed the winter at Mount Hope, where his wife Gudrid, the following spring, presented him with a son, who was called Snome. Now this same Snome, according to the genealogists, was one of the ancestors of Thorvaldsen.[1] "They are wonderful fellows, these *savans*," said the artist, laughing heartily. "How should we know, without them, whence we come, or whither we go?"

Thorvaldsen installed himself at the palace of Charlottenborg, in an apartment on the ground-floor appropriated to the Academy professor of sculpture. This apartment, the windows of which look out upon the botanical garden, had been ready for him since 1805, though he had occupied it only during a short stay in Copenhagen, in 1819. Before his arrival several rooms had been added to the suite, and the works which he had sent from Italy previous to his own coming were temporarily placed in them. The artist set himself to work to arrange these marbles and plasters, as well as those which came in the "Rota." He even thought of unpacking his rich collection of medals, antique vases, and engraved stones, but he had no time to put in order these numerous possessions. The sculptor no longer belonged to himself: he was the prey of the public. Every day a line of carriages, such as is never seen in Copenhagen except at the theatre on the evenings of some extraordinary performance, was stationed before the door of the Academy. All visitors

[1] The work containing the result of these researches in regard to the History of North America was published in 1837, under the title of *Antiquitates Americanæ*. The genealogical table annexed traces the pedigree of Thorvaldsen.

were received with affability; but the artist, who never hurried himself about completing his toilet, was generally surprised in his dressing-gown and slippers. Consequently he passed whole days in this costume, fulfilling the functions of cicerone to his own sculptures. Then every day he was obliged to dine out somewhere, and afterward go to some evening party. "I shall sink under it," he said to a friend.

What annoyed him the most in this kind of life was the impossibility of devoting himself to his work, being at first afraid that he should seem wanting in respect to his visitors, if he received them with moulding-tool or hammer in hand. Later, when he perceived how much pleasure they took in seeing him thus employed, he did not hesitate to continue his work as in Rome; and little by little his life assumed an aspect more in accordance with his tastes.

He rose early and breakfasted frugally, as had long been his habit, on two large tumblers of milk and two small rolls. But he continued to dine out every evening with a new host, without being able to accept all the invitations showered upon him.

Shortly after his arrival at Copenhagen, the administrative council of the *Frue Kirke* (Church of our Lady) wished to take advantage of the presence of the artist, who now determined to bring together in this church all his religious works. The "Christ and the Twelve Apostles,"[1] the "Preaching of John the Baptist," were not alone to ornament the *Frue Kirke*. Other great works were also planned: a frieze representing "The Entry of Christ into Jerusalem,"[2] in-

[1] The council notified him that it had devoted to this enterprise the sum of thirty-four thousand Danish crowns, which were at his disposal. The marble statue of "Christ," executed for the royal chapel, cost sixteen thousand crowns. For the "Ten Apostles," which the sculptor had had cut in marble at his own expense, he was paid two thousand crowns for each. The other two apostles, which he had always meant to remodel, were also ordered.

[2] The subject was chosen by Thorvaldsen.

tended for the peristyle; four statues of prophets, to be placed in niches each side of the great entrance; and marble statues of Luther and Melanchthon, for the porch.[1]

Thorvaldsen was now in his sixty-eighth year; but we forget his age when we see with what ardor he still projected great works in spite of the obstacles which the exigencies of Danish society threw in the way of their speedy completion.

His daily correspondence alone was no small occupation. The artist, as we have seen, had never been in a hurry to read letters any more than to answer them. He was now less disposed than ever to take this trouble upon himself. Fortunately, the Secretary of the Academy, Herr Thiele, his future biographer, a trustworthy friend, and a man of tact and judgment, did this service for him. Herr Thiele examined the correspondence, and gave the artist all the letters that required to be read immediately: the others he classified, and reported upon them periodically. Of this number were all requests for assistance. The ready money which Thorvaldsen had brought with him from Rome had so rapidly melted away in charitable gifts, that it soon became necessary to renew the supply. But, a second sum taking quickly the same road as the first, the artist was forced, by way of putting some check upon his liberality, to examine carefully the various requests. Upon Herr Thiele, who charged himself with this work, thus devolved the functions of both secretary and treasurer.

Though in his later years his habits of economy had degenerated into parsimony, Thorvaldsen was ever ready to generously assist the unfortunate. Superficial observers may, with a show of truth, accuse him of avarice; but they who have known the inmost secrets of his life emphatically deny

[1] The artist was working upon the bust of Luther at the time of his death. After that event, the project of erecting these two statues seems to have been given up. Two only of the statues of prophets were subsequently executed, — David and Moses, — by Messrs. Bissen and Jérichau.

this accusation. No doubt the old man has been heard disputing obstinately about the price of a pair of shoes: he has been seen stooping with difficulty to pick up a button. Meanwhile, let a poor woman leave his door satisfied with a generous gift, but showing by her mien and dress a still greater misery than he had at first recognized, and he hastens to recall her, and place in her hand another handful of crowns.

Nothing is more natural than this apparent contradiction. Characters are not wholly consistent, and we constantly see in human life contrasts which at first sight appear quite as strange. Thorvaldsen practised that excess of economy very common in old people who have known poverty in their youth, and who, having led a life of labor, have not seen their wants increase with their fortune. Such men are the more to be praised, when, parsimonious for themselves, they give freely of the fruit of their own toil to relieve the unfortunate.

But it was not the indigent alone who had recourse to the artist. As his influence was well known, every one who wanted a favor from the court, the ministers, or men in office, applied to him. He had therefore requests to present, petitions to indorse. The merchant, anxious to extend his business, begged Thorvaldsen to lend him the sum he needed, or be security for him. It was with great difficulty that the master could be dissuaded in such cases from lending his name; for the service seemed to him so easy to render, that he was almost ashamed to refuse; and, had it not been for the vigilance of his secretary and friend, he would often have become seriously involved in consequence of his willingness to oblige. A royal fortune would hardly have sufficed to satisfy the demands made upon him.

Very often, too, he was solicited only *ad pompam et ostentationem*, and we might give an entertaining account of all the letters he received from fathers and mothers begging him to stand godfather to their children. He usually consented to assume this responsibility, but generally forgot his promise: he would then make amends by sending some present.

Finally, all the Thorvaldsens, not only in the city and its environs, but in the whole kingdom, wrote or came to see him to explain carefully and at length the exact degree of relationship in which they stood to him. The artist was amused by all this, and repulsed no one. Among these importunities, the most numerous and least delicate were those addressed to him by people who wished to know when he would return to Italy, as they would like to bear him company. It was evident that they counted on having their expenses paid by so illustrious and generous a travelling-companion; and they even did not fail to insinuate that on this condition they would be willing to stay several years in the classic land of art.

With such constant calls upon him, and above all with so many social distractions, it is easy to understand how difficult it was for the artist to devote himself, as much as he liked, to the labor which still made the deepest joy of his life, as it had already made the glory of his name.

He felt that he could not free himself from all these impediments, except by quitting Copenhagen.

Let us not, however, blame the Danish people for an excess of zeal, under cover of which some annoyances may have been inflicted. If among the multitude of enthusiasts there were some without discretion, where are they not to be found? Let us rather dwell upon the extraordinary consideration shown to the great artist, the respect paid by his fellow-citizens to his old age. Such homage does no less honor to Denmark than to Thorvaldsen: it indicates the intellectual superiority of the nation, and its sincere fondness for the arts. In what other country do we see great artists so honored!

WINTER.

CHAPTER X.

Baron Von Stampe and his Family. — Thorvaldsen at Nysöe. — His Atelier at Stampeborg. — His Statue of Himself. — "Christ's Entry into Jerusalem." — "Christ bearing the Cross." — The Poet Andersen. — The Grand-Cross of Danebrog. — King Christian VIII. — Statue of Christian IV. — Wilkens.

THORVALDSEN.

Though Thorvaldsen was never married, he was better fitted for a domestic than a fashionable life; and before he had resided long in Copenhagen, he came to regard the households where he was kindly welcomed as his own, and made himself almost as much at home there as in his own apartments. That of the Baron von Stampe was especially attractive to him: the baron and baroness had several children; and the artist, treated by them with respect and affection, became, in one way, a member of the family.

They invited Thorvaldsen to pass the summer at their chateau at Nysöe. The barony of Stampe is a vast and beautiful domain, distant a quarter of an hour's drive from Prœstö. It is situated at the head of a bay bordered by great trees, and is in the midst of a richly wooded and farming country. To reach it by sea, from Copenhagen, requires a voyage of six or eight hours in the steamer, and by the land route the distance is still greater; so that it is quite secure from the incursions of troublesome visitors. Thorvaldsen was glad on more than one account to accept the invitation, seeing in it a means of escaping from duties which, though not without their charms, were still sometimes irksome.

To beguile the leisure hours of life in the country, he made for his amusement a few sketches in clay. The room adjoining the one he occupied on the ground-floor was given up to him for an atelier, and what was at first merely a pastime gradually became a serious occupation, to which he applied himself with all his native ardor.

Since his return to Denmark, he had been often urged by his friends to model a statue of himself. The Baroness von Stampe had frequently broached the subject to him, but without effect: he invariably refused, maintaining that it was too great a piece of vanity on the part of an artist to make any representation of himself. Profiting, however, by his sojourn at Nysöe, she, by constant perseverance, at length prevailed upon him to block out a small rough model; but he would do no more, alleging, as a pretext, that it was impossible to do anything more important in a room which was not high enough for him to work in with ease, and where there was no light from above. It was then that the baroness conceived a project which she was very careful not to reveal to her guest. With seeming indifference, she questioned him as to the size and arrangement he would consider indispensable for an atelier, and carefully noted his replies.

Thorvaldsen had left in Copenhagen an unfinished clay sketch of the celebrated Danish poet Holberg, with instructions to one of his pupils to keep it moist. He now thought it time to return thither and complete it. He accordingly left Nysöe, promising to be back in eight days. He had scarcely gone, when the baroness sent for a builder and workmen. She chose a suitable place in the garden before the castle; had, that very day, three great trees cut down; and set the men at work to build a small atelier. It was a busy time at Nysöe during that week; for it had been stipulated that, unless everything were finished within the eight days, nothing should be paid. When the artist returned, all was ready. It was a delightful surprise, and the occasion was celebrated by an inaugural fête. This took place in the month of July, 1839.

The atelier was so arranged that Thorvaldsen had no longer any pretext for not executing his statue: he was therefore obliged to yield. He had been working on it several days, very zealously, when he received from Copenhagen a letter from Oehlenschlaeger, whose bust he had promised to take. The poet was very anxious that the artist should fulfil his promise, and urged it vehemently, with the vanity of a famous man desirous to leave his features to posterity by the hand of an illustrious sculptor.

Thorvaldsen made merry over this with the baroness; and, notwithstanding his habitual good-nature, could not help ridiculing the poet a little. But suddenly he stopped laughing, and the letter fell from his hands. "It is very well for me," he said, "to jest at the vanity of others, when I myself, at this very moment, am engaged in raising a monument to my own vanity!" He threw down his tools with violence, and would have broken his statue. The baroness immediately called for help. She dragged the artist out of the atelier, locked it, and took possession of the key. She tried for a few days to convince him that he was wrong, by argument, but without success. Finding that, in this way, she obtained nothing, she had recourse to stratagem. We think it is Calderon who somewhere says: "Weep, woman, and you will obtain all you wish." The baroness pretended to be very much grieved, and began to cry. "Thorvaldsen cared nothing for her! He knew how much she wanted his statue, — her eagerness to build the atelier proved it, — but nothing could move him. He must have a very hard heart to behave in this way to so devoted a friend."

The old man, simple as a child, was taken in. Touched by this feigned distress, — "Well," he cried, "they may think what they please. My statue is not for posterity, but I cannot refuse it to a friend to whom it will give so much pleasure." He resumed his work directly, with the greatest ardor, as if he feared a return of his scruples, and finished the model in seventeen days.[1] The artist has represented himself in his working dress, one arm leaning upon his statue of "Hope."[2]

Henceforward Thorvaldsen was a constant guest at Stampeborg, dividing his time between Copenhagen and Nysöe. The first works composed in the atelier built for him by the baroness were — besides the statue of the master — the bust of the poet Oehlenschlaeger, and the sketch of "Christ's Entry into Jerusalem," a grand frieze, now over the principal entrance of the *Frue Kirke* in Copenhagen. Between the sketch and the finished work, which was subjected to many changes, there are marked differences.

Another sketch, no less important, was also made at Nysöe: that of the frieze representing "Christ bearing the Cross." On the preceding feast of Pentecost, the marble statues of the apostles had been set up in the *Frue Kirke*, in place of the plaster casts which had before temporarily represented them; and the statue of Christ was at the same time removed

[1] This anecdote was related to us by the baroness herself, when we had the honor of being received at her country residence, at Nysöe.

[2] In placing beside his portrait statue the archaic figure of his "Hope," Thorvaldsen's idea was to make the contrast strongly marked between the man, who was to be represented as living, and the marble statue, which ought, on the contrary, to be cold and motionless.

from the royal chapel, and placed in front of the choir. When all the statues were in their places in the church, it occurred to the architect Hetsch that a frieze placed in the apsis behind the "Christ" would have an excellent effect, serving to connect these detached pieces of sculpture with the building itself. Thorvaldsen, without troubling himself to ascertain whether the building committee would appropriate the necessary funds, eagerly embraced the suggestion of the architect, and agreed with him that the Passion of Our Lord, of which there was no representation in the church, should be the subject of this frieze. The model, sketched at Nysöe, and now in the Museum, differs in some respects from the frieze in the *Frue Kirke.* The latter was executed under Thorvaldsen's direction, by young artists in Herr Freund's atelier.

The poet Andersen, who was a frequent visitor at Stampeborg, and who happened to be there while Thorvaldsen was occupied with this composition, mentions in his autobiography that, one morning, upon going into the atelier, he saw the artist at work upon the figure of Pilate. Thorvaldsen was dissatisfied with the drapery, and asked Andersen's opinion. The baroness, who was present, and who had a religious respect for everything that came from the sculptor's hand, tried to prevent Andersen from criticising it; but the latter said frankly that the drapery seemed to him more Egyptian than Roman. "That is exactly my opinion," replied the artist, and immediately destroyed the sketch, much to the discomfiture of the baroness, who felt very angry with the poet.

Life at Nysöe was of a nature to charm the artist: the days flowed smoothly on, in a pleasant alternation of labor and leisure. The master rose early, and, by the time the clock had struck twelve, had frequently been at work seven hours. He did not like to be interrupted during these busy mornings, but, in the afternoon, was ready to walk in the beautiful woods that bordered the Bay of Prœstö, and receive and return the visits of the gentry of the neighborhood.

It was the custom, after dinner, for one of the daughters of the baroness to play for the sculptor his favorite airs. The old man, who was passionately fond of music, would then seat himself in a large arm-chair to listen at his ease, but generally fell asleep. After he had taken his nap, he would walk up and down the room, and end by saying: "Well, Herr Andersen, are not we children to be treated this evening to some little fairy tale?" The sculptor greatly enjoyed the poetic and delicate charm of the marvellous semi-sentimental stories in which Andersen excelled.

When night came he was always impatient to begin his favorite game of loto, which had become a sort of old man's mania with him; and care was taken by the family at the castle never to deprive him of this amusement. They were even glad to have him always win, for they knew that ill-luck annoyed him extremely, although they only played for the very smallest sums.[1]

The month of November, 1837, found Thorvaldsen still at Nysöe. The 19th was his birthday, and the family were making preparations to celebrate it, when he was notified by the Chapter of the Danebrog that the king had conferred upon him the grand cross of the order. Now, according to the statutes, whosoever has attained to this rank in the order must have his coat-of-arms suspended in its proper place in the Knights' Hall, in the palace of Fredericksborg. Thorvaldsen had never asked himself, no more than goodman Gottskalk, his father, whether he had a coat-of-arms or no; and in fact had none, so far as he knew. But from this day he appears to have sometimes given a thought to the matter; for there have been found scribbled upon fragments of letters a number of crude beginnings of sketches seeming to relate to this subject, amongst which, it was thought, could be recognized the god Thor, armed with his

[1] We were shown by Madame von Stampe the green silk bag that held the big pennies,—his winnings at loto, which he gave his servant to keep for him.

hammer. They were, after all, merely fugitive ideas, never seriously entertained; for in 1843 he had not yet sent the armorial bearings asked for. The Chapter reminded him of his neglect, but the artist took no notice of their communication.

After Thorvaldsen's death, Herr Bissen was called upon to satisfy the claim of the Chapter. He made use of the sketches we have mentioned, as suggestions; and thus it is that the sculptor's shield hangs in the ancient Hall of Knights, amid feudal coats-of-arms, emblazoned with the god of the North, and bearing the device, "Liberty and Love of Country."

Among the various works upon which the indefatigable old man was engaged during his sojourn at Nysöe was the sketch of a monument to the memory of Frederick VI, King of Denmark, who died the 3d of December, 1839: the monarch is represented clothed in the royal mantle, and seated on a throne. The artist expected the monument to be placed in the garden adjoining the palace of Rosenborg known as the king's garden.

Below the Castle von Stampe, and close by the atelier built for the sculptor, flows a little stream. Thorvaldsen used to take delight in daily throwing bread to the swans swimming on its surface, or disporting themselves on its grassy edge. The sight of these majestic birds suggested several compositions, illustrating the myth of Leda,—Jupiter changed into a swan and bearing Cupid on his back, Leda welcoming her kingly lover and Cupid flying away.

Christian VIII, who succeeded Frederick VI on the throne of Denmark, was anxious to have a statue of his ancestor Christian IV, a prince who had distinguished himself in the Thirty Years' War, and who bore the reputation of a skilful general, in spite of his defeat at Lutter, by Tilly, the lieutenant of Maximilian of Bavaria, then chief of the army of the Catholic league. He subsequently governed his country wisely, sought to promote the happiness of his people, and left behind him a venerated name.

Thorvaldsen readily promised the king to execute this statue, but, according to his custom, did not hurry himself in fulfilling the engagement. Several times Christian VIII reminded him of his promise; sometimes by his grand-marshal, sometimes by his officers, but always without success. One evening, meeting at a ball the Baroness von Stampe, the king begged her to use her influence with the artist in his behalf. But the baroness had no better success than her predecessors, and finding her arguments of no avail she again had recourse to a stratagem.

One day, when the sculptor had gone to walk, she, in his absence, took possession of the atelier, and began to model as well as she could a clay sketch, intended to represent the monarch. Upon Thorvaldsen's return, he was astonished at finding the baroness hard at work. "What are you about there?" he asked. "The statue of the king," replied the baroness. "Since I have pledged my word, and you will not do it, I must do it myself."

The artist laughed heartily, and began to criticise the work. "Do it better yourself, then," said the baroness, pretending to be piqued, "you who make fun of me. I defy you to find anything to alter in my statue." Thorvaldsen could not help taking up the clay to correct the proportions. When he had once begun, he finished the sketch, and afterward modelled the statue,[1] which was intended for a marble sarcophagus in one of the chapels of Roeskilde. It was cast in bronze; but its destination was afterward changed, and it is now in the little garden of the Rosenborg Palace.

[1] The sketch is in the Museum, but the small plaster model is at Nysöe. The officer sent by the king to see that the sculptor did not neglect the work expressed one day a wish to have the model. The artist, as an excuse not to give it to him, said he had promised it to Madame von Stampe. He told the story to the baroness, who took him at his word, and possessed herself of the plaster.

The greater number of the bas-reliefs which bear date of this period[1] are signed Nysöe. Thorvaldsen, however, divided his time between country life at Stampeborg and town life in Copenhagen. The ladies made it their pleasure to contribute to the adornment of his city home, and scarcely a day passed without his apartments at the Charlottenborg receiving some new embellishment, — an object of art, or some piece of feminine handiwork.

Everybody in Copenhagen now knew Thorvaldsen, from having visited him in his atelier: but the old man could not recollect the names of so many people, though he remembered their faces. He was often very much embarrassed, when obliged to ask to whom he had the honor of speaking. As he was invited everywhere, it sometimes happened that he did not know the name of his host. Herr Thiele relates in this connection the following anecdote: —

"I went," he says, "with Thorvaldsen, to a grand banquet given by Herr Mösting, Privy Counsellor and Minister of State. When we had left the company, and were coming home together, the master stopped and asked: 'Who is this Herr Steman?' — 'What Herr Steman do you mean?' — 'Why, the man whose house we have just left.' — 'You are mistaken: that is the Minister of State, Herr Mösting.' — 'Really!' exclaimed Thorvaldsen, stupefied: 'on my honor, I had no idea of it.'"

Thanks to his servant, however, the artist at last maintained a certain method in this business of dining out. At first, he was governed by the fancy of the moment. When

[1] Among others, "Diana imploring Jupiter to allow her to remain a Virgin;" "Cupid and Hygeia," modelled upon the occasion of the nuptial festivities of the King and Queen of Denmark.

"Perseus delivering Andromeda," a crowded composition, and utterly unlike the artist's usual manner; "The Pilgrims of Emmaus," for a church in the neighborhood of Stampeborg; "Jesus Blessing Little Children," intended for an infant asylum.

"The Genius of the New Year," composed for 1 Jan. 1841; "Jesus and the Woman of Samaria;" "Love Sleeping;" "The Sleeping Psyche;" and "Jesus in the Midst of the Doctors."

the hour drew near, he would look over the papers on his table, and, from among the four or five invitations which he was sure to find there, select one almost by accident. But such a system had numberless inconveniences; and, to avoid giving offence, Thorvaldsen was obliged to change it.

Wilkens, his servant, was a faithful, systematic fellow, who knew what was proper. He adopted the plan of writing down all his master's engagements in the order in which they were received; and, after that, when Thorvaldsen was urged to accept a verbal invitation, he would reply: "I cannot promise. See Wilkens: he will tell you whether I am disengaged. You must arrange it with him." The servant thus became a person of consequence. Great lords intrigued for the first place on his list: they flattered him and offered him money, but nothing could alter the legitimate order. Wilkens was an honest man, a slave to truth, and absolutely incorruptible.

In consequence of this arrangement, people frequently did not apply to the artist when they desired his company at dinner. They simply wrote their names on the servant's list. When the hour came, and while Wilkens was helping him dress, Thorvaldsen would ask, "Where am I going to dine to-day?" and as Wilkens always went with him, and came for him, it often happened that the old master, if he had neglected to inform himself beforehand, did not know who it was with whom he was dining. So true it is that great artists, as well as true poets, are very much like children, in that they easily allow themselves to be guided by others. Living, as they do, in a world of thought and imagination, they often behave with the *naïveté* of childhood when forced to descend to the level of every-day life.

Upon one occasion, Thorvaldsen received an invitation from the king himself. His majesty had come with the queen to the atelier, to see the model of the statue of Christian IV, to which Thorvaldsen was putting the finishing touches.

"Herr Counsellor," said the sovereign, graciously, as he was eaving, "I engage you to dine with me next Thursday." The artist gave an interrogative glance at Wilkens, who stood by the door. The poor servant, red with embarrassment, dared not reply. "Can I accept?" said his master to him: "is there any impediment?" Wilkens then committed the imprudence of pronouncing the name of Œrsted. "That's true," quickly replied the artist; and, turning toward the king, — "Your Majesty must deign to excuse me. I really cannot accept. Thursday happens to be the day of Œrsted's fête, and I have positively promised to go to Roeskilde." While the courtiers were half scandalized at this reply, the king said, with a kind smile, "I am very sorry, but I hope to be more fortunate another time."

When Wilkens, according to his custom, had come for his master to the house where he had dined, there generally ensued a series of nocturnal peregrinations through the streets of the city; for dinners could not satisfy everybody, and Thorvaldsen was also obliged to present himself at evening parties. He frequently attended two or three of an evening, while his servant waited for him; but if the artist were delayed, they were apt to enter the last house on their list just as all the other guests were leaving it. If, for fear of the same thing occurring two nights running, his domestic observed respectfully that everything went wrong the night before, Thorvaldsen, to console his faithful servant, would reply: "That is true, — we did arrive very late; but, at all events, we kept our word."

Among his constant visitors was an old man of unpretending exterior, who was in the habit of coming to see him almost every Sunday. Thorvaldsen always gave him a cordial welcome, made him sit by him on his sofa, where the two had a long and friendly conversation. Did the artist really enjoy this man's society? It is hard to say, though he did not fail to appear pleased. How much his visitor enjoyed himself was easily seen from the beaming expression of his countenance.

One Sunday, when the old man had gone, the sculptor asked his servant if he knew him; and, upon Wilkens replying in the negative, he told him that his name was Thorvaldsen; that he was an Icelander by birth, and toll-keeper of the Knippel bridge in Copenhagen. "Perhaps he wants some assistance?" said Wilkens. "Not at all: he assures me that he is in need of nothing, — wants absolutely nothing; but he thinks he is a relative of mine, which delights him greatly, and he takes pleasure in coming to see me. Let him come as much as he likes — the worthy man! I shall take good care not to undeceive him, since this mistaken belief makes him happy."

Unfortunately, Thorvaldsen's fits of melancholy sometimes impaired his kindness of heart. These moods, rare in his youth, became frequent in his old age, and were apparently almost causeless. At these times, his thoughts went back with pertinacity to those occasions in his life when he had been robbed, or been the victim of deception; and he would become misanthropical past all endurance. His habit was to ensconce himself gloomily in a corner of the sofa, and refuse to see any one. Even his art was distasteful to him. All efforts to rouse him from this unhappy state were useless, and in vain were his poor servant's endeavors to make him take some recreation. But, as soon as these melancholy fancies were dissipated, he felt sorry for whatever harsh words he might have uttered, and did his best to make amends.

The faithful Wilkens watched carefully over his master's health. He would have had him go out oftener in the daytime, and less frequently at night. After working hard all the morning, the old man required out-of-door exercise, which he took regularly at Nysöe, but not in Copenhagen. There, he always needed some inducement to go out, and to have one always ready taxed Wilkens's ingenuity to the utmost. If he could propose a visit to the atelier of an artist, success was almost certain; and, when once he was able to get his master out, he would contrive to take the longest way home. He frequently managed to pass through the street in which Thorvaldsen had lived in his boyhood, and then the old man would stop before No. 226, Aabenraa,— the house where he had resided with his parents before he went to Rome,—and look at it from top to bottom, point out to Wilkens the windows of his parents' chamber on the first floor, and that of the little closet where he had spent so many nights at work. One day, his servant, thinking that he would no doubt like to go into these rooms, proposed that they should enter the house; but hardly had the timid old man taken a step forward, when he turned hastily. "No," said he, "let us go. They will take us for suspicious characters." Suspicious himself, he thought naturally that other people were equally so.

The robbery in Rome, of which he had been the victim, had increased this natural distrust; and when he came to live in Copenhagen, he had had made a strong iron safe, to hold his collection of small valuables. For a long time it remained in his room unused, until, one day, Wilkens proposed to put the things into it. "No," said the old man, with a cunning smile, "all those things are very well where they are. Let them be. It would be a good joke if the thieves should come into my room and carry off the iron safe. I wonder who would be taken in then, they or I?"

This distrust was in part the cause of his parsimony; rendering him all the more difficult in his dealings with tradespeople. He had once a serious quarrel with a tailor whose bill he thought exorbitant. A misunderstanding in the discussion caused him to think that his confidence had been abused, and in his anger he uttered the word "cheating." The tailor, an honest man, was very much hurt, and went away saying that he would take nothing for his work. Struck by the dignified tone of the man, the artist called his servant, who explained the mistake. "Wilkens, this man is right," said Thorvaldsen, "and I owe him an apology. Let us go to him at once:" which he did, Thorvaldsen apologizing so heartily that the tailor was quite overcome. To make amends, he ordered on the spot a quantity of clothing which otherwise he would not have thought of getting; for he attached no importance to dress, and was never disposed to renew his wardrobe. His negligence in this respect was the despair of his servant, who had a keen sense of what befitted the dignity of the counsellor.

To aid a poor painter, the sculptor would pay three times the value of a picture.[1] Such generosity seemed to him the most natural thing in the world; but if Wilkens should say to him a few moments afterward, "The shoes of Herr Counsellor are so worn that the white lining shows," he would reply, —

"You have only to put on a little ink and it won't be seen."

"But, Herr Counsellor, that would look odd."

"Odd! does it hurt anybody? Has any one a right to prevent me?" the old man would rejoin, getting very angry.

The following anecdote is a still better illustration of the extreme concern of the worthy Wilkens for his master's dignity.

The artist had always been fond of the theatre, but the late dinners in Copenhagen entirely deprived him of this amusement. In order to enjoy greater liberty in this respect, he determined that as a rule he would dine at home if Wilkens's wife would prepare the meals. The honest couple tried so hard to please him, that he feared he was giving too much trouble; and this fancy so disturbed him, that he devised a plan which in his simplicity he imagined would work well.

[1] It is to such liberality we must attribute the number of mediocre pictures in the collection of the master.

He accordingly hinted to his servant that his wife would find it less inconvenient if they all took their meals together; an arrangement which seemed to him the more feasible as they also lodged in the palace. But Wilkens, with his respect for propriety, could not for a moment consider so monstrous a proposition, and tried by various pretexts to evade it. When Thorvaldsen proposed it more plainly, he opposed it chiefly on the ground of the difference of hours, as his wife and he dined much too early. "If that is all," replied the old man, "the thing is soon settled: let us compromise the matter. You dine a little later, and I a little earlier, and then we shall agree." Driven to the wall, Wilkens was finally obliged to give the true reason for his opposition. "What will the world think," he said, "when it hears that the counsellor dines with his servant?"

"The world! the world!" exclaimed Thorvaldsen. "There you are again with your world. Have I not told you a thousand times that I care nothing for what it thinks about such matters? Am I not free to live as I please? And besides, Wilkens, I consider that you are quite as good at your business as I am at mine;" and the master was so much offended that for several days he would not speak to his servant.

This indifference to social distinctions shows not only the simplicity of the artist's character, but how little he was elated by his great success in life. A king was his friend; had been, in Rome, almost his comrade. He had sat at the tables of the great, of princes, and of crowned heads, — had appeared at advantage there, — yet it seemed also very natural to him to sit at that of his faithful and honest Wilkens. "If he esteemed him, what mattered the rank?"

He still went into society, where his fame, his fine appearance, affability, and honorable character won for him universal good-will. Women were pleased with the courteous manners of this old man, whose long white hair so well set off his regular features, with their sweet and gracious expression. Above all, they liked to see him in his atelier, walking about in a long gray dressing-gown, and a black velvet cap on his white head.

When he was obliged to present himself at court, or at the house of one of the ministers, to select the decorations he should wear became a matter of much perplexity. His crosses and stars were so numerous that it was impossible to place them all on his breast. Nevertheless, he did not attach any undue importance to these distinctions. To him they were simply a collection,[1] interesting merely in the same way as his engraved stones and medals. These flattering marks of the esteem of kings had not made him vain, any more than fame and fortune had made him proud. His simplicity of character he retained to the last. If he sometimes spoke of his favorite works — though this was very rare — with a just appreciation of their value, he never did so in a conceited manner. As to the works of other artists, he was ever ready to admire and praise them sincerely: his complaisance in this respect was not politic, but real. If a work of art showed any spark of genius, he discovered it at the first glance, and took pleasure in pointing it out to others. The fits of misanthropy to which he was subject, and which obscured for the time his kindliness of heart, might render him unjust to his fellow-men, and mislead him as to their worth and character; but they never prevented his recognizing the talent of any artist or the merit of his work.

This fact proves that his misanthropy was an extraneous, not an inherent quality, and also that the jealousy of which artists are so often accused was entirely foreign to his nature. It always pleased the master when he could be useful to his brother artists; and numerous instances might be given of his kind disinterestedness. Here is one among a thousand:

[1] They were all arranged in one casket; and though he would never have thought of displaying them to persons of his own sex, he sometimes amused himself by showing them as pretty trinkets to ladies who visited him.

The King of Prussia gave a commission for a statue to Thorvaldsen. "Sire," replied he, "there is at this moment in Rome one of your faithful subjects, who is more capable than I of performing to your satisfaction the task with which you deign to honor me: permit me to solicit for him your royal favor." The sculptor thus recommended was Rodolph Schadow, who was then in embarrassed circumstances. By this act of kindness on Thorvaldsen's part, he received the commission, and executed a charming work, called "The Spinner."

THE GENIUS OF DEATH.

CHAPTER XI.

Departure for Rome.—Reception at Berlin, Dresden, Leipsic, Frankfort, Mayence, and Stuttgart.—Banquet given at Munich.—"La Société des Hommes sans Gêne."—Visit to King Louis.—Sojourn in Rome.—Return to Denmark.—The Artist and his Museum.—"The Genius of Sculpture."—Death of Thorvaldsen.—His Funeral.

THE ANGEL OF BAPTISM.

THORVALDSEN had come back to his native country with the intention of ending his career in Denmark; but, on leaving Rome, he had promised himself that he would return once more, were it only to make a brief stay, to the city where the most important period of his life had been passed. Some unfinished works were awaiting him in his old atelier, around which clustered the memories of forty-two years of his prolific artistic life.

Only an opportunity was needed to decide him to undertake the journey; and this the sculptor found when the Baron von Stampe announced his intention of going to Italy with his family. The friends resolved to travel in company across the continent; Thorvaldsen wishing to see again those of his works which now ornamented the public squares of some of the larger cities of Germany. They set out the 21st of May, 1841.

The extraordinary festivities occasioned by the artist's return to his country find a natural explanation in the just admiration of compatriots for a fame which flattered their national pride. The ovations following one upon another during the whole journey of the Danish sculptor through Germany present a spectacle which to-day may appear strange.[1]

In Berlin, the royal family invited Thorvaldsen to pass the evening at the Chateau Schönhausen (May 30, 1841). A few days later (June 3), the artists of that city gave him a grand banquet at Jagor's restaurant, when, to show unmistakably that he is the hero of the occasion, they place his bust in a bower of green leaves, together with Rauch's famous statue of Victory, so arranged that the goddess seems to be setting her crown upon Thorvaldsen's head.

In Dresden, the King of Saxony hastened to invite him to be present at a special performance at the new theatre (June 12). A court carriage came for him at the hotel and took him to the theatre, where he had a seat in the royal box. Hardly does he appear when all present welcome him with cheers; and, as if this were not enough, at the end of the play the curtain again rises, and, by way of epilogue, an actress comes forward to salute him in the name of dramatic art.

Mendelssohn, whom we have lately seen arriving in Rome, young and buoyant, and delighting the sculptor by playing the piano in his atelier, was now living in Leipsic. Thorvaldsen remembered this on arriving in that town, and the

[1] "The Kunstblatt" of 1841 has published the most circumstantial account of this journey through Germany.

composer was overjoyed by a visit from his old friend. He arranged a musical fête in his honor, followed by a banquet at the *Hôtel de Saxe*, while in the evening students carrying torches came singing in chorus under the artist's windows.

From Leipsic Thorvaldsen went to see Goethe's monument at Frankfort, and Gutenberg's at Mayence. He arrived at the latter city in the evening (June 29th). The municipality, apprised of the presence of the sculptor, escort him to the sound of music, and by the light of torches. The next day the president of the grand-ducal government of Hesse comes for him with a numerous suite to conduct him to the statue of the Inventor of Printing: the monument is decorated for the occasion with garlands, the square is filled with people, speeches and cheers abound. The following day the theatre gave a special performance in honor of "the honorary citizen of the city, the Chevalier Thorvaldsen."

At Stuttgart there were similar ovations. The Square in which stands the Schiller monument was illuminated with Bengal lights on the night of the master's arrival (July 6th); and he was serenaded by the Society of Friends of Song, and enthusiastically cheered by the crowd. Early the next day a deputation from the magistrates and the college of burghers came to pay their respects to the man who had endowed the city with so fine a monument, and to present him with the thanks of the corporation. The diploma of honorary citizenship is given him the following day at a grand repast at Silberbourg Palace. At midnight all the company form a torchlight procession, and conduct him back to his hotel.

Thorvaldsen now proceeded to Munich, where he saw again his statue of Maximilian I in the Wittelsbachplatz. There is in this city a club of *savans*, who call themselves *Société des Hommes sans Gêne.* They gave the sculptor (July 15th) a banquet in a truly characteristic German style.

One of the members, Schelling, begins by wishing the artist a long life. So far there is nothing out of the way; but now follows a series of Germanic eccentricities. Martius calls upon the spirits of nature and tropical heat (it was the month of July) to glorify this happy day. Steiglitz chants in Greek verses the joy of *les hommes sans gêne*, at having among them a master in classic art. A dead language will not serve the orientalist Naumann: he celebrates the fame of Thorvaldsen in five living languages successively, — German, English, French, Armenian, and Chinese! It was a great honor, to be sure, for the sculptor, who made no pretensions to being a *savant*. But this is not all: a discourse follows, much enjoyed and applauded, in which the orator, treating of art and industry, portrays "the wonderful and laughable quarrel of Thorvaldsen with the devil." (What had the devil to do in the business?) Weichselbrenner is more serious: he delivers an essay on the artist's works, passing them all in review, and rapidly sketching the story of his life.

Is this all? Not quite! The biographer from whom we borrow these particulars states that Förster proposed a toast in rhyme "to the wine-cask crowned with myrtle and laurel, always full of fine and generous wines," &c. But enough of this. Nevertheless, we have not come to the end of the chapter of eccentricities. The traveller was allowed scarcely time to breathe. The Society of Friends of the Arts, two days afterward, organized a fête where allegory was the order of the day. In a mythological interlude, Mercury appears enveloped in a fur mantle, in ironical allusion to the heat of the weather, and announces that the "Final Judgment," a burlesque in one act, in prose, is now to be represented. It relates to a quarrel supposed to be going on between different cities, as to which has the right to claim Thorvaldsen. Schiller pleads the cause of Stuttgart, Gutenberg of Mayence. Maximilian I advances on horseback as the advocate of Munich. Christian IV, the champion of Copenhagen, is not disposed to yield his rights. Nor are orators wanting to maintain those of Rome, Warsaw, and other cities. But now Juno, who sits beside Jupiter, grows so excited in listening to this debate, that she takes part in it herself, and declares that Olympus ought rather to claim so great an artist. The king of gods knits his awful brow, the quarrel angers him: in a tremendous voice he pronounces his decision, "Thorvaldsen belongs to the whole universe!"

King Louis, the master's illustrious friend, was not at this time in Munich, but at the baths of Brückenau. As soon as he was informed of Thorvaldsen's arrival, he hastened to write to him, July 17, 1841.

"I have most earnestly desired to see again at Munich my old and excellent friend Thorvaldsen, the greatest of all the sculptors since the most flourishing times of Greece, and to do him the honors of my capital, where the most beautiful monument which has come from his hands excites general admiration. The equestrian statue of the elector Maximilian I has never been surpassed.

"Not being able to give you in person the cross of the Order of Merit of St. Michael which I proposed to confer upon you, I have ordered the minister of my household and of foreign affairs to present it to you. Pray accept it as a token of the good intentions of him who knows how to appreciate what the world owes to you."

Thorvaldsen was unwilling to leave Bavaria without seeing King Louis; and this prince having shortly after repaired to his castle of Hohenschwangau in the Tyrol, the sculptor hastened there to visit the royal family. He had just received a very friendly letter from the King of Denmark, charging him to present his compliments to his old friend the King of Bavaria. These two princes, in their youth, had become acquainted at Rome.

The triumphal journey of the artist through Germany had greatly fatigued him: entering Switzerland by Lindau, he went to Zurich and Lucerne, and stayed a month in that neighborhood, to rest awhile before crossing the St. Gothard into Italy. He merely passed through Milan, Genoa, and Leghorn, and remained only two days in Florence, in spite of the cordial reception he received from the artists in that city. The 12th September he arrived in Rome.

The next day, a deputation, headed by the president, the ex-president, and vice-president of the Academy of St. Luke, came to offer him the congratulations of the artists in Rome. His return was also celebrated, some days later, by a grand banquet. The first two months of Thorvaldsen's visit were entirely taken up in renewing his intercourse with old friends. His health was not so much benefited by the climate of Italy as he had hoped; and he was troubled for the first time with pain in his chest, which affected him seriously enough to occasion the following remark, in a letter written November 8th, 1841: "Thorvaldsen thinks he is attacked by phthisis, and that he will die of it." It was under this impression that he made up his mind to return, the following spring, to Copen hagen. He prolonged his stay, however, beyond that time, passing the greater part of the year 1842 in Rome, and not returning to Denmark until October.

He was, during the interval, principally occupied with his religious works, — among others, a series of small bas-reliefs illustrative of the life of Christ: "The Adoration of the Shepherds," "The Flight into Egyyt," "Jesus in the Midst of the Doctors," "The Baptism of Christ," "Christ's Entry into Jerusalem."

These subjects must have been intended to form part of a more complete series, as drawings have been found, made at the same period, and now preserved in the museum, representing "The Marriage of the Virgin," "Joseph's Dream," "The Adoration of the Magi," "The Circumcision," "The Resurrection," "The Daughter of Jairus," "Jesus tempted by the Devil," "The Buyers and Sellers driven from the Temple,"

"The Canaanite Woman," "The Treason of Judas," "The Entombment."

The model for a new group of "The Three Graces," ordered by the King of Würtemburg, was also made in Rome. It differs in many respects from the one already mentioned.

Thorvaldsen was long in deciding upon the route he should take in returning home. The fear of new ovations, or, as he wrote, "the annoyance of exhibiting one's self all through Europe, like a curious animal," made him think of going by sea. Then he changed his mind: he would cross France to see Paris, going from Leghorn to Marseilles, and re-embarking at Havre. But this plan was again modified. During the voyage from Leghorn to Marseilles, he reflected that, if he went by way of Paris, he should find himself tempted to remain there some time, in order to see properly that great city, where he had never been. On the other hand, he was anxious to get back to Copenhagen, for he had heard that his museum was finished. Determined by this last consideration not to prolong his absence, he stopped two days only at Marseilles (5th to 7th of October, 1842), and went thence directly to Strasbourg.

Passing rapidly through Manheim, Mayence, Frankfort, Cassel, Hanover, and Hamburg, he arrived at Kiel, where a frigate of the royal navy, the "Frederick VI," was waiting to convey him to Copenhagen. His first care upon arriving was to go to his museum, which had been built according to the plans of the architect Bindesböll. A public subscription defrayed the greater part of the expense; and the city, with the royal approbation, made up the rest. The edifice was begun in 1839; and the exterior, including the roof, was finished in 1841.

It was here that the city council and the committee of public works received Thorvaldsen, the day after his return. He went over the whole of the great building, which had been hung with garlands for the occasion, expressing everywhere the liveliest interest, until he reached the inner court, the spot where he was one day to be buried, — for the edifice erected to perpetuate his fame was also to be his tomb, — and to those present it seemed as if the future had already begun for the master. The sculptured marble alone was to remain, the man was to return to the dust. Bending toward the earth his venerable head, the old man remained for a few moments absorbed in thought; but soon the artist roused himself and walked on with head erect. Yes: he would live again in his works, which were all to stand there around his mortal ashes, ever living witnesses of his immortal genius. Did such thoughts pass through his mind? Those around him were filled with emotion, but no one dared question him.

Thorvaldsen was now in his seventy-second year. His mind had lost none of its power: there was still the same productive energy, the same creative facility. His execution alone was unequal. Henceforward we find no longer in his modelling that perfect finish which excites our admiration in a great number of his former works; especially in those executed in Rome, in the fulness of his power and of his fame. It would not be just, therefore, to judge the artist by his last productions, though many of them are still worthy of his genius: for instance, the colossal bust of Frederick VI, made for the monument erected to this prince in Jutland, on the hill upon which stands the Chateau Skanderborg, and the four bas-reliefs ornamenting the pedestal, — "The Abolition of Serfdom," "The Institution of the Provincial States," "The Protection of Science and the Arts," "The Administration of Justice."

A charming medallion, representing the angels keeping Christmas in heaven, also belongs to the end of the year 1842. The King of Denmark was so delighted with it that he ordered directly a copy in marble. The bust of the Baroness von Stampe is of the same period.

The following year, the artist executed the model for the colossal statue of Hercules. In spite of the imperfections of this work, the vigor of mind it displays, considering the master's age, is astonishing. He also made the sketch for the statue of Æsculapius, intended as a companion to the above. Both were cast in bronze, for the façade of the royal palace of Christiansborg, in Copenhagen.[1]

A number of medallions appeared at the same time, — the Genii of Sculpture, Painting, Architecture, Poetry, and Harmony; afterward, "The Three Genii of the Arts of Design." In 1844 the artist made repetitions, varied, of most of these works.

But we must mention particularly, on account of the attention it excited in Denmark, a more important composition, the bas-relief known as "The Genius of Peace." The Genius is kneeling, holding a dish, out of which a lion and an eagle are eating together, while beside him is a dog. This was thought to be an allusion to the approaching marriage of the prince royal of Denmark to a Russian grand-duchess, and was mentioned in the political journals. Wilkens having reported their comments to his master, — "Since it is so," said Thorvaldsen, "I shall add the Phrygian cap to my composition;" and the same day he placed this emblem on the head of the allegorical figure, and also on a liberty-tree.

Among the figures representing genii, by means of which he was accustomed, in his later years, to symbolize philosophic ideas and the various phases of art, the Genius of Sculpture naturally interested him more than any other. At Nysöe, in 1843, he had portrayed him seated before a bas-relief representing the birth of Minerva, — thought springing from the brain and taking form. But this composition, though a happy one, had not satisfied him; and he returned once more to this subject, placing the Genius on the eagle's back, at the

[1] See Catalogue.

foot of the statue of Jupiter. This new bas-relief pleased him no better; and the 20th of March, 1844, he drew in chalk on a slate a third design, now in the Copenhagen Museum, in which the Genius, with the audacity of conscious power, is perched upon the shoulder of Olympian Jove himself. This was the sculptor's last composition, for we have now reached the end of this long and prolific career.

At about five o'clock in the morning of Sunday, March 24th, the artist, feeling unwell, rang for his servant. He had passed a bad night, and had not been able to sleep. Wilkens tried to calm him, begging him, however, to keep his bed. But he rose, took a book, and settled himself upon his sofa; and soon afterward, overcome with fatigue, fell asleep. When he awoke, at about eight o'clock, he took his glass of milk and roll as usual, and passed the whole morning in work.

The Baroness von Stampe having invited him to dinner, he excused himself, and replied that he intended to stay at home. This lady came to press her invitation, and found him occupied in modelling the bust of Luther. He yielded to her entreaties, and laid down before the bust his handful of clay, thrusting into it his moulding-tool. The unfinished work is preserved under glass in the Museum, and the impress of the master's hand on the morsel of clay is still visible.

He left the house with Madame von Stampe, paid a few visits, and went to the baron's to dine. He talked gayly, was amused by a humorous article in a newspaper, and said sportively, in speaking of his museum, "Now I can die when I choose, — Bindesböll has finished my tomb." A few moments afterward, on his way to the theatre, he met this architect, and they exchanged a friendly greeting.

One year precisely before this epoch, the poet Andersen, greatly moved by the news of a recent tragic occurrence, came to relate it to Thorvaldsen. Admiral Wulff, celebrated in Denmark as the translator of Shakespeare and Byron, was taken ill at the Theatre Royal during the play. He was driven home in a carriage, but upon arriving at his door was found dead by the driver. "Well," exclaimed the sculptor, with an energy which amazed Andersen, "is not that an admirable way to die, and one to be envied?"[1]

It was just a year from that time that Andersen met the artist on his way to the theatre. Thorvaldsen urged him to come with him; but the poet, impatient to commit to writing some new work of his imagination, refused. Thorvaldsen entered the theatre alone, and took his usual seat in the parquet. A lady, coming in afterward, was obliged to pass before him. In order to make room, he rose; and the lady, turning to thank him, saw him stooping down. "Have you lost anything, sir?" she asked. Thorvaldsen did not reply. It was now seen that he was ill, and people ran to his assistance. He was carried in great haste to the Charlottenborg Palace, which adjoins the theatre, and laid on his sofa. A physician hastened to open a vein; but no blood came. The great artist had ceased to live.

The next day the sad news spread quickly through the whole city, filling it with dismay. The funeral ceremonies took place on Saturday, March 30, 1844, and were marked by a royal pomp. The whole nation, so to speak, followed the venerated master to the tomb. He was laid in state, in the hall of antique sculpture in the Charlottenborg Palace. There, in a coffin richly decorated with wreaths,[2] with face uncovered, and brow crowned with laurel, he lay, surrounded by the masterpieces of ancient Greece, whose spirit lived again in his works.

It was here that the deputations met to join the friends of the deceased. When they were all assembled, the artists intoned the chant of farewell, and the coffin was closed. On its lid was engraved the master's statue of himself: on the

[1] We had this anecdote from Herr Andersen himself, when we called upon him in Copenhagen.

[2] To M. Dotezac, French Minister to Copenhagen, who was present at the ceremony, I am indebted for some of these details.

pall lay his chisel, amid branches of laurel and palm. Among the wreaths was one of flowers, woven by the Queen of Denmark.

A doctor of theology, Professor Clausen, delivered an address, and the procession began its march through the New Market, East Street, Amakplads, Vimmelskaftet, and New Streets. Every house was hung with black, the crowd was grave and silent: not a sound was heard, save the tolling of the funeral knell from the towers of all the churches, and the chanting of choirs stationed in the belfries.

From the windows, women cast flowers before the coffin, borne by forty artists. As soon as the cortège approached the *Frue Kirke*, the king in person, accompanied by the prince royal, advanced to meet it at the entrance of the church. There, in the presence of Thorvaldsen's religious works, was celebrated the funeral service. The prior of the cathedral, the Rev. Herr Tryde, preached a sermon; and after the ceremony the crowd dispersed slowly and quietly. They felt that the whole nation had met with a grievous loss.

The remains of the illustrious sculptor rested nearly four years in a chapel of the *Frue Kirke*, awaiting the completion of the interior of the museum; and it was not until Sept. 6, 1848, that the body was laid in the vault, in the centre of the Thorvaldsen Museum. There, amid the rich collection of the master's works, repose to-day his mortal remains.

MERCURY.

PART II.

WORKS OF THORVALDSEN.

FIGURE, FROM THE FRIEZE, "THE TRIUMPH OF ALEXANDER."

CHAPTER I.

Influence of the French School upon Art in Denmark, from the time of Louis XIV. — The Academy of Fine Arts in Copenhagen. — Revival of Art in Italy under Winckelmann.

PSYCHE.

A PUPIL of the Copenhagen School of Fine Arts, Thorvaldsen produced his works under the influence of the theories advanced by Winckelmann at the close of the last century. It is impossible, therefore, to form a just estimate of his worth and individuality as an artist, without giving at least a short account of the state of art in Denmark at the time of the sculptor's birth, and of the reaction which had spread through Italy when he, a mere youth, took up his abode there; for, however great may be an artist's individuality, he cannot remain unaffected by surrounding influences

The progress of the fine arts in Denmark is closely connected with the history of the French school. Poussin studied in Rome; also Lebrun, the painter of Louis XIV, and the real founder of the French Academy in that city. During the last half of the seventeenth century, all through Europe, in Italy, Germany, and the North, the influence of the French school was dominant.

Everywhere in these countries, in churches, palaces, castles, we meet either with immense paintings in the florid style of Lebrun, or with statues which recall, by their ambitious elegance, the manner of the Coustous.

To Lebrun succeeded Mignard; and after him came Watteau, Boucher, the painters of *fêtes champêtres;* Lancret, Pater, the sculptor Clodion, and many others. In sculpture, as in painting, grace, as the chief end in view, came to be substituted for the grand style of the age of Louis XIV, with its conventional dignity, its imposing and sometimes exaggerated splendors. A new style, full of mannerisms and elegant artifices, was now the fashion, — a style already very far removed from the point of departure of the French school, but which, being in perfect harmony with the thought and taste of the period, wielded an influence felt everywhere throughout Europe.

In the North, from the reign of Louis XIV, these changes can be even more distinctly traced than elsewhere. Born in Copenhagen, Thorvaldsen was not uninflnenced by the general current of thought, as we might at first suppose. When he came into the world, the arts, and especially sculpture, were cultivated with success in Denmark.[1]

It is true that previous to the reign of Charles V (1670–1699), the Danish painters were influenced by the Dutch school; but, by the end of the seventeenth century, French ideas were disseminated among them, and held thenceforward absolute supremacy. The national genius, let us remark, yielded easily to French influence, while it rejected that of countries less remote.

[1] It is well known what an important part the countries of the North formerly played in the political affairs of Europe. There are still vestiges in the city of Copenhagen of the ancient magnificence of her kings. A visit to the Rosenberg Castle, which contains so many valuable relics of the past, vases, precious stones, objects of art of all kinds, is sufficient to convey an idea of the former splendor of the Danish court, — to-day so dignified in its simplicity.

This taste for the rich and brilliant, this love of beautiful things, we ought to add, was already diffused in the time of Christian IV (1588–1648).

During the reign of Christian V, a French painter, Jacques d'Agar, was settled in Copenhagen as portrait painter to the court; and another artist, French also, the sculptor Abraham Cæsar L'Amoureux, executed in 1688 the equestrian statue of the king. This statue, already referred to in the biography of Thorvaldsen, was cast in lead, and erected in the centre of the Place Royale (Kongens Nytorv). The monarch tramples under the feet of his horse a demon representing envy, which writhes with hate and base anger. This work, though not wanting in force, is both sensational and pretentious.

Frederick IV and Christian VI protected the arts.[1] In their reigns the French school took root in Denmark. Under the sway of Frederick V (1746–1766), the palace of Charlottenborg was arranged for the use of the Academy of Fine Arts. At the same time an entire new quarter of the city, Fredriksstaden, was laid out in Copenhagen; and here the leading nobles vied with each other in erecting sumptuous mansions. The principal square in this quarter was called *Amalienborgs Plads*, from an old castle on the same site, which had been destroyed by fire in 1689.

An equestrian statue of the king, also the work of a French sculptor, J. F. J. Saly, stands in this square. It has a fine general appearance; certain parts, especially the head of the horse, being very well executed.

Saly, who resided in Denmark until 1774, produced other works of merit, and had an important influence over the growth of the Academy, of which he became director. C. F. Stanley, A. Weidenhaupt, N. Dajon, sculptors born in

[1] Frederick IV (1699–1730) had a true perception of the beautiful. Fredericksberg and Fredensborg furnish proof of how well he understood the principles of art. These palaces are skilfully planned to harmonize with their sites and the natural scenery of the surrounding country. Frederick IV was, above all, the patron of painting. His successor, Christian VI (1730–1746), was passionately fond of luxury. The palace of Christiansborg (destroyed by the fire of 1794) and numerous country-houses and hunting-boxes, among them Hirsholm and the Hermitage, testify to the splendor with which he surrounded his court.

Denmark, who have left behind them justly honored names, studied at the Academy during his administration.

The Danish sculptor, who after Saly was held in the highest estimation, was Johannes Wiedewelt, who succeeded him as director of the Academy. He belonged to a family of artists, his grandfather having been an architect and his father a carver. To decorate the prow and stern of vessels with figure-heads and rich carvings was already the custom in Denmark. The father of Wiedewelt pursued this avocation in the shipyards of Holmen; and here his son, like the young Thorvaldsen afterward, made his first essays.

Under the direction of his father, Wiedewelt acquired a certain degree of aptitude; and when Saly came to Copenhagen, in 1753, he was travelling to complete his art education at the royal expense. He first went to Paris, where he studied with William Coustou the younger; thence to Rome, where he lived on intimate terms with Winckelmann, who directed his attention to the antique. This intimacy had a decided influence upon Wiedewelt, who from that time began to study the Greeks and Romans with enthusiasm. The relations between him and the illustrious *savant* were founded on true friendship, and they corresponded constantly until the death of Winckelmann.

Upon his return to Copenhagen (1758), Wiedewelt was made member of the Academy, and the following year professor. He was also charged with a large number of works. In the magnificent cathedral of Roeskilde, the burial-place of the Danish kings, the sarcophagus of Christian VI and the great monument of Frederick V, enriched with figures larger than life, are both by Wiedewelt. Several statues in the garden of Fredensborg Castle are also by his hand, besides richly decorated marble vases, and four large groups in sandstone of mythological subjects. Wiedewelt executed a great number of busts and mortuary monuments. Many of them were destroyed, either when the castle was burnt in 1794, or during the bombardment of Copenhagen in 1807. But his finest and most characteristic work has fortunately been preserved. It is a statue in marble of a woman, and represents Fidelity. It is placed with three other statues around the obelisk to Liberty, erected in 1792 in front of the west gate of the city. This monument commemorates the abolition of serfdom.

An intelligent artist, Wiedewelt possessed the inventive faculty and composed with great facility. His sojourn at Paris and Rome, his relations with Winckelmann, had contributed to enrich his mind with extensive knowledge. Nevertheless, his talent, though developed under such happy influences, was wanting in flexibility; and the artist did not succeed in putting life and expression into his figures, which are executed with learned accuracy, but with a certain stiffness.

The tendencies of style observable in the works of this sculptor testify to the authority exercised over him by Winckelmann: they already indicate the working of the new ideas which later were to become dominant with Canova and Thorvaldsen.

In his old age, Wiedewelt gradually gave himself up to a profound melancholy, and finally, in 1802, put an end to his life.[1]

Weidenhaupt, a pupil of Saly, acquired a fair reputation, especially as professor of the Academy. He left an *écorché*, which was highly esteemed, and used for a model until within a few years. A pensioner of the Academy, Weidenhaupt went to Paris, where he studied from 1762 to 1765.

[1] Among the pupils of Wiedewelt, we ought to mention J. J. Holm, a young artist of talent, who soon gave up sculpture for the engraving of medals. He was, however, surpassed in this art by Peter Gianelli, of Copenhagen, who engraved several medals of true artistic value. One, commemorating the abolition of the slave trade in the Danish colonies in 1792, is specially remarkable. He died early in this century. His brother, Dominic Gianelli, who obtained the great gold medal in 1799, subsequently took up his abode in England. He sent in 1820 to the Academy in which he had studied a portrait bust of the Duke of Gloucester.

Under the direction of Pajou, he worked upon a marble Saint Augustine, intended for the *Hôtel des Invalides.* In Rome he was attracted to the antique, and modelled reduced copies of some of the most celebrated statues. These copies, which have unfortunately disappeared with time, had great success in Copenhagen exhibitions.

"Agriculture," one of the marble figures adorning the obelisk to Liberty, was executed by Weidenhaupt. It is only just to say, that in this statue, as well as in other studies by the same artist, there is a marked and sustained effort in the direction of the simplicity of Greek art.

Nicholas Dajon, born like Weidenhaupt in Copenhagen, and a pupil of Saly, also worked on the monument to Liberty. The two female figures, "Courage" and "Patriotism," are from his chisel; but they are inferior to the other two. He succeeded better in a very rich mortuary monument, ornamented with two marble female figures of life-size, in a cemetery in Copenhagen.

Thorvaldsen received lessons at the Academy from this sculptor. When, in 1819, the pupil returned to Copenhagen, already covered with glory, the old master was almost forgotten. He died in 1823.

It does not enter into our plan to follow out the history of art in Denmark:[1] we have attempted only to show by a few

[1] In Sweden, also, the influence of the French school was felt, and in a more persistent manner than in Denmark. The younger brother of our celebrated Bouchardon settled in this country, where he was without a rival. He died in 1762. Larchevêque, who was director of the Royal Swedish Academy, and who died in 1778, was a mannered artist. He had for a pupil Sergel, the best of the Swedish sculptors, of whom the Marquis de Chennevières has given an interesting notice in the "Revue Universelle des Arts" (May, 1856). Sergel, who made an excellent "Sleeping Fawn," was Canova's predecessor in Rome. It was there he formed himself, not altogether escaping, however, the influences of the French school, — of which his charming group of "Love and Psyche" is an evidence. We cannot forget that it is to Sergel we owe the tomb of Descartes, in the church of Adolphus-Frederick, in Stockholm. After this artist, the most famous Swedish sculptors were Byström and Fogelberg, contemporaries of Thorvaldsen. The first, of serious and rather cold turn of mind, sought inspiration from the antique: the other was a pupil of Sergel, but he also studied under Guérin and Bosio in Paris. Gustave Planche has devoted a very care-

illustrations, how this country, after having yielded to the general influence of the art movement in Europe, especially in France, formed its own Academy, and to indicate the conditions under which Thorvaldsen made his first art studies.

We must not exaggerate the influence in Denmark of the principles brought from Italy by Wiedewelt, the friend of Winckelmann. They were not always adopted by his successors. It was not at Copenhagen, therefore, but in Rome, in presence of the masterpieces of antiquity, that Thorvaldsen finally found his proper path.

When he arrived in Italy, the art revolution was definitely accomplished. It had commenced in the Peninsula about the middle of the seventeenth century: in the eighteenth, Mengs, a German, settled in Rome, encouraged it, and Winckelmann ensured its triumph. By a fortunate coincidence, the discoveries of Pompeii and Herculaneum favored this great movement. Thoroughly familiar with the beauties of the Greek language, admiring Sophocles and Demosthenes, and enthusiastic over Hesiod and Homer, Winckelmann had long studied the antiquities of the German Museums before going to Italy. At the time he arrived in this land of promise for the artist and scholar, Antiquity herself, rising up from beneath the ashes and lava which had preserved her, stood ready to reveal herself, unveiled and glowing, to her enthusiastic lover.

The works of Winckelmann on the antique have long been well known. The great influence they have had upon artists has reformed the taste for the meretricious and affected, and induced a return to the severe beauties of Greek art. Had they no other merit, these works would, on this account alone, be worthy of the respect of all judicious

ful article in the "Revue des Deux Mondes," 1855, to this artist, who was very fond of the traditions of the Scandinavian mythology. To Fogelberg we owe the statues of the gods, Odin, Thor, and Balder. His works were published in 1856 in Paris by M. Casimir Leconte.

minds. Nevertheless, as they have had, generally, less happy results in painting than in sculpture, they have lost some of the popularity they enjoyed at the beginning of this century.

Perhaps, also, the fault lies in the excessive zeal of some artists, who, confounding the letter with the spirit, have overshot the mark, and gone far beyond the ideas of Winckelmann, — substituting absolutely for an intelligent study of nature a servile copying of the relics of antiquity. These artists have given birth only to imitations.

The learned German says: "The treatise in which we have discussed the art of the Egyptians, Etruscans, and other nations, may enlarge our ideas, and lead to correctness of judgment; but this on Greek art will attempt to base them on the Unity of Truth (the one and the true) as a standard of opinion and a rule in execution. [1]

There are to be found in the works of Winckelmann just and wise teachings. The great admirer of the Greeks was fully persuaded that in their art those masters were in possession of truth; and when he describes their methods, he incidentally lays down precepts of high value. To what was owing the superiority, incontestable in sculpture, of these Greek artists, so happily endowed with a natural aptitude for feeling and appreciating beauty? Above all, to the daily study they made of the naked figure.[2]

But, if the Greeks had constantly before their eyes the naked figure, they did not content themselves with copying it; they chose from many models what pleased them most,

[1] Winckelmann, vol. ii, p. 4. Lodge's Translation.

[2] The gymnasia and other places where the young exercised naked, in athletic and other games, and which were the resort of those who desired to see beautiful youth, were the schools wherein the artist saw beauty of structure; and, from the daily opportunity of seeing it nude and in perfection, his imagination became heated, the beauty of the forms he saw became his own, and was ever present to his mind. At Sparta, even the young virgins exercised naked, or nearly so, in the games of the arena. Winckelmann, vol. ii, p. 43. Lodge's Translation.

And from this choice composed a harmonious whole, superior, consequently, to each model taken separately. "They purified their images from all personal feelings, by which the mind is diverted from the truly beautiful."[1] "This selection of the most beautiful parts, and their harmonious union in one figure," again observes Winckelmann, "produces *ideal beauty*, which is therefore no metaphysical abstraction."[2]

The idealistic doctrine to-day has numerous opponents; nevertheless, if it does not insist upon absolute truth, it does not forbid the study of the beautiful in nature, that being in fact the basis on which it rests.

The search after the beautiful in nature, and the creation of the ideal, did not comprise all the æsthetic doctrine of the Greeks. The artist who follows their precepts must also devote himself to expression and action. "An observance of propriety in expression and action," again remarks Winckelmann, "ought therefore to be inculcated at the same time with the principles of beautiful forms, because it is one of the constituents of grace."[3] Still, moderation is necessary in expression as in action; for if beauty, like limpid water drawn from the clearest springs, loses its purity by the admixture of foreign elements, expression ought only to be admitted so far as it does not alter the features of the face. So, also, the action of the limbs should never be so strongly emphasized as to break the harmonious equilibrium of the body.

Such is the essence of the teachings of Winckelmann. Thorvaldsen is one of the artists who have most faithfully endeavored to put these theories into practice, and in sculpture he may be said to be their most complete and truest expression. It is impossible, therefore, to separate his works from the principles which may almost be said to have produced them.

1 Winckelmann, vol. ii, p. 47. Lodge's Translation. 2 Ibid. p. 48.
3 Vol. ii, p. 112. Lodge's Translation.

ACHILLES AND PRIAM.

CHAPTER II.

Theories of Winckelmann and Thorvaldsen. — Figures of Manhood: "Jason," "Mercury," "Vulcan," "Hercules." — Youthful Figures: "Bacchus," "Ganymede," "Cupid," "Apollo," "Adonis." — Goddesses: "Venus," "The Three Graces," "Psyche," "Hebe." — Statue of the "Young Dancing-Girl," and that of "Hope." — The Ægina Marbles.

ADONIS.

THE works of Winckelmann, which were destined to exercise so important an influence upon art, remained for a long time almost unknown to artists. The principles propounded by the *savant* were first appreciated only by archæologists; but when, little by little, they had penetrated beyond this narrow circle, they effected a complete revolution in ideas. David, on his return from Italy, brought them to France, where they were the more readily welcomed, as the study of the republican institutions of Greece and Rome was then in vogue; and whatever related to them, whether in politics or art, was assured of a great popularity. Canova, whose genius was pliant and facile, succeeded in giving to his work a certain semblance of antique art. He very soon became the most celebrated sculptor, not only of Italy, but of Europe; and when the Empire, in its turn, evoked the memories of the Rome of the Cæsars, he was still more highly considered.

At the time of Thorvaldsen's arrival in Italy, the revolution was accomplished; but we must not conclude that the artist did no more than yield to the influence prevailing around him. It was under the guidance of a purely personal feeling that he was immediately attracted by the most beautiful, the most severe monuments of Greek art; and, though he participated in the general movement, he played a part in it peculiar to himself. Circumstances also favored him. Scarcely had the young Dane taken the first step on the road which was to lead him to fame, when he encountered a fervent disciple of Winckelmann. Doubtless he owed much less to the wise counsels of this friend than to the clearness of his own judgment, but his modesty made him rely with respectful confidence upon the knowledge of Zoëga. Warmly encouraged by the learned archæologist in his enthusiastic admiration for the grand style of antique statuary, Thorvaldsen abandoned himself without reserve to his tastes, and went resolutely on in the direction in which his talent was to receive its full development.

In Rome he found a vast field open to investigation, and innumerable models for his studies. In spite of the ravages of time, of civil wars, invasions of barbarians, devastations, Rome was still the heiress of Antiquity; and the excavations carried on in Italy, and pushed as far as Greece, added every day new treasures to her store.

Before attempting any original work, Thorvaldsen strove to imbue himself with the spirit of the Greek artists; and, "*les œuvres de force* attracting him by preference, he took for the model of his first important copy one of the Dioscuri of Monte Cavallo, — the Pollux, — which he executed with a sort of religious respect. Under the profound impression[1]

[1] "'Emotion received should be transmuted into our own being,' says truly Mme. de Staël; and the truer this emotion is, the less will it inspire a servile imitation."

left upon him by the study of this antique, he produced the "Jason," a statue so lofty and severe in style, that we can scarcely believe that it marks the *début* of a young artist.

"When Jason appeared," says Pindar,[1] "all the people were struck with astonishment. They took him for Apollo, Bacchus, or Mars." For the type of his "Theseus," Canova chose Apollo. To represent Jason, Thorvaldsen selected the more manly figure of Mars. The hero still wears his long floating hair, as he wore it, according to the poet, when he entered Athens for the first time. It escapes from his helmet in thick curls. He is represented in all the vigor of manhood, and his noble attitude recalls the Hercules of an antique mosaic in the Villa Albani.[2]

The Greeks gave more expression and action to heroes than to gods. According to their principles, too much action was incompatible with the sublime serenity of divinity; but it was permitted to the artist to put more animation into figures representing human beings. "In heroes, — that is, in men to whom antiquity attributed the highest excellence of human nature, — he [the Greek artist] advanced even to the confines of the divine nature, without passing beyond them, and without blending the very nice distinctions which separated the two."[3] The "Jason" is an application of this principle.

With the Greeks, the representations of their divinities corresponded to the ideas they had previously conceived of them. The admirably well-balanced imagination of this people, unlike the generality of the Oriental idolaters, was incapable of giving birth to monsters, but, on the contrary, produced types of perfect and superhuman beauty, which very soon became recognized objects of worship. These

[1] Ode iv.
[2] Discovered in 1760, and described in the *Monumenti*, No. 66.
[3] Winckelmann, vol. ii, p. 86. Lodge's Translation.

figures of the gods are instinct with thought: not the face alone, but the whole body, from head to foot. Whenever Thorvaldsen represented these divinities, he necessarily conformed to the Greek tradition, adopting the established type[1] for each. Still, while he constantly employed the refining processes practised by the sculptors of antiquity, he at the same time endeavored not to lose sight of nature; and, in the larger number of his statues, we find evidence of careful anatomical study of living models.

Thorvaldsen, in following with a wise moderation the system of deification of the human form, has produced in his "Mercury" a work commingled of the real and the ideal. It is one of the finest pieces of modern sculpture, and will compare favorably with the antique statues. "Mercury Argiphontes,"[2] says Nagler, truly, "is a most happy expression of manly beauty at the age of thirty. It resembles in character and in its proportions the famous Greek hero known as the "Fighting Gladiator." To create such a work, Thorvaldsen began by copying nature. As we have already said, the very pose of the figure was given him by a porter, whom he accidentally saw in the Corso. The porter is become a god, owing to the exquisite choice of forms, idealized with an intelligent discretion without losing any of their truth; and owing, also, to the nobility which characterizes the expression of the countenance. It is not human guile, it is divine intelligence which is reflected on the brow and beams in the eye of Mercury. The action, or, to speak with more exactness, the preparation for action, is sufficient to

[1] "As the ancients," says Winckelmann, "had mounted gradually from human to divine beauty, each of the steps of beauty remained through which they passed in their ascent." And, farther on, he adds, in regard to the process of making a hero into a god, that "the effect has been produced rather by subtraction than addition; that is to say, by the gradual abstraction of all those parts which, even in nature, are sharply and strongly expressed, until the shape becomes refined to such a degree that only the spirit within appears to have brought it into being." Vol. ii, pp. 86, 90. Lodge's Translation.

[2] "The Slayer of Argus."

give movement and flexibility to the body and limbs; but it is restrained and reveals a god, capable of vigorous and yet effortless activity.

In the statue of "Mars," the muscles are more strongly marked. It was proper to give to the god of war a more pronounced appearance of exterior force than to Mercury. Both these divinities display the characteristics of youth united with those of manhood. Mars and Mercury are beardless, and their short and curly hair falls over their forehead.

The statue of "Vulcan" belongs to the period of developed manhood.[1] The Greeks, it is known, endowed divinities of this age with a character in some respects immutable, so that they can be recognized by the conventional cast of the features and the cut of the hair and beard. The countenance of Vulcan is characterized by that calm ruggedness proper to the blacksmith-son of Jupiter: he has the heavy beard and thick bushy hair of the king of gods; his head is covered with the workman's cap; his tunic, after the prescribed fashion for this god, always occupied with hard labor, is unfastened on the right shoulder, leaving the chest bare. The general attitude of this figure reminds us very much of an Hephaistos on an altar in the Vatican.[2]

In regard to the statue of "Hercules," it should not be judged severely, when we remember that Thorvaldsen was seventy-three years old when he modelled it. It is certainly inferior to the works above mentioned, though it still bears the marks of a master-hand.

The Greek sculptors saw in Hercules two different persons. One is the hero "who had to contend against monsters and fierce men, and had not yet reached the end of his toils:"

[1] Sometimes, but very rarely, the ancients represented Hephaistos (Vulcan) with the features of youth.

[2] Mentioned by M. Theil, in his Dictionary.

he is represented with protuberant muscles. The other is the demi-god, "whose body had been purified by fire, and who had been raised to the enjoyment of the happiness of Olympus. The former is represented in the Hercules Farnese, and the latter in the torso of the Belvedere."[1]

Thorvaldsen selected the man Hercules. He has not represented him, as the Greeks sometimes did, in the glory of youth, with features which leave his sex almost doubtful, so that his beauty resembles that which the complaisant Glycera required a young man to have in order to be worthy of her favors.[2] He has given him, on the contrary, a robust and even heavy figure. We notice the weight rather than the strength of the colossus. The hand which holds the club does not seem to grasp it with vigor; nor does the head much resemble that of Hercules, subduer of monsters, to whom the Greeks always gave a low brow, with thick, coarse hair bristling over the forehead, like the shaggy locks between the horns of the bull.[3]

Among the youthful figures treated by Thorvaldsen, we note those of Bacchus, Ganymede, Love, Apollo, and Adonis, which have very distinctive characteristics. The Greeks gave to Bacchus a mixed type of beauty, compounded of both sexes, and "drawn from the conformation of eunuchs."[4] The ancient artists, who represented this god in his youth, always rounded his limbs to the point of feminine elegance, and developed his hips to almost womanly proportions; for, according to the fable, Bacchus was brought up as a girl.[5]

Following this tradition, Thorvaldsen has given much feminine delicacy to his "Bacchus." The god is leaning negligently against the trunk of a tree, and turning his head

1 Winckelmann, vol. ii, p. 78. Lodge's Translation.
2 Winckelmann.
3 Winckelmann, vol. ii, p. 157. Lodge's Translation.
4 Ibid. vol. ii, p. 73.
5 Ibid. vol. ii, p. 73.

languidly toward the cup which he is lifting to his lips. The brow is crowned with vine-leaves; and the hair, gathered together, and knotted on the top of the head like a woman's, is allowed to partly escape and fall over the shoulders, — an arrangement common to Apollo and Bacchus, and to them alone of all the divinities.[1] There is something soft and easy in the contour of this figure, a voluptuous flexibility in the action of the body. The rounded abdomen and projecting hips approach to the feminine type: the muscles and knee-pans, scarcely marked, are those of young boys.

Ganymede has none of this blending of forms. He is a youth remarkable for the delicacy of his limbs, the want of prominence in his muscles, the softness and roundness of his flesh. His hips are not developed like those of Bacchus. The son of Tros unites in himself all the beauties which nature is capable of giving to young boys. It is thus he appears in the statues of Thorvaldsen and in the group where the artist has represented him kneeling before Jupiter, metamorphosed into an eagle. The young Trojan is performing, for the first time, his duties as cup-bearer to the god. The way the eagle regards him indicates the cause of the jealousy of Juno. This group is grand in style, well balanced, and fine in execution.

The "Ganymede" is only an embodiment of idealized human beauty. To represent Love, the artist should, according to the principle of the Greeks, strive for a higher aim, — a divine ideal. "Love Victorious" has all the graces of youth, joined to an exceeding delicacy. Though the forms have something of the blending of the two types, as in the "Bacchus," they have more loftiness and purity, and reveal a god of a superior order. The conqueror of gods and men, leaning on his bow, is looking at the point of one of his arrows with an expression of malice and pride which is almost cruel.

[1] Winckelmann, vol. ii, p 185. Lodge's Translation. Also see p. 68.

In the group of "Cupid and Psyche," the figure of the god is firm and slender, and copied more directly from beautiful living models. This composition is a masterpiece of true grace and simplicity. In drawing from the same sources as the Greek masters, the sculptor has approached nearer to them, perhaps, than he could have done by the mere imitation of their works; and has given to his figures all the originality of his own genius. Psyche stands looking thoughtfully at the cup of immortality: she hesitates before putting it to her lips, she does not yet dare to confront this immense unknown. Cupid encourages her with tender persuasions, and smiles sweetly at the *naïveté* of the young girl. In this work, there is something superior to the beauty of form: it is the extreme delicacy of the sentiment and of the philosophic idea. In representing Cupid and Psyche, Canova satisfied himself by grouping together two beautiful figures in an attitude of tenderness and soft languor. Thorvaldsen has done more: he has expressed a thought.

Among the Greeks, the figure of Apollo is the highest type of ideal beauty, whose most complete expression is the Apollo Belvedere. In our judgment, Thorvaldsen did not here attain to his ideal. The figure of his "Apollo" is nearer akin to the mixed beauty of Bacchus, a less noble divinity. The face is wanting in that distinction of feature which might be dispensed with in Apollo, shepherd of Admetus, but which must be always retained in the god of Parnassus

Adonis not being a deity, the sculptor had only to copy skilfully what he saw in nature, and give to his figure a simple and antique attitude. His "Adonis" is a youth in the full bloom of manly beauty, copied with scrupulous fidelity from the finest living models. Here are still all the graces of adolescence, but with no false refinement to disturb the purity of the figure, or compromise its noble simplicity. This work, which has some resemblance to the "Apollo Sauroctonos" of antiquity, is, however, entirely original in execution. Thorvaldsen borrowed from the Greeks the perfect form of the head, the arrangement of the hair, the repose of the attitude, the careful balance of the figure ; but the pensive expression of the young shepherd, and the evidences of a loving study of nature, give to the marble the personal imprint of the artist. No traveller visiting the Glyptothek of Munich can fail to be sensibly impressed, not only by the elegance and severe style of this work, but also by the deep feeling pervading it.

If we extend this comparative method of study to the female figures of Thorvaldsen, we shall still find the artist a pupil of the Greeks, and, imbued with their principles, applying with an independent genius the rules which guided these masters.

The Greeks, in expressing beauty of form in their goddesses, do not seem to have followed closely the distinctions to which they so rigidly adhered in their gods and heroes.[1] The faces of the goddesses have all a character of their own ; but the forms, which, moreover, are usually draped, have seldom any distinguishing difference except that of age.

To Venus and the Graces belong the nearly exclusive privilege of being habitually represented nude, though we have almost the right to say that, in the first period of Greek art, this license was not permitted. The Venus of Melos, which belongs to the finest epoch of antiquity, is partly draped.

When Thorvaldsen was modelling his "Venus," he could not have known of the statue found in the Island of Melos in 1820, and directly afterward taken to Paris. But he must have studied the Medicean, the Capitoline, and the Venus of Troas ; and he seems to have been inspired by the more youthful beauty of the first. He has not given his figure that attitude of modest embarrassment which characterizes the three antique statues : still, there is nothing in the severe beauty of the "Venus Victrix" of the Danish sculptor which

[1] Winckelmann, vol. ii, p. 91. Lodge's Translation.

can excite an equivocal thought. The admiration which she inspires is similar to that which those philosophers might feel, for whom "Love is the colleague of Wisdom."[1] The goddess, with her left hand, is already taking up the garment which, before presenting herself to Paris, she had laid on the trunk of a tree. The right arm is drawn near the body by a movement which, though graceful, is lacking a little in freedom; the hand holds the apple, the prize of victory. The head, slightly inclined, is expressive of gratified pride and divine serenity in her triumph.

Thorvaldsen did not usually give a large development to the bosom in his figures of women. The outlines of his "Venus" are elaborated with a finished delicacy; the movement of the hips, thighs, and legs is graceful without affectation; the feet and hands are executed with extreme nicety.

In the group of the "Three Graces," Thorvaldsen seems to us less happily inspired. The type of feminine beauty adopted by him is not that usually chosen by the Greeks, which was both strong and delicate. In trying to idealize his figures, he has only succeeded in making them thin. The faces express the innocence of youth, and the virginal bosoms are rounded and finished with extreme delicacy; but the less developed contours of the lower part of the bodies have a certain hardness and angularity of outline.

In accordance with the theory of Mengs, that a group should always have the pyramidal form, the artist has made the head and shoulders of two of his figures incline: the third, on the contrary, is upright, and stiff in attitude. One of the three sisters presents her full face: the others are in profile. Consequently, we do not see the back of any of them. This arrangement did not permit the artist to please by a simultaneous view of the feminine form in all its aspects. Jean Goujon, Raphael, the greater number of ancient sculp-

[1] Τᾶ σοφίᾳ παρέδρους ἔρωτας. Euripides, Media, v. 843.

tors,[1] appear, on the contrary, to have preferred the opposite arrangement, which is much more satisfactory to the eye.

In spite of the praise which this group has received, — it has even inspired the poetic mind of a king,[2] — there is no doubt that Thorvaldsen was not fully satisfied with his work, and in 1842 he executed a new model, different from the first. But the perfection to which he could not attain in the fulness of his powers was not to be reached in his old age, and the second work seems to us even inferior to the first. Nevertheless, the sculptor tried to give more ease to the middle figure, whose attitude he changed. The right foot only is resting on the ground, while the left is raised. The movement — a little unnatural — of the second goddess is also modified. To get rid of the angular outline of the lower part of the body, the artist turned the right-hand figure three-quarters round, making it face nearly to the front; so that its posture does not vary sufficiently from that of the central figure. Finally, notwithstanding the excellent intentions for which this new attempt is to be commended, the group of 1842, though carefully finished, is inferior to the other in delicacy of workmanship. In both compositions, the goddesses are wanting in fulness of outline.

To Psyche undoubtedly belongs the slender and delicate form of extreme youth. This charming subject has been twice treated by Thorvaldsen: first in the group of which we have already spoken, and afterward in a pretty statue, representing the gentle victim of the vengeance of Venus bearing from the infernal regions the mysterious box given her by Proserpine. She stands in a pensive attitude; her drapery has fallen below her hips, leaving exposed the upper part of the body. By a movement indicative of innocent

[1] See Seneca, De Beneficiis, i, 3.

[2] King Louis of Bavaria wrote a poem, in which he celebrated with enthusiasm the "Three Graces" of Thorvaldsen, and criticised severely Canova's group. (Nagler.)

curiosity, the young girl lays her right hand on the cover of the box; but she hesitates. We can imagine nothing more delicate. It is a charming creation, with no sign of effort.

Hebe has been twice represented by the artist. In the first model, the young goddess is clothed in a double tunic: the garment, unfastened on the shoulder, leaves the right breast bare. The drapery is elegant and severe. But this exposure of the bust was considered a fault; and ten years later Thorvaldsen, in modelling a repetition of this first statue, covered the bosom entirely, to better express the modest grace which belongs to the goddess of youth.

We must not conclude our examination of these female figures, without saying a word about a charming statue of a young girl, whose tunic, slipping over her right arm, exposes a bosom hardly yet developed. By a *naïve* movement, she raises her dress on both sides, and begins to dance. Her hair is knotted simply on the top of her head. This composition is full of freshness and buoyancy. It is a very characteristic work, strongly imbued with the artist's individuality.

The statue of "Hope," on the contrary, is wholly archaic, — a skilful and intentional imitation of early Greek art. The attitude of the goddess is impassive: in one hand she holds a flower ready to scatter its seed, in the other a fold of her long tunic, — a movement conformed to antique tradition. The severe fall of the drapery, under which the body is discreetly but strongly indicated; the placidity of the face, admirable in its purity of feature; the hair, whose long curls fall over the shoulders; the brow, encircled with a wide bandeau in the form of a diadem, — all recall the hieratic prototype of Greek antiquity,[1] and reveal the profound studies

[1] Bröndsted thus describes the figures imitated by Thorvaldsen, and which he supposes to be Graces and Hours: "The temple of Ægina," he says, "had as *acroteria*, above the apex of the pediment, a large flower-like ornament, carefully executed in marble, and covered with paintings, and, on each side, two small female figures standing a little lower, on the slope of the cornice, and supported by small pedestals.

which, shortly before modelling it, the artist had to make for the restoration of the famous Ægina marbles.

The Ægina marbles, which ornamented the pediment of the Temple of Jupiter Panhellenius, appear to belong to a transition period, and to be connected with two epochs: in the first, which was entirely hieratic, the figures were motionless, like the statue of "Hope"; in the second, without losing their gravity, they borrowed from human life, when they represented it, a certain degree of movement and greater diversity of attitude. It is this which has made a critic say that "the statues of Ægina seem still to adhere to the dogma, with regard to the immobility of their countenances, while they emerge into the world of art by the movement of their limbs. The Greek and Trojan heroes have the heads of gods and the bodies of athletes."[1]

The assiduous labor bestowed by Thorvaldsen upon the Ægina marbles during a whole year, — this struggle *corps à corps*, if one may so express it, with Greek antiquity, — contributed largely to the perfect development of his talent. The effects of this thorough study can be more directly traced in those works produced shortly after the time the artist was thus employed, — the statue of "Hope," "The Young Shepherd and Dog," and the group of "Ganymede and the Eagle."

These two little statues were robed, and had each a flower in one hand, while with the other they held up the hem of their garments. I am inclined to take these four little figures of the two pediments for the two earliest Hours, Thallo and Karpo, and for the two most ancient Graces, Auxo and Hegemone. (Comp. Pausan. ix, 35, 1.) Still lower, at the ends of the pediment, were griffins, very well formed; of which were found enough fragments in the excavations of 1811 to justify their restoration, so successfully accomplished by Thorvaldsen." — *Voyages en Grèce*, livraison 2, note on p. 159. Paris, Didot, 1830.

[1] M. Viardot, Musées d'Allemagne.

ALEXANDER IN HIS CHARIOT, FROM THE FRIEZE, "THE TRIUMPH OF ALEXANDER."

CHAPTER III.

Heroic and Mythological Bas-Reliefs. — Anacreontic Subjects. — The "Shepherdess with the Nest of Loves." — The "Four Ages of Life."

HEBE.

The superiority acquired by Thorvaldsen in bas-reliefs seems not to be questioned. His great frieze, the "Triumph of Alexander," would of itself suffice to render an artist famous.

When the sculptor conceived this vast composition, he had probably not yet seen the casts of the bas-reliefs of the Parthenon. The marbles were not brought to England from Greece until 1814. Drawings of them, however, had been made as early as 1674,[1] by a Flemish artist employed by the Marquis de Nointel: these had been often engraved, and there is no doubt Thorvaldsen consulted them. But the imitation was not servile, as jealous artists have maintained: on the contrary, it was perfectly independent. This is especially notable in the groups of Macedonian cavaliers, which recall the Athenian horsemen in the Panathenæan Procession. Most of the lat-

[1] See Stuart and Landon, Antiquities of Athens.

ter wear the tunic and chlamys, which the Danish artist has retained, and properly so, in his warriors of Alexander's train. He has also given them breastplates. The attitudes these cavaliers assume, whether in curbing or urging on their steeds, are skilfully varied; and the action of both horses and horsemen are in the severe style of antique work.

In the representation of so important an historic event as the entry of Alexander into Babylon, the artist has followed, as far as the dimensions of the frieze would permit, the narrative of Quintus Curtius. If it were not possible for him to give the walls the great height spoken of by the historian, he has peopled them with citizens eager to salute their new king. Alexander, in accordance with the account given by Quintus Curtius, stands in his chariot, surrounded by his guards, and followed by his army. At the side of the hero, holding the reins, is a Victory; while another allegorical figure, Peace, presents to the conqueror an olive-branch and a horn of plenty. In that part of the frieze in which the Babylonians are represented coming to meet their new master, the narrative of the Roman writer has been scrupulously followed.

"Mazæus," writes Quintus Curtius, "with his adult children, came as a suppliant to meet Alexander, and surrender to him the city and himself. Bagophanes, keeper of the citadel and of the royal treasury, not to be outdone in devotion by Mazæus, had the path of the conqueror strewn with flowers and garlands, and silver altars erected upon each side of the way, upon which incense burned, with a thousand other perfumes. Following him were rich presents, droves of cattle and horses, lions and leopards; then the magi chanting their national hymns. Behind them came the Chaldeans and the poets of Babylon, musicians also, with the instruments of their country. The office of the latter was to chant the praises of their kings; that of the Chaldeans, to explain the course of the stars and the periodic revolutions of the seasons."

Quintus Curtius, we believe, is the only historian of antiquity who has preserved for us the account of this event. Though there is a great mixture of truth and fable in his works, it is probable that he derived these details from some Greek historian whose writings have not come down to us. However this may be, Thorvaldsen, instead of composing an imaginary scene, preferred to follow the Roman narrative.

His frieze is in much higher relief than the "Panathenæan Procession." The sculptural decorations of the Parthenon varied in this respect, the "Panathenæan Procession" being in the lowest relief of all.

The rapidity with which Thorvaldsen in the first instance had to execute his frieze forced him, as we have said, to neglect perfection of detail. The work was to be placed at a sufficient height to allow the artist to devote himself principally to the attitude of the figures, and the general harmony of the composition. But when the work was cut in marble, not only did he complete what had been neglected in the plaster, but introduced several happy changes.

In the Museum of Copenhagen there are four different models of the principal figure,—Alexander in his triumphal chariot. In the first, the attitude of the hero more nearly resembles the exaggerated style of Lebrun's paintings than the beautiful simplicity of antique bas-reliefs. There is more of arrogance than of noble pride in the pose of the conqueror, who holds high his lance in his right hand, while he rests his left on his hip. The artist himself was dissatisfied with this figure, and changed it almost entirely. In the second model, the conqueror is resting his left hand on his chariot, and turning his head toward his army.[1] In a third, he leans against the chariot with his right hand, and still turns his

[1] The model executed in marble for the Duke of Sommariva, and engraved at the head of this chapter.

head. The last and fourth variation, simpler and in our opinion the finest, represents Alexander looking straight before him, with the same action of the head and throat that we find on all his medals. The hair, turned off from the brow, falls in waves on each side, according to the mode adopted by ancient artists in their representations of the conqueror who called himself the son of Jupiter Ammon.

Thorvaldsen delighted in subjects drawn from the heroic age of Greece. Although entirely ignorant of the language of Homer, he was profoundly impressed by the grandeur of the poet, — a grandeur not derived from magnificence of diction merely, but from elevation of thought and dramatic action. The beauty of the style he undoubtedly lost in translations, but they supplied him with all the details of the drama; and he has interpreted the poet with a vigor and simplicity only equalled by Flaxman.

"The Abduction of Briseis" was his first subject. Achilles yields to the command of Agamemnon, his heart swelling with resentment. The heralds hesitate, embarrassed and full of respect for the son of Peleus.[1] He directs Patroclus to deliver to them the beautiful girl, who follows sorrowfully. Achilles turns away with anger, calling upon gods and men to witness the outrage.

The Homeric inspiration is still more striking in a smaller bas-relief, — "Hector and Paris."

> "There entered Hector, dear to Jove; he bore
> In hand a spear eleven cubits long:
> The brazen spear-head glittered brightly, bound
> With a gold circle. In his room he there
> Found Paris, busied with his shining arms, —
> Corslet and shield; he tried his curvéd bow;
> While Argive Helen with the attendant maids
> Was sitting, and appointed each a task.
> Hector beheld, and chid him sharply thus: —
> 'Strange man, a fitting time indeed is this,

[1] Iliad, b. i, l. 331. Bryant's Translation, l. 415–440.

To indulge thy sullen humor, while in fight
Around our lofty walls the men of Troy
Are perishing, and for thy sake the war
Is fiercely blazing all around our town.
Thou wouldst thyself reprove him, shouldst thou see
Another warrior as remiss as thou
In time of battle. Rouse thee, then, and act,
Lest we behold our city all in flames.' "[1]

The hero, stately and strong as an oak, stands erect and motionless. He fixes a severe look upon his brother, who appears confused at his base inaction. The valor and virtue of Hector, the self-indulgence of Paris and Helen, are expressed with so much energy and delicacy, that this bas-relief is inferior in neither strength nor beauty to the one representing "Priam begging Achilles for the Body of his Son."

Thorvaldsen made a repetition of "Hector and Paris"; but the second model, in which there are some changes, is not equal to the first. To follow more faithfully the text of Homer, which describes Helen seated, surrounded by her women and directing their work, he has added two female figures, placed behind Paris, who appear to be deriding his weakness. The artist, in thus adding to the poet, has certainly overshot the mark. In Homer, Helen might reproach her ravisher for not being a gallant warrior, but her maids would not have dared to turn the prince into ridicule by offering him a distaff. The addition of these two figures, and the want of decorum in their attitude, by taking from the composition part of its truth, has also detracted from the grandeur and simplicity which made it a work of the first order. This is, however, the only error of the kind committed by the artist.[2]

[1] Iliad, b. vi, l. 414 *et seq.* Bryant's Translation.

[2] It is true that the ancients, less scrupulous in this respect than the moderns, strove first of all to explain the scene, often to the injury of the verisimilitude. In the greater part of Thorvaldsen's bas-reliefs, the figures speak for themselves by their attitudes, without any other explanation. See "Cupid leaving Psyche," "Hylas carried away by the Nymphs."

One of the most touching scenes in the Iliad is the interview between Hector and Andromache at the Scæan gate. The hero, on the point of leaving for the battle-field, meets his wife, accompanied by the nurse bearing the young Astyanax. After having taken a tender farewell of his wife, —

> "Mighty Hector stretched his arms
> To take the boy; the boy shrank crying back
> To his fair nurse's bosom, scared to see
> His father helmeted in glittering brass,
> And eyeing with affright the horse-hair plume
> That grimly nodded from the lofty crest.
> At this both parents in their fondness laughed;
> And hastily the mighty Hector took
> The helmet from his brow and laid it down
> Gleaming upon the ground, and, having kissed
> His darling son and tossed him up in play,
> Prayed thus to Jove and all the gods of heaven: —
> 'O Jupiter, and all ye deities,
> Vouchsafe that this my son may yet become
> Among the Trojans eminent like me,
> And nobly rule in Ilium. May they say,
> "This man is greater than his father was."'"[1]

Hector, raising his son in his arms and invoking the gods, has his body inclined backward. Andromache, by a movement of loving sadness, leans her forehead against her husband's head. Paris, armed for the fight, comes to join his brother.

The mind of Thorvaldsen, which interpreted the Homeric scenes with so much loftiness and truth, lent itself with equal facility to the expression of the graceful fancies of the minor Greek poets. To interpret Anacreon was to him a pastime, an every-day amusement. It is singular that the artist should have given colossal proportions to the first composition taken from the odes of this poet,—the group

[1] Iliad, b. vi, l. 597–615. Bryant's Translation.

of "Cupid and Mars," — to which he had intended to add two other figures, Venus and Vulcan; but a little later composed instead a bas-relief, representing the whole scene of the forty-fifth ode: —

" In his smithy at Lemnos the husband of Venus
For Cupid was forging some arrowlets small,
His mother, fair Cypris, the points dipped in honey,
Which Eros, the rogue, had made bitter with gall.

Just then from the battle great Mars, home returning,
Came by with a ponderous dart in his hand;
He sneered at the lightness of Cupid's small arrows,
And thought that such weapons a gnat might withstand.

The little god handed him one of his arrows,
And said as he gave it, 'I think you will find
That mine is the heavier. Please you to try it.'
(Fair Venus, meanwhile, standing, smiling, behind.)

So Mars took the arrow; but presently groaning,
'Take it back! take it back!' he cried with a sigh.
'Take it back! take it back! for me it's too heavy,'
'You've got it, pray keep it,' was Cupid's reply."

The artist has expressed extremely well in his bas-relief the astonishment of the god of war, and the malice of Cupid. Venus, by a graceful movement, turns to look at Mars, while Vulcan continues his work.

The sculptor has been quite as successful in his rendering of the fortieth ode of Anacreon, — " Cupid stung by a Bee." Here the god is represented as an innocent child, unconscious of the pain caused by his arrows. He runs to Venus in tears to tell her "that he has been wounded by a little winged serpent"; and his mother replies, "If the sting of a bee hurts you so much, think how much they must suffer whom you have pierced to the heart with your arrows!"

In another work, it is, on the contrary, the pitiless conqueror of the world, the sly and cruel god, who penetrates into the dwelling of Anacreon. For the proper appreciation of the ingenuity of the composition, and the skill of the sculptor, it is necessary to cite the entire third ode: —

'’T was noon of night, when round the pole
The sullen Bear is seen to roll;
And mortals, wearied with the day,
Are slumbering all their cares away:
An infant, at that dreary hour,
Came weeping to my silent bower,
And wak'd me with a piteous prayer,
To save him from the midnight air.
'And who art thou?' I, waking, cry,
'That bid'st my blissful visions fly?'
'O gentle sire!' the infant said,
'In pity take me to thy shed;
Nor fear deceit: a lonely child,
I wander o'er the gloomy wild.
Chill drops the rain, and not a ray
Illumes the drear and misty way!'
I hear the baby's tale of woe;
I hear the bitter night winds blow;
And, sighing for his piteous fate,
I trimm'd my lamp, and op'd the gate.
’T was Love! the little wandering sprite,
His pinion sparkled through the night!
I knew him by his bow and dart,
I knew him by my fluttering heart.
I take him in, and fondly raise
The dying embers' cheering blaze;
Press from his dank and clinging hair
The crystals of the freezing air,
And in my hand and bosom hold
His little fingers, thrilling cold,
And now the embers' genial ray
Had warmed his anxious fears away.
'I pray thee,' said the wanton child
(My bosom trembled as he smiled),
'I pray thee let me try my bow,
For through the rain I've wander'd so,

That much I fear the ceaseless shower
Has injur'd its elastic power.'
The fatal bow the urchin drew;
Swift from the string the arrow flew;
Oh! swift it flew as glancing flame,
And to my very soul it came.
'Fare thee well,' I heard him say,
As laughing wild he wing'd away;
'Fare thee well, for now I know
The rain has not relax'd my bow;
It still can send a madd'ning dart,
As thou shalt own with all thy heart.' "[1]

Thorvaldsen has represented Anacreon seated, and has placed near the poet his lyre, with the thyrsus and amphora of Bacchus. The old man is warming and drying the wet child, who regards him with cool maliciousness, while plunging an arrow into his heart. The antique grace of the bas-relief is in such perfect harmony with the subject, and the philosophic idea of the Greek poet to whom Plato gave the name of Sage is so happily expressed that nothing is wanting to this exquisite work, — to our thinking the most agreeable of Anacreontic compositions.

"Love bound by the Graces" is another charming fiction. The god, with hands tied, is bound to a tree by chains of roses. The three sisters, lying on the grass, are playing with his arrows. But Love appears so little offended by their sport that he remains a quiet prisoner, without making any effort to free himself. And in fact, according to the thirtieth ode of Anacreon, when Venus, informed of the captivity of her son, hastens to ransom him, the released Cupid refuses to leave the society of the Graces.

Amatory bas-reliefs by Thorvaldsen are very numerous; but in all these works, even in the most trifling, the intention is never lascivious. At most, we find one or two

[1] Translation by Thomas Moore.

compositions scarcely finished, representing satyrs and bacchantes, in imitation of the figures painted on the so-called Etruscan vases, which could possibly be called equivocal.

In his lightest, as well as in his severest creations, the artist always appears as much occupied by the idea as by the form; and thus he often succeeds in imparting a serious grace to his compositions, without rendering them insipid, through too much sweetness. This observation applies equally to his bas-reliefs and statues.

"The Shepherdess with a Nest of Loves" is a charming creation. The young girl has before her every shade of the tender passion, — faithful love, passionate love, and fickle love, who flies away as fast as his wings will carry him. This composition was suggested to the sculptor by an antique fresco, discovered in Pompeii, in the house called Homer's (*Casa Omerica*). In this painting, a young woman is holding a nest, and looking with delight at three babies just come out of the egg.[1] The artist intended, doubtless, to represent Leda contemplating her three children, — Helen, Castor, and Pollux. If Thorvaldsen's work bear some resemblance to the antique by the character and style of the figures, the thought is not the same, and the execution wholly different.

The idea of the bas-relief of "The Ages of Love" is taken from a fresco, found at Stabiæ. In the antique painting, "The Sale of Loves,"[2] the figure of the saleswoman is quite commonplace. But the Loves — sons of Mars, of Jupiter, or of Mercury — have distinct characteristics. Thorvaldsen has carried this idea further, and represented with much delicacy and ingenuity all the philosophic story of the great passion which reigns over the human race. To the infant, Love is the unknown, exciting curiosity. The little girl questions

[1] Compare the bas-relief of Thorvaldsen with the copy of the painting in the "Real Museo Borbonico," vol. i, pl. xxiv.

[2] Real Museo Borbonico, vol. i, pl. xxiv.

him with a timid and innocent look; the young maiden soon makes him the object of her modest adoration; then follow the transports of passion, succeeded quickly by disenchantment; the wings of Love are drooping. The god alights in conquering attitude on the shoulder of the grown man, who bends beneath his weight; and when the old man calls him with a trembling voice, the mischievous child flies away, deriding him who invokes him.[1]

The bas-reliefs of Thorvaldsen, considered collectively, form a work distinguished by its infinite variety. To turn alternately from Homeric subjects to the lighter suggestions of fancy seems to have been mental diversion only for the sculptor. We have endeavored to point out the distinctive characteristics of the great number of compositions which attest a mind largely receptive of the beautiful, and rich in creative power. Such a union of grace and strength, combined with so fruitful an imagination, has been seldom vouchsafed to any artist.

[1] Compare the song of Béranger, "La Fuite de l'Amour."

REBECCA AND ELIEZER.

CHAPTER IV.

Thorvaldsen considered as a Sculptor of Sacred Subjects. — The Christ and the Twelve Apostles. — Friezes. — The Pediment of the *Frue Kirke* of Copenhagen. — Sepulchral Monuments.

THE CHRIST.

WITH regard to the religious works of Thorvaldsen, most of which are collected in the *Frue Kirke* at Copenhagen, there is much diversity of opinion, though no one disputes their admirable severity of style. It was at Rome that most of these were modelled; and before the artist had completed his first sketch, his opponents were already striving to demonstrate that it would be impossible for him to give the Christian idea its adequate expression.

At this period, the so-called school of "Nazarenes" was flourishing in Italy. The imitators of Overbeck had pushed to exaggeration the tendencies of their master. This painter, while studying Raphael, the pupil of Perugino, had allowed himself to be carried away by his personal feeling for Fra Angelico. His imitators went as far back as Giotto, and, to secure the *naïveté* of their model, they even borrowed his processes of painting. Thorvaldsen could not lay claim to the approbation of this school, which was indeed bitterly hostile, and openly denied to him the possession of the religious sentiment. On the other hand, the Lutheran Church, which, from the severity of its principles, welcomes only with reserve works of art in houses of worship, accepted Thorvaldsen's, as being by their austerity the most reverent artistic expression of revealed religion.

Upon entering the *Frue Kirke* at Copenhagen, we are struck by the imposing aspect of the colossal figure of the Christ, surrounded by the twelve apostles. Thorvaldsen followed the counsel of Winckelmann: his Christ is as beautiful as Raphael's or Leonardo da Vinci's.[1] The hair of the Saviour is parted in the middle, after the fashion of the inhabitants of Nazareth. The face is not perhaps in perfect harmony with the general character of the statue. The Man-God is standing; and we are almost surprised to see that gentle head, so pure and delicate in drawing, bowed down upon a breast as broad as that of Hercules. The strong arms are stretched out with a loving gesture, as though calling to him all who are sorrowful and heavy laden; but the stout legs attach to the earth the Master of the world; and we ask ourselves if

[1] "Modern artists ought to have formed their figures of the Saviour conformably to the ideas which the ancients entertained of the beauty of their heroes, and thus made him correspond to the prophetic declaration, which announces him as the most beautiful of the children of men. But the idea of most figures of him, beginning with Michel Angelo, appears to be borrowed from the barbarous works of the Middle Ages, and there can be nothing more ignoble than the face in such heads of Christ. How much more noble the conceptions of Raphael are may be seen in a small original drawing, in the Royal Farnese Museum at Naples, which represents our Saviour's burial, and in which his head exhibits the beauty of a young hero without beard. . . . But if such a face should possibly appear to the artist a scandalous innovation on the customary representation of the Saviour with a beard, let him study the Saviour of Leonardo da Vinci." Winckelmann, vol. ii, pp. 89–90. Lodge's Translation.

this can be that same Christ, that diaphanous figure which glided over the surface of the waters.

The Christ is placed in front of the chancel, and the apostles are arranged in opposite rows down the nave. St. Peter and St. Paul are nearest their divine Master. Upon the Saviour's right, after St. Peter come Matthew, John, James the Less, Philip, and Thaddeus. On the left, next to St. Paul, are Simon Zelotes, Bartholomew, James the Greater, Thomas, and Andrew.

To each of these figures the artist has given a distinct individuality. St. Peter expresses faith, St. Paul the power of the Gospel; there is more of gentleness and love in the features of St. John; an austere resignation is imprinted upon the countenance of St. Simon. Nevertheless, in attitude and disposition of drapery, in the severity as well as beauty of the types, the apostles are less like saints and martyrs than philosophers and sages.

"The Angel of Baptism" has a more Christian aspect. There is an expression of ecstasy mingled with the conventional serenity of the face which is more allied to religious sentiment. Kneeling in the centre of the nave, this angel holds a large shell-shaped vase for holy water.

These great works do not compose the whole of the interior adornment of the *Frue Kirke*. Behind and above the altar is the frieze representing our Lord on the road to Calvary, extremely well composed, but somewhat feeble in execution. Upon the walls of the side aisles are two other friezes, "The Baptism of Jesus" and "The Lord's Supper." Above the alms-chest is a small bas-relief illustrative of Christian charity; and, opposite, "The Guardian Angel."

When Thorvaldsen made the model for the Supper, the Copenhagen world was astonished at first, and almost shocked, at the sight of so unconventional a composition. The Saviour is represented standing, while his apostles, kneeling, are grouped around him; an arrangement which implies that the institution of the eucharist took place after the Master and his disciples had risen from the table. But people soon became reconciled to this new idea, which after all has nothing in it precisely contrary to the traditions of the Church.

The portal of the *Frue Kirke* is surmounted by an immense frieze, "Christ's Entry into Jerusalem"; and, lastly, the pediment is composed of an admirable composition in terra cotta, "The Preaching of St. John the Baptist." Following the wise method adopted by the Greeks[1] to give greater play of light and shade, Thorvaldsen did not content himself with carving this pediment in half-relief: he has, on the contrary, composed it of entirely detached figures. This work is stamped with the character proper to the Biblical scene. The subject was more suited to the sculptor's turn of mind. It was not God himself he had to portray, but simply him who is the forerunner of God. The hour of struggle and martyrdom had not yet struck, and Christianity existed only in the mind of the Precursor.

[1] "After the proofs furnished us by the superb discovery of eighteen figures from the two pediments of the temple of Ægina, the vast groups of more than forty colossal statues of the two pediments of the Parthenon, the description by Diodorus of the sculptures in the pediments of the temples of the Olympian Jupiter at Agrigentum, and that which Pausanias gives of the groups which once stood in the pediments of the temples at Olympia, Tegea, Thebes, Delphi, etc., — after all these proofs, what can be more certain than the fact that the Greeks, in the finest period of their architecture, always placed in the pediments of their great peripteral temples, whether hexastyle or octostyle, entire figures and never bas-reliefs? And how could this fact, re-established by purely historical methods, be better supported, or how could the question, why did the Greeks lay down and practise such a rule, be better answered, than by our every-day experience; which teaches us that only figures entirely detached from the background and sculptured in complete relief are capable of producing the proper effect, when seen at a considerable height, whilst all sculptures in low relief are wanting in that most material point, depth of shadow and the decision of contour which results from it, — matters indispensably necessary if a figure placed at any considerable elevation is to be seen clearly and distinctly." Thus says Bröndsted (Voyage en Grèce); and he adds that this rule is not now followed (1830), because "we are always accustomed in our schools to confine ourselves to the imitated models of the Romans," whilst we neglect the axiom of the Greeks: "The capital ornament, the great pediment adorned with sculptures, should stand out boldly, like a vast diadem, sharply and artistically carved, crowning the whole edifice."

"The Preaching of St. John the Baptist," a complex work, merits an attentive examination. The character of the figures, the idea they express, the contrasts between them, — all contribute toward the harmonious general arrangement of the composition. The Baptist is in the centre: his attitude is noble, natural, and decorous. He stands upon a rock, which raises him above his audience. He speaks, and points to heaven. It is not by a fiery eloquence that he is seeking to persuade: his words are simple, because they proclaim the coming of the Word of Truth. The conviction which takes possession of the minds of his hearers expresses itself in the several attitudes of each. It is profound in the man nearest St. John, who is deep in thought while waiting to be baptized; simple and spontaneous in the women; irresistible in the youth, who already manifests an impatient fervor. The doctor, habituated to discussion, does not receive so readily the new ideas: he only yields after mature reflection. The Pharisee, in his pride, protests against words which astonish, but do not touch him; while the sportsman, whom accident has brought to the spot, gives himself up unresistingly to his emotion. His dog is occupying the attention of two children; whilst the last person in the scene, a shepherd, looks on with indifference. The most beautiful part of the composition, to our mind, is a group of two figures on the right of the Saint. A young man, already converted, leans upon the shoulder of his father, and watches with an unspeakable expression of sweetness and pious satisfaction the impression produced by the Baptist's words. The father's manly face is uplifted, he seems struck with astonishment; and we feel that he will say presently, like the Pauline of Corneille, "Je vois, je crois, je suis désabusé."

Throughout the whole composition the emotions of the mind are more deeply marked on the countenances of the auditors than is usually permitted by the rules of Greek art.

The arrangement of the pediment is skilfully studied with

a view to harmony. The figures, whether standing or leaning, seated or lying down, whether differing in age, height, or costume, form (according to the rule of Mengs) a pyramid, though their heads are not ranged in a perfectly straight line, which would be both monotonous and unnatural.

Two figures designed for a part of this immense composition have been left out: one, a Roman soldier, leaning against a rock; the other, a Jew sitting on the ground. Though both are fine, it is not strange that Thorvaldsen excluded them. We do not see how they could have been added without destroying the harmony of outline of the pediment. As it now stands, the "Preaching of St. John the Baptist" is an admirable work. There is true feeling in the figures, and the composition is happy and skilful; while the grand thought that should be dominant in the scene is very correctly expressed.

The philosophic rather than the strictly Christian character of Thorvaldsen's religious works is more strikingly manifested in his sepulchral monuments, — in the tomb of the Duke of Leuchtenberg, for example. Eugène de Beauharnais, step-son of Napoleon I, and Viceroy of Italy, remained devoted to the Emperor in adversity as well as in prosperity, and refused to purchase at the price of treason the throne which the allied sovereigns offered to guarantee to him. The monument erected in the Church of St. Michael in Munich represents the prince on the point of descending into the tomb, upon the door of which is inscribed his device, — "Honor and Fidelity." He is in Roman costume, and has laid aside his helmet and breast-plate, retaining only his loyal sword. He presses his left hand to his heart, and presents to the Muse of History the only thing which remains to him, — his crown of laurel. Standing beside him on the left is the Angel of Death, upon whom is leaning the Genius of Immortality. There is nothing particularly religious in this composition, but it expresses with grandeur a noble sentiment.

The absence of the Christian idea is no less striking in the beautiful marble placed over the tomb of Prince Potocki, in the cathedral of Cracow, which represents the young hero clothed in the antique costume. It might be taken for a Marcus Aurelius.

In the mausoleum of the illustrious and able defender of the church, Cardinal Consalvi, the artist has succeeded in expressing happily the Catholic idea; but in the monument of Pius VII there is, perhaps, an aiming after grandeur and force hardly in keeping with Christian humility. Here we find, also, as in the tomb of the Duke of Leuchtenberg, a species of compromise between the Catholic dogma and Greek mythology,—a result of carrying the doctrines of Winckelmann to extremes, a common mistake of artists at this period. Canova, in the tombs of Clement XIII and Clement XIV, had already expressed grief, gentleness, and moderation under the figure of slightly clothed and almost pagan genii.[1] Thorvaldsen, having to personify wisdom and strength, also went back to heathen sources. The Greeks worshipped these virtues under the forms of Minerva and Hercules; and the artist has scarcely done more than appropriate, with a change of name and attribute, these types.

Wisdom bears on her breast the ægis, but a cherub's head has been substituted for the Medusa; a crown of laurel replaces the helmet; the Bible serves for the shield. At her side is the symbolic owl.

As Hercules could not be transformed into a woman for the second statue, Iole replaces him, clothed in his lion's skin, which covers her head, and falls over her shoulders; but, disdaining brutal force, she tramples under foot the club,

[1] Etudes sur les Beaux-Arts, by M. H. Delaborde.

and crosses her arms on her breast to express by this attitude her trustful resignation to the will of God.[1]

In his large number of bas-reliefs intended for tombs, genii most frequently figure, while the symbols of the Christian faith are rarely employed. Many of these bas-reliefs might ornament a Roman mausoleum, as they seldom convey any religious thought but the immortality of the soul. The monument of the Baroness Chandry, however, presents to view the figure of a woman pressing a cross fervently to her breast. Draped in her shroud, with uplifted head, she seems to spring toward heaven, rising in air with the lightness of an impalpable form.

Thorvaldsen had been educated in the Lutheran faith: he lived at Rome in an atmosphere of Catholicism, at a time of great political agitation, and when, as it is well known, all beliefs were shaken. The mind of the artist was affected by these uncertainties, and the result was indifference. A friend once remarking to him that his want of religious faith must make it difficult for him to express Christian ideas in his works, — "If I were altogether an unbeliever," he replied, "why should that give me any trouble? Have I not represented pagan divinities? — still, I don't believe in them."

In speaking thus, the sculptor, in our opinion, has given the key to the character of his works. They are the product of his fine intellect: his heart bore no part in their creation.

Thorvaldsen held fast to his artistic faith, even when

[1] Stendhal, in his "Promenades dans Rome," speaks several times of Thorvaldsen, and, generally, in no friendly spirit. He judges of the merit of the artist only from the tomb of Pius VII. He says of this monument: "I saw it in an advanced state in his atelier (1828). There are, as usual, three colossal figures, the Pope and two Virtues. Pius VII is represented seated, and giving the benediction. With a little audacity, he might have been represented standing, and replying to the anger of Napoleon. One of the Virtues is 'Wisdom,' reading a book; the other is 'Strength of Character,' clothed in the lion's skin, with crossed arms, and eyes raised to heaven. If this work is superior to all the commonplace tombs we find in St. Peter's, we must thank the revolution effected in art by the illustrious David. That great artist *a tué la queue du Bernin*, — has given the finishing blow to Bernini and his train. (I ask pardon for this *mot* of a great painter, — one of my friends.)"

illustrating Christian subjects. He never abjured his worship of severe beauty, as the Greeks understood it. We find in his statues one reminiscence only of Gothic art. The mediæval sculptors often produced a pleasing spiral effect in the borders of their draperies. We recognize a similar effect in the figures of the apostles. Was it the instinct of his race which here revealed itself? We are more inclined to think that the artist found similar examples in some antique works in which they exist, and that his clear-sighted mind saw the use to which they might be put. In fact, Thorvaldsen's style is wholly derived from the Greeks; and even in his Christian subjects he followed the heirs of those great masters, who, having settled in Italy, were the first to reproduce in mosaic the Christ, the Virgin, and the Apostles.[1] The Danish sculptor was acquainted with these Greco-Latin mosaics. The style of the great school of antiquity had doubtless much degenerated in the hands of the artists executing them. Nevertheless, those artists, still in love with beauty, had not altogether lost the tradition of it.

The worship of the beautiful in form is, we need not say, no obstacle to the expression of religious feeling. But, for the work to be thoroughly stamped with this feeling, the man must put into it all the fervor with which his soul is filled. Thorvaldsen had not the enthusiasm which comes of faith: aiming, above all, at beauty, if he ever animates his figures, it is with philosophic thought; and his works are more fitted to satisfy the mind of the thinker than the heart of the Christian.

[1] Such works exist at Rome, in the churches of St. Cosmo and St. Damian, St. Praxedes, St. Prudentiana, St. Paul without the walls, and St. Maria Maggiore.

THE ARMS OF ACHILLES.

CHAPTER V.

Thorvaldsen's Rapidity of Conception. — Severity of his Judgments upon his own Works. — The Fire of First Inspiration tempered by Reflection. — Creative Genius. — Canova. — Bartolini. — Error of Mme. de Staël. — The Scandinavian Genius of Thorvaldsen applies the Principles of Greek Art.

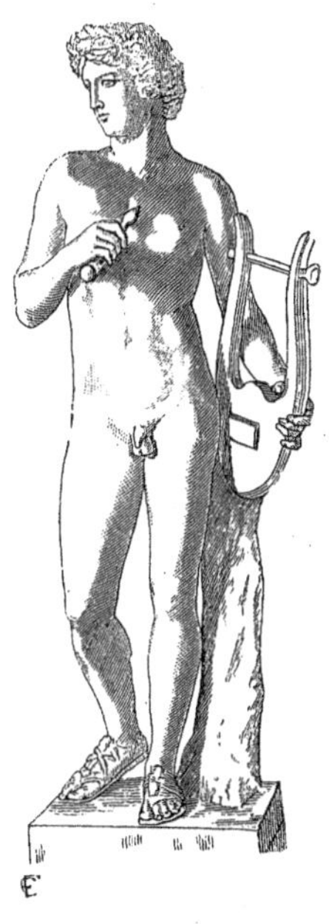

APOLLO.

THE first impression upon visiting the Thorvaldsen Museum in Copenhagen is amazement at the great productiveness of the artist. The vast galleries, the long corridors, the numerous rooms of this Etruscan palace, the lofty walls, and even the staircase, are all filled and lined with statues and bas-reliefs; and the catalogue which guides the stranger through this immense museum, enclosing, also, the modest tomb of the sculptor, contains no less than six hundred and forty-eight numbers. In presence of such a wealth of original compositions, it is difficult to understand how any critic could represent Thorvaldsen as a patient imitator, entirely wanting in imagination.

As we have already seen in the history of his life, the Danish artist was especially distinguished for the creative power of his mind. The accident of his birth, in the first place, but, much more, a strong vocation, made him a sculptor. That which was toil to his father was the pastime of his childhood. While still very young, he was gifted with extraordinary natural facility, composing and sketching upon the spur of the moment with all the unconsciousness of youth. Throughout his whole career, he found in himself this innate resource; but far from abusing it, even in his youth, he was distrustful of this precious gift.

His fears, his school-boy terror, when competing for the Academy prize, are proofs of this. From the beginning he seemed to understand all the difficulties in the way of the artist who would devote himself seriously to his profession.

The same feeling led him when he first went to Rome to study the antique with such indefatigable patience, and made him always dissatisfied with his first essays, which he destroyed as soon as made.

In all the plenitude of his power, and even of his fame, Thorvaldsen continued to be severe toward himself. He was quick in conception, and composed with great facility. When he wished to celebrate, for instance, the birthday of his friend the Baroness von Schubart, a few days sufficed him to design and execute the charming bas-relief of "The Dance of the Muses."

Conception with the master, therefore, was ever rapid, the first execution easy; but the disciple of Winckelmann possessed too refined a taste to be easily satisfied, and consequently he thought long over his works, retouched, matured his plan, and in many instances made a new composition. In his mind's eye, he saw an ideal so lofty and perfect that he could not easily attain to it: hence, his hesitations, his severity with himself when other artists would have been proud of their work. Nevertheless, with a thorough comprehension of the extent of his abilities, when he believed he had touched the goal he stopped.

Nothing is more interesting than to study the collection of small, rough models in one of the rooms on the first floor of the Copenhagen Museum. In them the observer beholds the mind of the artist wrestling with his subject: he is present, as it were, at the birth of the idea, and sees its first expression; then come the retouchès, the successive alterations, up to the final completion of the work.

"The Christ" is one of the subjects upon which the sculptor was the longest engaged. In the first sketch, which is undraped and purely anatomical, the upper part of the body is inclined backward by a very marked movement. The head is raised, the eyes uplifted to heaven.[1] "The Christ" is advancing, he stops, looks up to heaven, and pronounces a benediction. Such must have been the first idea of the sculptor.

In the second sketch, the figure is draped, and smaller. The attitude is almost the same, but calmer, and the inclination of the head backward is less violent.

Then comes a model in plaster, larger and in a more advanced state of completion. The head is erect, the eyes looking forward. Both arms are extended by a simple action, as though inviting men to come to their Redeemer. The face has emerged from the formless block of the first studies: it is calm and noble. The drapery is long, and trails on the ground. The body, meagre in the first sketches, is now fully developed, and the chest is broad. Still, in its finished state, the statue, in some important points, differs widely from this model. Both feet rest on the ground by a powerful action; while the head, slightly inclined forward, is expressive of sweetness and benevolence.

The attitude of "The Christ" was definitely settled in a rough model, which is not in this collection. This is the

[1] This figure has no arms, but, from the action of the shoulders, it is probable that the right arm was to be raised, and the left extended. The body rests on the left foot, the right foot is thrown back, and lifted from the ground.

story, as related to us by the Danish professor who was with Thorvaldsen in his studio at Rome, at the time: —

> "The master and I were going out to a party, and, just as we were crossing the threshold, he turned back, and I followed him. He stopped in front of his 'Christ,' and looked at it some moments, without uttering a word. The clay statuette had the head erect, one of the arms raised, the other extended. Suddenly, the artist advanced with a firm step, like a man who has just made up his mind, and seizing the arms bent both down by a quick movement. With a few hasty touches, he soon reshaped them, and taking a few steps backward, cried out, 'There is my "Christ"! That is the way it shall be.' He then hurried me away, and we left the atelier."

Thorvaldsen did, however, make some further alterations in this masterly work; but the general attitude which gives to the figure of Christ the benignant majesty of the Olympian Jupiter remained unchanged from this moment.

This anecdote seems worth preserving, because it paints to the life the artist's character, and exhibits also the turn of his mind, and his method of working. His first conceptions were perfectly free, and not wanting even in a certain impetuosity, as can be shown by the attitudes of many of his sketches.[1] It was only by reflection and study that he succeeded in tempering this violent action, and thus gave to his statues that calm and grand aspect which he admired in the Greek style, and which has sometimes brought upon him the accusation of coldness.

Thorvaldsen's genius was eminently creative: he displayed the utmost ardor in his manipulation of the clay, in his efforts to extract from it the form which his mind had conceived, to give to it the impress of his thought. When it seemed to him that it sufficiently expressed his idea, he himself made the plaster cast, which generally he finished with care, and consigned to his workmen as a model: it was

[1] Compare also the attitude of Achilles in the two variations of the bas-relief of the "Abduction of Briseis"; that of Alexander, &c.

their task to translate it into marble. This work was done under his own eye, in his ateliers: he constantly superintended it, very often retouching and sometimes finishing it with his own hand.[1]

This manner of working gave artists, envious of his success, occasion to say that no doubt he knew how to model tolerably well, but that he could not cut the marble. Once when such remarks were repeated to him, "Bring me a block of Carrara or Paros," he said, "take away my chisel, tie my hands, and I will make a statue come out of it with my teeth."

Nothing, indeed, could be more unjust than such a criticism; and the "Adonis" of the Glyptothek of Munich, which was wholly executed by the artist, according to the agreement made with Prince Louis of Bavaria, is its most eloquent and unanswerable refutation.

Ought we to regret that Thorvaldsen did not, as in this case, finish in marble with his own hands all his works? If the artist had, in every instance, undertaken this labor, we might have been the richer by a few statues perfect as the "Adonis,"[1] but we should have lost, perhaps, more than one of the best creations of the master.[2]

Thorvaldsen and Canova have been so often compared,

[1] The marbles executed by his pupils are not always done as carefully as the models of the master. Thus, to form a correct judgment of Thorvaldsen's work, it is necessary to see the collection of plaster models in the Copenhagen Museum.

[2] Is it not reasonable to suppose that the greatest sculptors of Greece pursued the same course in this respect as the Danish artist? One writer even asserts that they were accustomed to divide their works into several pieces, so as to employ a greater number of assistants: —

"Who does not know (and we could cite here examples and authorities) that the great artists of antiquity, intrusted, as they were, with immense works, almost beyond the conception of modern times, made use of the expeditious method of cutting up their models, which they delivered, thus divided, to their workmen, in order to accelerate the work, and render their subalterns more useful, to whom, as it often happened, they abandoned entirely the execution of certain accessories, which, in the finest works, are sometimes treated with a great deal of negligence, and little sentiment?"—Bouillon's *Musée des Antiques*, vol i *La Vénus de Mélos*, treatise by J. B. Saint-Victor.

that it is not possible to conclude a sketch of the Danish sculptor without saying something also of his illustrious rival. In every age, such comparisons have always been instituted; and, in comparing Canova and Thorvaldsen, we have the advantage of regarding them from the same starting-point, as both artists seem to have been influenced by the same traditions.

A great French sculptor of our time, — David d'Angers, — comparing the talent of the two artists, has declared his preference for the Italian master, because he does not feel himself so quickly touched by the work of the Danish sculptor, whose eminent beauties, he says, only reveal themselves after long study.

We can oppose to this judgment that of another sculptor, of equally great merit, who said to us not long ago: —

> "Before Canova's works, I always feel on the defensive. I fear to allow my judgment to be taken captive by the excessive grace of the figures, and by the extreme skilfulness of the execution, which often conceals real faults. The pretty little taper-fingered hand of the Princess Borghese, in the character of Venus, may be charming; but it is full of airs and affectation, and is surely neither natural nor antique. With Thorvaldsen, on the contrary, I do not fear any such artifices: my mind is tranquil. I prefer him to Canova for his greater breadth of style, and because his work is truer and more correct."

If, in some of the works of the Danish sculptor, we perceive hands a little coarse, feet rather large, this very fault is a proof that Thorvaldsen was very far from trying to captivate the taste by any excessive refinement.

In following the art movement which was the result of Winckelmann's theories, Canova is, in reality, neither Greek nor Roman. His work, though worthy in other respects of the admiration which it excites, is full of the petty artifices of his Italian predecessors, and has, as it were, only put on the antique garb.

To Canova nature was pleasing and coquettish, rather than

grand and powerful; and if he claim kindred with the antique, it is by his imitation of the artists of the third period of Greek art, who are to Phidias what Guido is to Raphael.[1] He was attracted by preference to those suave qualities characteristic of the epoch when grace was all-powerful, and he generally succeeded better in delicate compositions than in figures of force. The beautiful forms of his groups have something undulating about them which charms the eye, and leads the mind to tender thoughts, — a penetrating influence over the senses which brings back memories of Cytherean Greece.

There is nothing of this sort about Thorvaldsen's work; and therefore those who are in the habit of contrasting the two artists find him cold, after Canova. The Danish sculptor was more austere, more philosophic in his quest of the beautiful. As to his illustrious contemporary, the Florentine Bartolini, he also belongs to the school of artists who followed Winckelmann, in their worship of the Greek antique. His horror of imitation, however, rendered him more indedependent than either Canova or Thorvaldsen, and he went first of all to nature for the form and expression of his figures.

An eminent critic, whose opinions are authority in matters of art, has devoted to Bartolini a most interesting paper, in which we find this estimate of Canova and Thorvaldsen: —

"Considered in itself," says M. Henri Delaborde,[2] "the manner of the author of the 'Madeleine,' 'The Danseuses,' and the 'Venus' of the Pitti Palace, is more pleasing than beautiful. It originates in the artist's desire to conform himself to antique examples; but these examples Canova has weakened, in adjusting them to suit the rather narrow limits of modern taste. He mixes up the Greek simplicity with a pretentious grace, an equivocal elegance, — in a word, he treats antiquity as he does nature: he tries to embellish both. In sheltering somewhat his personal responsibility under a semblance of classic

[1] Winckelmann. [2] Etudes sur les Beaux-Arts.

art, he succeeds in adroitly counterfeiting a resemblance, but does not express with dignity a truth.

"Thorvaldsen had talent and aspirations of a wholly different order. Although he sometimes strives for elegance, and attains it, as, for example, in his 'Night,' or his 'Mercury Argiphontes,' he generally aims only at grandeur, and this end he sometimes attains. His 'Lion of Lucerne,' his bas-reliefs of the 'Triumph of Alexander,' and many of his allegorical figures, are distinguished for imagination and force."

Thorvaldsen exerted much influence upon almost all the sculptors who came to Rome in his day. To association with him, Rauch is indebted for the purity of his style: the German artist established subsequently a school where the principles of high art were taught. From this school issued Rietschel,[1] of Dresden; Drake[2] and Albert Wolff,[3] of Berlin; Blaeser, of Cologne, — who all tried to keep art in the path traced out by their masters. Schadow and Schwanthaler were friends of the sculptor, and they profited by his counsels. At Copenhagen, Thorvaldsen's influence has been kept alive by Bissen; at Rome, by Tenerani,[4] Louis Bienaimé, Pierre Galli,[5] and Emile Wolff.[6]

[1] Rietschel executed a large number of public works. He died four years ago.

[2] Drake is a countryman of Rauch: like him he was born in the principality of Waldeck. At the Universal Exposition of Fine Arts, held in the Champ de Mars (1867), he obtained one of the grand prizes for his equestrian statue of King William of Prussia.

[3] Albert Wolff has executed several public monuments in Germany.

[4] Tenerani, now (1867) seventy-eight years old, lives in Rome. He has recently completed the monument to Pope Pius VIII in St. Peter's.

[5] Galli is the last pupil who worked with Thorvaldsen. It was he who, during the absence of the sculptor, had charge of the atelier. He executed, for the Torlonia Palace, a series of medallions, sketched only by the master. (See Catalogue.) Later he composed a large number of small statues and bas-reliefs, which now decorate the loggia of the Vatican, and merit the esteem of men of taste. His larger statues are less happy.

[6] Emile Wolff is settled in Rome, where he enjoys a deserved reputation. He has followed religiously the principles of his master, for whom he cherishes a deep and touching veneration. Among his numerous works, we cite the statue of Prince Albert, in the Isle of Wight; "The Wounded Amazon," at Eaton Hall, the residence of the Marquis of Westminster; "Victory" on the Schlossbrücke, in Berlin; "The Four Seasons," bas-reliefs, of which one — "Winter" — has been repeated more than fifty times in marble.

Thorvaldsen has therefore founded a school in Germany as well as in Italy; but, Mme. de Staël[1] to the contrary notwithstanding, the artist is not German. He belongs to the Scandinavian race: its genius and character were his. This race of the extreme north, somewhat rude, simple and proud, kind and hospitable, has in all ages delighted in noble things. The poetry of its earliest bards was warlike and chaste. It has believed always in the immortality of the soul,—in a future life broader and grander than the earthly, where warriors would love and fight after the fashion of gods. With us, the long days of summer are accepted as a right; but, with the Scandinavians, these same days, so niggardly counted out, are welcomed as a benefaction of Nature; and when the grass is green, and the meadows enamelled with flowers,—when the sun gilds the tops of the lofty pines, and the breeze gently ripples the surface of the great lakes, the North holds high festival, and the entire people celebrate the joyous season with wild and tender hymns, in tones full of freshness and force.

It was, indeed, the pure and vigorous sap of the Scandinavian race which flowed in the veins of the Danish artist, and which he infused into Greek art, by a graft upon its stoutest and strongest branch. But he was not a parasite plant: on the contrary, he gave to the tree his own strong support. If Thorvaldsen idealized his figures by the use of Greek processes and according to the æsthetic principles developed by

[1] In her book on Germany, Mme. de Staël says: "A Dane, Thorvaldsen, educated in Germany, now rivals Canova in Rome. His 'Jason' resembles him whom Pindar describes as the handsomest of men. He holds a lance in his hand, and the repose of conscious strength characterizes the hero." It is so far from being true that Thorvaldsen was educated in Germany, that it was not until 1819, when he was fifty years old, that he first set foot in that country. Mme. de Staël's error comes undoubtedly from an article by A. W. Schlegel in the "Jenaer Allgemeine Zeitung" (1805, Intell., n. 120, p. 1006). "Thorvaldsen, to whom in one way we can lay claim, for though born a Dane he speaks our language like a native, and his culture is wholly German." Herr Thiele truly remarks that the artist, who did not visit Germany until he was already old, never could have spoken German as correctly as this writer maintains.

Winckelmann, he sought for his models in nature: he drew directly from the fountain head. It was the *grand tournure*, the distinction of style, he essayed to borrow. His works will maintain a high rank in the esteem of men, not only because they are the most complete expression, and one of the highest, of the tendencies of the age, but also because they are the product of an original mind, — of a genius true and individual.

CATALOGUE

OF

THORVALDSEN'S WORKS.

We have not thought it necessary in this Catalogue to follow the chronological order, however interesting that arrangement might prove. In a list of works as numerous and varied as those of Thorvaldsen, the classification by subjects seemed to us to offer greater advantages, as tending to avoid confusion and facilitate research. Besides, the first part of the volume, the biographical part, has already given an almost complete chronological classification; and, to leave nothing to be desired on this point, care has been taken to place at the end of each description in the Catalogue the date when the work was produced. The valuable labors of Messrs. Thiele and Müller have been of great assistance in the performance of this task, and, thanks to them, scarcely a date is wanting.

[In translating the Catalogue, the French measures, metres and centimetres, have been reduced to English feet, inches, and hundredths.]

FAÇADE OF THE THORVALDSEN MUSEUM, COPENHAGEN.

SACRED SUBJECTS.

I.
STATUES AND GROUPS.

CHRIST AND THE TWELVE APOSTLES.

Colossal statues; marble. *Church of Our Lady (Frue Kirke), at Copenhagen.* Height: The Christ, 11 ft. 5.40 in.; St. Peter, 7 ft. 11.27 in.; St Matthew, 7 ft. 11.66 in.; St. John, 8 ft. 1.24 in.; St. James the Less, 7 ft. 10.09 in.; St. Philip, 7 ft. 8.91 in.; St. Judas Thaddeus, 7 ft. 9.69 in.; St, Paul, 7 ft. 11.27 in.; St. Simon Zelotes, 8 ft. 1.24 in.; St. Bartholomew, 8 ft. 0.85 in.; St. James the Greater, 7 ft. 11.66 in.; St. Thomas, 8 ft. 0.06 in.; St. Andrew, 7 ft. 10.48 in.

The Christ. (See wood-cut, p. 219.) — The Saviour is standing, the arms outstretched, the upper part of the body slightly inclined forward. His hair, parted in the middle, falls in ringlets over his shoulders. He is draped in a wide mantle, leaving the right side of the breast uncovered. Modelled at Rome in 1821.

St. Peter. — The saint turns his head to the right, and holds in his right hand the keys of Paradise; with his left hand he gathers the folds of his mantle around his breast. He wears a sleeved tunic fastened at the throat by a clasp. Modelled at Rome in 1821.

St. Matthew. — Holds a stylus in the right hand, and with the left supports a tablet which rests upon his knee. His right foot is raised and placed upon a rock. On the right of the saint, an angel designates him as an evangelist, whilst a purse lying on the ground recalls his previous occupation as a publican. His dress consists of the sleeved tunic and the mantle. Rome, 1821.

St. John. — He raises his eyes to heaven as though waiting for a revelation, and prepares to write upon a tablet. His mantle is thrown over his shoulders and is kept in place by a clasp at the throat; it is open in front and shows the whole of the tunic. At the feet of the saint is the eagle. Rome, 1824.

St. James the Less. — The features of his face suggest his relationship to Christ. He leans in meditation upon a long traveller's staff. His dress is the mantle and sleeved tunic. Rome, 1823.

St. Philip. — He carries his head slightly inclined to the right, and seems overcome with grief. His right hand is protruded from the folds of his mantle and holds a cross. Rome, 1823.

St. Judas Thaddeus. — St. Jude is in a standing posture, and is clothed in a sleeved tunic. His hands are clasped and raised to the height of his face. A long lance terminating in an axe, the instrument of his martyrdom, leans against his left arm. Rome, 1842.

St. Paul. — The saint is represented with a long beard and in the act of preaching, his right arm raised and the left resting upon his sword. He wears the sleeved tunic, and his mantle hanging from his shoulders is thence brought under his right arm and the end thrown over the left forearm. Rome, 1821.

St. Simon Zelotes. — St. Simon leans with a grave and pensive countenance upon a saw, the instrument of his martyrdom. He gathers together, and holds up with both hands joined, the folds of his mantle, which is open in front, showing the tunic. Rome, 1823.

St. Bartholomew. — The apostle wears an ample sleeved tunic. His mantle is thrown over the right shoulder and the end held in his left hand. He has a thick beard, and holds in his right hand the knife by which he suffered martyrdom. Rome, 1823.

St. James the Greater. — The saint is in the act of walking, and holds in his right hand a long traveller's staff. The folds of his mantle are held up by the left arm so as not to impede his steps. His inner garment is a sleeved tunic, and he has also a broad-brimmed hat. Rome, 1821.

St. Thomas. — The artist has endeavored to characterize the face of St. Thomas by an expression of doubt. The apostle is in meditation: he presses the forefinger of his left hand against his cheek, and in his right holds the square, emblem of the exact sciences. He is amply draped in his mantle, which envelopes him almost entirely.

His right arm, however, is covered only by the sleeve of the tunic. Rome, 1821.

St. Andrew. — The saint holds a scroll in the left hand, and with the right the end of the cross. He wears the tunic, and a mantle hangs from his left shoulder. Rome, 1841 and 1842.

The Apostles St. Andrew and St. Thomas, modelled for the second time by Thorvaldsen in 1841–42, and executed in marble for the *Frue Kirke*, had been previously represented by the artist, unsatisfactorily to himself, in attitudes differing from those above described. St. Andrew (height, 7 ft. 11.66 in.), modelled at Rome in 1823, is wrapped in his mantle, and leans with his left arm upon the cross: he wears no tunic, the right arm and a part of the breast are nude. St. Thaddeus (height the same), modelled at Rome, 1827, turns his head to the right and clasps his hands on a level with his breast.

The Thorvaldsen Museum has the plaster models of the *Christ* and the *Twelve Apostles*. In grouping them together in the *Hall of the Christ*, the directors rightly selected the plasters of St. Andrew and St. Thaddeus, which date from the years 1823 and 1827, as belonging to the same period with the others, and placed the two figures modelled in 1841 and 1842 in another gallery.

The Museum also contains many interesting manikins *(maquettes)*, made as studies for these large figures. Of the Christ there are two small sketches, one (height, 25.19 in.), which is draped and wanting the forearm, has the head very much thrown back; the other (height, 21.25 in.) is draped, and the head is not carried so far back. There is, besides, a statuette in plaster (4 ft. 7.90 in.), finished by Tenerani; the head is erect, the right foot thrown back and raised from the ground, and the arrangement of the drapery different from that finally adopted. The execution is delicate, but lacking the master's firm touch. There are in the same hall sketches of St. Matthew (height, 1 ft. 6.50 in.); St. James the Less (1 ft. 8.07 in.); St. Thomas (1 ft. 8.47 in.); St. Bartholomew (1 ft. 8.07 in.), with the hand holding the knife brought nearer to his breast; St. Simon (same height), with the hands crossed on the breast, and without the instrument of his martyrdom; St. Paul (1 ft. 7.29 in.); St. John (1 ft. 7.68 in.), the face turned to one side, having at his feet a cup and a serpent, and behind him the eagle; St. Andrew (2 ft. 2.37 in.); St. Thaddeus (two sketches, 2 ft. 3.95 in. and 2 ft. 7.10 in.). These three last sketches were for the models made in 1841–42.

There is a bronze of the statue of Christ in the Church of the Peace at Potsdam. (See p. 89 *et seq.*, 220 *et seq.*, and p. 231.)

The Angel of Baptism. (See wood-cut, p. 169.)

Statue; marble. *Frue Kirke, Copenhagen.* Height, 4 ft. 8.29 in.

The angel, crowned with flowers, kneels upon one knee and holds a large shallow shell, intended to contain the baptismal water.

Rome, 1827. The plaster model is in the Thorvaldsen Museum. (See p. 221.)

The Angel of Baptism.

Statue; marble. *Executed for Lord Lucan.* Height, 5 ft. 10.86 in.

This figure is the same as the preceding, but the attitude is different: the angel is standing.

Rome, 1823-24. The plaster model is in the Thorvaldsen Museum, where there is also a sketch; height, 19.68 in.

The Preaching of St. John the Baptist.

Group; terra cotta. *Pediment of the Frue Kirke, Copenhagen.* Height of the St. John, 7 ft. 10.48 in.; breadth of pediment, 41 ft. 8.78 in.

St. John stands upon a rock in the centre and above the rest of the composition. He is in the act of preaching; his right hand is raised, and the left holds a staff surmounted by a cross. The shell with which he dips water for baptism hangs by his side. He wears a tunic of camel's hair, unfastened on the left side, and has a broad mantle thrown over his shoulders.

The figures on his right (the spectator's left) are: —

A Young Man absorbed in Meditation. He stands with his left foot upon the rock, his left elbow resting upon his left knee and his head supported by his left hand. His tunic is unfastened at the right shoulder, and his cloak is wrapped around his right arm.

An Old Man and his Son. The father, with head uplifted, looks toward the preacher and listens attentively. His arms hang naturally, and his hands meeting in front hold together the folds of his cloak. The son, who stands behind him, leans upon his shoulder.

A Mother and her Young Child. The child puts his little arms upon the shoulder of his mother, who kneels upon her right knee.

A Doctor. He is seated upon a rock, his body bent and his hands crossed upon his breast; he is wrapped in a large cloak, and wears the Israelitish head-dress.

A Young Man reclining. His elbow resting upon a rock, he turns round in an attentive attitude.

On the opposite side of the pediment are: —

A Youth. His posture is upright; he wears a tunic, but is taking off his cloak, in preparation for baptism. His attitude is animated, and indicates an impulsive temperament.

A Pharisee. His head is covered by a cap, and he wears a rich cloak. His bearing is haughty, and he looks with disdainful pride toward the Baptist.

A Hunter. Laden with game and followed by his dog, he stops to listen as he passes by.

Two Children. Their whole attention is given to the hunter's dog. But the boy checks his sister and makes signs to her to keep silent.

A Mother and her Child. The woman is seated and listening.

The child, undraped, leans against his mother's knee, — his attitude resembling that of the infant Jesus in the picture by Raphael, known as *La Belle Jardinière*. The woman's head is a reproduction of the portrait of Vittoria Cardoni. (See p. 89.)

A Shepherd. This recumbent figure terminates the pediment. He plays only an incidental part in the scene, to which he is morally a stranger.

This pediment was modelled at Rome in 1821–22. (See pp 89. and 222.) The plaster models are in the Thorvaldsen Museum. Two other figures, *A Jew seated* and a *Roman Soldier*, which were to form part of the composition, were suppressed. (See, farther on, DIVERS SUBJECTS.)

The Museum has also the first miniature model *(maquette)* of *The Preaching of St. John*. Some of the figures differ from those in the finished work.

II.

BAS-RELIEFS.

§ 1. — *Subjects from the Old Testament.*

ADAM AND EVE.

Plaster. *Thorvaldsen Museum*. Height, 3 ft. 3.37 in.; length, 4 ft. 11.05 in.

Adam and Eve are seated side by side. Abel, pursued by Cain who tries to snatch an apple from him, seeks protection in his father's lap. Eve appears grieved at this first quarrel between her children. On the left the serpent is seen to creep upon an altar.

Rome, 1838. The Museum has also a plaster sketch, 14.17 by 15.35 in.

ELIEZER AND REBECCA. (See wood-cut, p. 218.)

Plaster. *Thorvaldsen Museum*. Height, 3 ft. 1.79 in.; length, 6 ft. 1.62 in.

Abraham's servant is drinking from the pitcher which Rebecca offers to him. A boy behind him carries a box containing the jewels intended for Isaac's betrothed. On the right are two camels led by a camel-driver; on the left, two women, who have come to draw water at the spring.

Has the inscription: NYSÖE, 26 January, 1841.

THE JUDGMENT OF SOLOMON.

Bas-relief; sketch. *Thorvaldsen Museum*. Height, 1 ft. 3.74 in.; length, 6 ft. 7.52 in.

Solomon sits on his royal judgment-seat, surrounded by his courtiers. On the left is the mother of the dead child, and near her the body of her son; on the right, the mother of the living child in despair appeals to the king. Solomon stretches out his arm to check the soldier who is on the point of dividing the young victim.

Sketch of a bas-relief projected, but not executed, which was to have ornamented the pediment of the Town Hall of Copenhagen.

Heliodorus driven from the Temple.

Plaster. *Palace of Charlottenborg.* Height, 3 ft. 8.88 in.; length, 5 ft. 8.89 in.

Heliodorus, surrounded by his guards, is struck down whilst car rying off the treasures of the temple in obedience to the orders of the king. A horseman in rich armor appears, whose horse strikes with his forefeet the envoy of Seleucus, whilst two young men of great strength and beauty, one on each side, chastise him with rods. On the left is the High Priest kneeling, and surrounded by other priests. On the right, behind the affrighted guards, a woman and her child cry out in wonder at the power of the Most High. (2 Maccabees, iii.)

Copenhagen, 1791. Obtained the small gold medal (the prize for sculpture) at the Academy of Fine Arts. (See p. 9 *et seq.*)

§ 2. — *Subjects from the New Testament.*

The Institution of the Lord's Supper.

Bas-relief; marble. *Frue Kirke, Copenhagen.* Height, 3 ft. 2.58 in.; length, 7 ft. 6.58 in.

Christ stands before the table at the left extremity of the composition: he raises his eyes to heaven and blesses the cup. The Apostles kneel before their Master, except one who rises in amazement. St. John and St. Peter are nearest to Christ. St. Thomas, in an attitude expressing doubt, has not yet clasped his hands. Judas is going away.

The plaster model, made at Copenhagen in 1820, is in the Thorvaldsen Museum. (See p. 221.)

Christ's Entry into Jerusalem.

Bas-relief; plaster. *Frue Kirke, Copenhagen.* Height, 4 ft. 1.99 in.; length, 43 ft. 9.58 in.

Christ is riding upon an ass led by St. John. He raises his right hand. Behind him walks St. Peter, who stretches his arm toward him. Then follow the other disciples, and after them the lame and the blind man cured by the Saviour. At the other end of the frieze, the people, coming toward Christ, scatter flowers and spread garments in the way, or wave branches. Women prostrate themselves in adoration. Near the gate of Jerusalem a Pharisee is conversing with a doctor. Two boys pass near them shouting "Hosanna," and a man points out to his wife the new King of the Jews.

Nysöe, 1839–40. The plaster model is in the Thorvaldsen Museum (height, 2 ft. 1.98 in.; length, 24 ft. 1.76 in.).

Christ bearing the Cross.

Bas-relief; plaster. *Frue Kirke, Copenhagen.* (Frieze above the altar, in the choir.) Height, 6 ft. 2.80 in.; length, 65 ft. 7.40 in.

Christ stands in the centre of the frieze, bearing the cross which Simon the Cyrenean endeavors to hold up. The Saviour turns round toward the kneeling woman. He is preceded by two executioners: one drags the rope fastened to the cross; the other, with his assistant, carries the ladder, the hammer, and the nails. A man is leading the two thieves with their hands tied behind them: the younger looks toward the Saviour, and seems to repent; while the other, hardened in vice, fixes his eyes on the ground. At the head of the procession a mounted centurion, followed by horsemen and Roman foot-soldiers, gives the order to move faster. One of the horsemen carries the order to the executioner. A soldier armed with a lance keeps back the crowd, and a number of Jews are beginning to ascend the hill of Calvary.

At the opposite end of the frieze, behind the group of kneeling women, Joseph of Arimathea is sadly watching the fainting mother of the Saviour who is upheld by St. John and Mary Magdalen. Three Pharisees on horseback come next, and one of them sternly commands the Virgin to be thrust aside and the way to be cleared. Roman foot-soldiers bring up the rear of the procession. Some of the Jews are collected around the house of Pilate, who is washing his hands, unwilling to be stained with the blood of the just.

Nysöe, 1839. The plaster sketch is in the Museum (height, 2 ft. 1.98 in.; length, 25 ft. 2.36 in.). It differs in some points from the finished work above described Pilate wears an Israelitish dress, afterward changed for a Roman costume. Two disciples walking in front of Joseph of Arimathea have been replaced by a woman leading her child. (See p. 154 *et seq.*)

Christ's Charge to St. Peter.

Bas-relief; marble. *Chapel of the Pitti Palace, Florence.* Height, 2 ft. 1.19 in.; length, 5 ft. 10.86 in.

Christ points out the sheep to St. Peter, and commands him to feed his flock The Apostle, holding the keys, kneels before his Master.

St. John stands behind St. Peter. The other Apostles stand on either side.

Rome, 1818. The Museum has the plaster model, and also a plaster cast taken from the marble.

SAINT PETER HEALING THE PARALYTIC.

Bas-relief; plaster. *Palace of Charlottenborg.* Height, 3 ft. 10.85 in.; length, 5 ft. 9.29 in.

St. Peter and St. Paul stop at the entrance of the temple. St. Peter takes the paralytic man by the right hand, and invoking God raises up the mendicant and cures him. The people coming into the temple are filled with astonishment. (Acts iii.)

Copenhagen, 1793. Obtained the grand prize at the Copenhagen Academy. (See p. 12.)

THE HOLY WOMEN AT THE SEPULCHRE.

Bas-relief; plaster. *Purchased by Prince Louis of Bavaria for a church in Munich.* Height, 3 ft. 7.70 in.; length, 8 ft. 6.36 in.

Mary, the mother of James, Mary Magdalen, and Salome bring perfumes to the tomb of Jesus. They find the stone taken away. An angel stands before the open sepulchre and points to heaven.

Rome, in 1817. This composition and the next are not to be found in the Thorvaldsen Museum. There are in the galleries two vacant spaces waiting for them. Shall they remain unoccupied? King Louis I honored the artist with his friendship, and professed the greatest esteem for his talent. Will his grandson one day show a taste for sculpture, and allow casts to be taken from the two bas-reliefs, so that there may be no gaps to be regretted in the collection of the master's works?

THE ANNUNCIATION.

Bas-relief; plaster. *Purchased by Prince Louis of Bavaria for a church in Munich.* Height, 3 ft. 7.70 in.; length, 6 ft. 6.74 in.

The Virgin is seated with hands clasped. The Angel Gabriel flies toward her, and presents to her a lily.

Rome, 1819. See the preceding.

BAPTISMAL FONTS.

Bas-reliefs; marble. *Church of Brahe-Trolleborg in Fionia.* Height, 2 ft. 3.95 in.; breadth, 1 ft. 9.65 in.

These baptismal fonts are square in shape, and four bas-reliefs ornament the four sides: on the front face, St. John baptizing Christ; on the right, Christ seated blessing little children; on the left, the Virgin seated with the infant Christ in her lap, and the little St. John standing beside her. Faith, Hope, and Charity are represented by three angels soaring together.

Modelled at Rome, in 1807, to the order of the Countess von Schimmelmann, cut in marble in 1808, and placed in the church in 1815. The plaster models are in the Museum, where there is also a repetition, with variations, of the left-hand bas-relief. Thorvaldsen executed in 1827 a duplicate in marble, intending to present it to the Church of Myklabye, in Iceland, of which his ancestor, Thorvald Gotskalksen, had been pastor. The composition was now surmounted by a wreath of flowers, and above the angels was engraved this inscription: —

OPUS HOC ROMÆ FECIT
ET ISLANDIÆ
TERRÆ SIBI GENTILICIÆ
PIETATIS CAUSA DONAVIT
ALBERTUS THORVALDSEN
A. M.D.CCC.XXVII.

It is supposed that this copy, before it reached Iceland, was sold by the artist to a Norwegian merchant, who had the inscription effaced. Thorvaldsen, however, immediately had another copy made at Carrara.

The Baptism of Christ.

Bas-relief; marble. *Frue Kirke, Copenhagen.* Height, 3 ft. 1.79 in.; length, 7 ft. 4.97 in.

Christ standing on the bank of the Jordan with hands clasped and head bowed receives the water of baptism which St. John pours upon him. Two angels are placed behind St. John, two others are flying in the air. On the margin of the river an Israelitish family are preparing for baptism.

Copenhagen, 1820. Plaster model in the Museum.

Christ blessing Children.

Bas-relief; sketch. *Thorvaldsen Museum.* Height, 1 ft. 5.71 in.; length, 2 ft. 5.92 in.

Christ, standing, calls to him the children whom one of his disciples wishes to send away. St. John and another disciple are on the left.

Modelled at Nysöe, 1840, for the asylum called by the name of Frederick VI, at Copenhagen.

Jesus Teaching in the Temple.

Bas-relief; plaster. *Thorvaldsen Museum.* Height, 2 ft. 9.46 in.; width, 2 ft. 5.13 in.

Jesus, at the age of twelve years, stands in front of two doctors, one of whom, seated, has a roll of papyrus on his knees; the other standing, his hand upon his mouth, listens and reflects.

Nysöe, 1841.

Christ and the Woman of Samaria.

Bas-relief; plaster. *Thorvaldsen Museum.* Height, 2 ft. 6.31 in.; width, 2 ft. 4.34 in.

Christ leans upon the curb of the well. The Samaritan woman, coming to draw water, rests her hand upon her pitcher and pauses in an attentive attitude.

Nysöe, 1841.

The Annunciation.

Bas-relief; plaster. *Thorvaldsen Museum.* Height, 2 ft. 2.77 in.; length, 4 ft. 1.99 in.

The Virgin is seated; she lays down the work on which she was engaged upon a basket beside her. Her eyes are cast down, and she raises her right hand to her face. The angel Gabriel advances toward her with a lily in his hand, and the Holy Spirit descends upon her in the form of a dove.

Rome, 1842.

Adoration of the Shepherds.

Bas-relief; plaster. *Thorvaldsen Museum.* Height, 2 ft. 1.98 in.; length, 4 ft. 1.21 in.

The Virgin mother is kneeling before the new-born Child. On the right are four shepherds in the act of adoration; one of them plays upon the flute, another upon the bag-pipe. St. Joseph is on the left near the manger, where an ox and an ass are feeding. Three little angels hover above the head of the infant Saviour.

Rome, 1842.

The Flight into Egypt.

Bas-relief; plaster. *Thorvaldsen Museum.* Height, 2 ft. 3.16 in.; length, 4 ft. 1.21 in.

St. Joseph walks before with a staff in his hand, followed by the Virgin carrying the infant Jesus. An angel hovers by Mary's side, pointing out the way and protecting the fugitives from the fury of Herod's soldiers. On the left, one of these soldiers snatches a child from its mother and is about to kill it.

Rome, 1842.

Jesus in the Temple.

Bas-relief; plaster. *Thorvaldsen Museum.* Height, 2 ft. 2.77 in.; length, 4 ft. 1.21 in.

Jesus is standing in the midst of the doctors; one of them, seated, holds open a scroll upon which the Child places his finger. He is interpreting the Scriptures. On the left, the Virgin, coming in with St. Joseph, recognizes her Son and crosses her hands in token of adoration.

Rome, 1842.

The Baptism of Christ

Bas-relief; plaster. *Thorvaldsen Museum.* Height, 2 ft. 2.77 in.; length, 4 ft. 1.99 in.

Christ is bending before St. John Baptist, who pours the water upon his head; his feet are in the stream. The Jordan is personified by a recumbent old man leaning upon an urn. Three little angels hover above the Saviour, and the Holy Spirit descends in the form of a dove. Behind the Baptist, a man, a young girl, and a child are undressing to be baptized also.

Rome, 1842.

Christ's Entry into Jerusalem.

Bas-relief; plaster. *Thorvaldsen Museum.* Height, 2 ft. 1.59 in.; length, 3 ft. 0.61 in.

Christ is mounted upon an ass, which is led by St. John. Coming to meet him, are a man who is spreading a carpet, a woman scattering flowers, and a child carrying a palm branch.

Sketch modelled at Rome in 1842.

Christ at Emmaus.

Bas-relief; silver *repoussé* work. Altar-piece, *Church della Santa Annunziata, Florence.* Height, 2 ft. 1.19 in.; length, 11 ft. 6.58 in.

Christ seated at the table takes the bread and blesses it. By this action the disciples, placed on either hand, recognize him as the Saviour. A curtain is suspended behind him, above which are seen the tops of trees.

Rome, 1818. Plaster model in the Museum.

Christ at Emmaus.

Bas-relief; plaster. *Thorvaldsen Museum.* Height, 4 ft. 0.03 in.; length, 5 ft. 0.62 in.

The scene is laid in a room at the end of which is a double window. Christ is on the right. The disciples have risen from the table and are on the left. One is kneeling with clasped hands; the other stands with his hands crossed over his breast.

Modelled at Nysöe in 1840, and designed as an altar-piece for a church near Stampeborg. It was afterwards cut in marble at Rome, by the sculptor Holbech.

The Resurrection.

Bas-relief; sketch. *Thorvaldsen Museum.* Height, 1 ft. 4.14 in.; length, 6 ft. 2.80 in.

Christ with outstretched arms issues from the tomb, stepping upon the stone which has been rolled away from the entrance. Two angels stand in adoration on either side of the Saviour. One of the guards flies in terror, another grasps his sword; the rest are asleep. In the distance, the holy women are seen coming.

Rome, 1835. This bas-relief, intended for the pediment of the chapel of the palace of Christiansborg, was never more than sketched.

The Four Evangelists.

Four medallions; marble. *Thorvaldsen Museum.* Diameter of each, 1 ft. 8.86 in.

The evangelists are borne aloft: St. Matthew, by an angel; St. John, by an eagle; St. Luke, by an ox; St. Mark, by a lion.

Rome, 1833. The plaster models are also in the Museum.

Saint Luke.

Medallion; plaster. *Thorvaldsen Museum.* Diameter, 1 ft. 8.86 in.

The saint, standing with a stylus in his hand, is writing the gospel upon a tablet which rests upon his knee. The winged ox lies beside him, and the evangelist places one foot upon the animal.

Sketch modelled at Rome, about 1833.

Saint Luke.

Medallion; plaster. *Thorvaldsen Museum.* Diameter, 1 ft. 8 86 in.

The saint, in conformity with the tradition, is painting the portrait of the Virgin. Behind him is the winged ox.

Sketch modelled at Rome, probably in 1833.

§ 3. — *Angelic and Symbolic Figures.*

Three Angels keeping Christmas.

Medallion; plaster. *Thorvaldsen Museum.* Diameter, 3 ft. 4.55 in.

The angels are soaring among the stars on Christmas night. One is playing upon the harp, the others sing the birth of the Saviour. Little cherubs playing upon different instruments hover around the angels.

Modelled at Nysöe in December, 1842, as a Christmas present to the family of the Baron von Stampe.

ANGELS OF THE LAST JUDGMENT.

Three bas-reliefs; plaster. *Thorvaldsen Museum.* Form, oval. No. 1: height, 3 ft. 3.37 in.; width, 2 ft. 2.37 in. Nos. 2 and 3: height, 2 ft. 8.28 in.; width, 1 ft. 6.89 in.

The first angel stands facing the spectator; a star glitters above his head; he holds his trumpet in his right hand. The second places his left hand on his breast, and holds his trumpet in his right. The third holds in his left hand the scroll upon which are written the actions of men; the sword of chastisement rests upon his right shoulder.

These three bas-reliefs, intended for a cemetery, were modelled at Rome in 1842.

THE GUARDIAN ANGEL.

Bas-reliefs; marble. *Frue Kirke, Copenhagen.* Height, 2 ft. 3.55 in.; width, 1 ft. 7.68 in.

The angel, in token of protection, places his right hand on the shoulder, and the left on the head, of a child praying.

Copenhagen, 1838. The plaster model is in the Museum.

THREE ANGELS.

Two bas-reliefs; bronze. Altar-pieces, *Cathedral of Novara.* Height, 1 ft. 2.56 in.; length, 2 ft. 1.19 in.

These two compositions, forming a pair, represent each three little angels flying, bearing garlands and scattering flowers.

Rome, 1833. Models in the Museum.

THREE ANGELS.

Two bas-reliefs; marble. *Thorvaldsen Museum.* Height, 1 ft. 2.96 in.; length, 1 ft. 5.32 in.

One of these bas-reliefs represents three little angels standing, leaning upon each other, singing and holding a long strip of parchment unrolled. In the other, the angel who is in the middle is seated upon an altar, and is playing upon the cithern; the two others are standing, one with a harp, the other with a flute.

Rome, 1833. Intended for the Cathedral of Novara, but replaced by the foregoing compositions. The plaster models are also in the Museum.

FIGURES OF ANGELS.

Bas-relief; marble. *Dome of the Chapel of Christiansborg.*

These are three little angels standing and holding garlands. They are repeated a great number of times, ornamenting the whole interior cornice of the dome.

Copenhagen, 1820. The model is in the Museum.

Faith, Hope, and Charity.

Bas-relief; plaster. *Thorvaldsen Museum.* Height, 1 ft. 5.71 in.; length, 2 ft. 9.85 in.

Charity is represented by an angel sitting upon a raised seat and spreading his wings over two figures on either side of him whom he encircles with his arms. One is a woman kneeling in prayer, — Faith: the other, a woman seated and holding a flower in her hand, — Hope.

Rome, 1836.

Christian Charity.

Bas-relief; marble. *Frue Kirke, Copenhagen.* Height, 2 ft. 3.55 in.; width, 1 ft. 6.50 in.

Charity is represented under the figure of a woman carrying a child in her arms, and making another go before her.

Rome, 1810. First cut in marble the same year for the Marquis of Landsdown. A second copy was made later to be sold for the benefit of a poor Norwegian, who died before the charitable plan was carried out. It is this copy, doubtless, which, together with the plaster model, is now to be seen in the Museum. The copy which is placed over the Poor's Box in the church is consequently the third which has been taken in marble.

III.

SEPULCHRAL MONUMENTS.

Mausoleum of Pius VII.

Marble. *Clementine Chapel, St. Peter's, Rome.* Height of statue of Pope, 9 ft. 7.74 in.; Wisdom, 9 ft. 8.14 in.; Strength, 9 ft. 11.68 in.; Two angels seated, 4 ft. 8.29 in. and 4 ft. 10.26 in.; The Pope's Arms (bas-relief): height, 2 ft. 4.34 in.; length, 6 ft. 9.10 in.

This monument is square in shape. It is surmounted by statues of the Pope, and of two angels placed one on each side of the Pontiff. To the right and left of the door of the mausoleum are the statues of Wisdom and of Strength. The Holy Father, seated upon the pontifical throne, raises his right hand to give the benediction. The tiara is placed upon his head, and he wears the cope and the alb:

upon the border of the latter are represented the instruments of martyrdom of the Apostles. Divine Wisdom is represented under the figure of a woman, standing, wearing the ægis of Minerva, and holding the open volume of the Holy Scriptures: the owl is at her feet. Another woman, her head and shoulders covered by the lion's skin of Hercules, typifies Divine Strength: she tramples under foot material strength, symbolized by the club, and with arms crossed upon her breast looks up to heaven. On the right an angel, seated, points with his finger to the hour-glass which has numbered the days of the Pope; on the left another angel has just closed the book in which he has recorded the actions of Pius VII. Over the door of the mausoleum two little angels support the arms of the Pontiff, surmounted by the tiara and the keys of St. Peter.

Erected at the expense of Cardinal Consalvi. Modelled at Rome, 1824-1831. The plaster models are in the Thorvaldsen Museum, as well as a sketch of the whole mausoleum (height, 3 ft. 6.51 in.), and a sketch of the statue of the Pope (height, 1 ft. 5.71 in.). In this first composition, which was not adopted, the Pontiff has laid aside the tiara, and holds in his hand the palm of martyrdom. Two angels were to have held a crown of stars above his head. (See p. 92 *et seq.*)

Monument of Cardinal Consalvi.

Bust and bas-relief; marble. *Pantheon, Rome.* Height of bas-relief, 1 ft. 10.44 in.; length, 4 ft. 0.03 in.

In the bas-relief the cardinal presents to the Holy Father six kneeling provinces; the first two are Ancona, with a rudder, and Bologna, with a shield.

Rome, 1824. (See p. 96.)

Mausoleum of Eugène de Beauharnais.

Group; Carrara marble. *Church of St. Michael, Munich.* Height of statue of the Prince, 9 ft. 1.44 in.

Eugène, wearing a tunic open on the right side, and a cloak thrown over his shoulders, stands before the closed door of his tomb. He places his left hand on his heart, and holds in his right a laurel wreath which he presents to the Muse of History. The Muse, seated, is writing upon a tablet the exploits of the hero. On the other side, the Genius of Death carries his extinguished torch, and sustains the Genius of Immortality, whose eyes are raised to heaven. At the feet of the prince lie the iron crown of Italy, his armor, helmet, sword, and baton of command. Between the capitals of the columns which form the door of the tomb is inscribed the motto of Eugène de Beauharnais, — *Honneur et Fidelité*. On the socle of the mausoleum is the following inscription upheld by two angels: —

HIC PLACIDE OSSA CUBANT
EUGENII NAPOLEONIS
REGIS ITALIÆ VICES QUONDAM GERENTIS
NAT. LUTET. PARISIOR. D. III. SEPT. MDCCLXXXI.
DEF. MONACHII D. XXI. FEBR. MDCCCXXIV.
MONUMENTUM POSUIT VIDUA MŒRENS
AUGUSTA AMALIA
MAX. JOSEPH. BAV. REGIS FILIA.

Modelled at Rome in 1827; erected in 1830. (See pp. 105 and 112.) The Museum has the plaster model of the statue of the prince, and the sketch of the group of the two genii (height, 1 ft. 4.92 in.).

Monument of Christian IV, King of Denmark.

Statue and bas-relief; bronze. *In the Garden of Rosenborg, Copenhagen.* Height of statue, 7 ft. 1.43 in. Height of bas-relief, 1 ft. 10.44 in.; length, 2 ft. 7.10 in.

This monument consists of a statue of the king and a bas-relief. The monarch stands, wearing the costume of his time, holding his hat in his right hand, and resting his left upon his sword. He wears the insignia of the Order of the Elephant. The bas-relief, composed to illustrate the king's motto, *Regna firmat Pietas*, exhibits three genii personifying *Strength*, *Government*, and *Piety*.

The statue was modelled at Copenhagen in 1840; the bas-relief, at Nysöe in 1842. The statue, which was intended to be placed, with the bas-relief, upon the sarcophagus of Christian IV at Roeskilde, the burial-place of the Danish kings, has changed its destination, and has since been set up in the little garden surrounding the castle of Rosenborg, at Copenhagen. The Thorvaldsen Museum has the plaster models of the statue and of the bas-relief, and a sketch of the statue (height, 2 ft. 1.59 in.). There is also a small model in plaster belonging to Madame von Stampe. (See p. 157.)

Mausoleum of Prince Vladimir Potocki.

Statue and bas-relief; marble. *Cathedral of Cracow.* Height of statue, ft. 0.25 in. Bas-relief, height, 2 ft. 11.43 in.; width, 2 ft. 6.70 in.

The young prince is represented as an antique hero. His open tunic shows his breast; his cloak is thrown over his left shoulder; his right hand rests upon his hip, his left upon the pommel of his sword. At his feet lie his helmet and breastplate: upon the latter is sculptured the Polish eagle. In the bas-relief, the Genius of Death, crowned with poppies, is seated and asleep; his right hand resting upon his extinguished torch, his left holding a garland of oak-leaves. (See wood-cut, p. 168.)

The statue was modelled at Rome in 1821 (see pp. 81 and 225), and the bas-relief in 1829. The Thorvaldsen Museum has the plaster models, as well as a marble copy of the bas-relief, *The Genius of Death.*

MAUSOLEUM OF CONRADDIN.

Statue; marble. *Church of the Madonna del Carmine, Naples.* Height, 7 ft. 0.25 in.

The last of the Hohenstaufens is standing, his shoulders covered by the royal mantle, and his right hand resting upon the hilt of his sword. He wears the Neapolitan crown; and his helmet, the crest of which is surmounted by an eagle's head, lies behind him.

Modelled at Rome in 1836, to the order of King Louis of Bavaria. The marble left unfinished at the artist's death was completed by the Bavarian sculptor, Peter Schöpf, and the statue set up in 1847. The Thorvaldsen Museum has the model in plaster and a sketch (height, 1 ft. 9.65 in.). Another sketch belongs to Herr Thiele.

MAUSOLEUM OF THE PHYSICIAN VACCA BERLINGHIERI.

Medallion and bas-relief; marble. *Campo Santo, Pisa.* Diameter of medallion, 1 ft. 6.89 in. Height of bas-relief, 3 ft. 4.55 in; length, 6 ft. 6.74 in.

The medallion is a portrait of the celebrated oculist. The bas-relief represents Tobit healing his father. The young man holds a cup containing the lotion of fish-gall which he applies to his father's eyes. The angel is withdrawing; and the mother, leaning upon the table, watches her son. The dog sits looking toward his young master.

Rome, 1828. (See p. 108.) The plaster models are in the Museum.

MONUMENT OF RAPHAEL.

Bas-relief; plaster. *Thorvaldsen Museum.* Height, 8 ft. 0.61 in.; length, 4 ft. 3.18 in.

The god of Love supports the tablet which the artist is drawing, and presents to him a rose and a poppy, emblems of pleasure and of eternal sleep. Raphael, in the costume of his time, one foot resting upon a Corinthian capital, is seated upon the altar of the Muses and Graces. Fame brings him a palm-branch and a wreath of laurel, while the Genius of Light brandishes his torch.

Rome, 1833. Intended for the tomb of Raphael, but the plan was not executed.

SEPULCHRAL MONUMENT OF AUGUSTA BÖHMER.

Three bas-reliefs; marble. *Near Wurzburg, Bavaria.* Height, 2 ft. 7.10 in.; width, 2 ft. 0.01 in., and height same; width, 1 ft. 6.11 in.

On the front, Augusta Böhmer, while giving drink to her mother, is stung by a serpent in the heel, — an allusion to the young girl's death. On the sides, Nemesis notes this act of filial devotion; the Genius of Death, his head covered with poppies, leans upon his inverted torch.

Rome, 1811. Ordered by the philosopher Schelling, whose wife, Caroline Schelling, a writer of some reputation, was the mother of Augusta Böhmer. The young girl had been an actress at Weimar (Müller). The *Genius of Death* was executed separately for the tomb of Herr Donner at Altona. Plaster models in the Museum.

Sepulchral Monument of Philip Bethmann Holweg.

Three bas-reliefs; marble. *Cemetery at Frankfort.* Height, 2 ft. 11.43 in.; length, 4 ft 7.11 in., and height same; width, 3 ft. 1.40 in.

This young man, who had risked his life at a fire in Vienna, died shortly after, in Florence, in consequence of this act of devotion, and in spite of his brother's care. He is represented in the principal bas-relief at the moment of expiring, and giving to his brother the civic crown, the reward of his courage. The Genius of Death, holding poppies in his hand, leans upon his shoulder. The bas-relief on the left represents the mother and sisters of the young man overwhelmed with grief; the one on the right has a figure of Nemesis, and beside her the River Arno and the Lion of Florence.

Rome, 1814. Plaster models in the Museum.

Sepulchral Monument of the Baroness von Schubart.

Bas-relief; marble. *Leghorn, Cemetery of the Protestant English Church.* Height, 1 ft. 11.62 in.; length, 3 ft. 1.40 in.

The husband is seated upon the edge of the couch upon which his wife is lying: he takes her hand and raises his arm in an attitude of grief. The Genius of Death stands at the head of the bed.

Rome, 1814. Plaster model in the Museum.

Sepulchral Monument of the Children of the Princess Helena Poninska.

Bas-relief; marble. *Cathedral of Cracow, Chapel of the Jagellons.* Height, 3 ft. 2.58 in.; length, 5 ft. 2.20 in.

A brother and sister, led by a Genius whose torch is not yet extinguished, are leaving their weeping mother, who strives to detain them.

Modelled at Rome in 1835, to the order of the princess, whose children had died within a short time of each other. The plaster model and a sketch are in the Museum.

Sepulchral Monument of the Countess Pore.

Bas-relief; plaster. *Thorvaldsen Museum.* Height, 2 ft. 11.43 in.; width, 3 ft. 0.22 in.

The husband of the deceased, seated, raises his arm and holds upon his knees the funeral urn. The daughter approaches her father to console him, and lays her hand upon his shoulder. The son, a mere child, embraces the urn which holds the ashes of his mother.

Rome, 1817. We do not know whether this bas-relief was ever executed. Compare it with the second bas-relief of the monument of Philip Bethmann. *(Vide supra.)*

Sepulchral Monument of the Countess Berkowska.

Bas-relief; marble. *Upon the tomb at . . . ?* Height, 2 ft. 6.70 in.; width, 3 ft. 3.37 in.

The Genius of Death is leading the countess, and extinguishes his torch against the stone which marks the limit of the life of the deceased. Her son prays to heaven, and tries to detain her.

Rome, 1816. Ordered by the son of the countess. Plaster model in Museum.

Sepulchral Monument of the Baroness Chandry.

Bas-relief; marble. *Upon the tomb in England.* Height, 4 ft. 1.21 in.; width, 3 ft. 2.58 in.

A young woman is soaring toward heaven, holding in her hands a cross which she presses against her breast; the Genius of Death raises his eyes, and leans upon his inverted torch.

Rome, 1818. The marble sent to England in 1828 (Thiele). Plaster model in Museum. (See p. 226.)

Sepulchral Monument of Lady Newboock.

Bas-relief; plaster. *Thorvaldsen Museum.* Height, 2 ft. 5.92 in.; length, 2 ft. 6.70 in.

A column upon which the cross is sculptured supports a cinerary urn. The mother of the deceased, in mourning weeds, kneels beside the ashes of her daughter. Opposite, the Genius of Death, holding poppies in his left hand, bends his head and leans upon his inverted torch.

Rome, 1818.

Sepulchral Monument of Mademoiselle Jacobi.

Statue; marble. *At Altona.*

An angel is kneeling in prayer with his arms crossed upon his breast. The torch of life beside him is not quite extinguished.

Nysöe, 1839. Sketch in the Museum (height, 1 ft. 5.71 in.).

Sepulchral Monument of an English Lady.

Bas-relief; marble. *On the tomb in England.* Height, 3 ft. 1.40 in.; length, 4 ft. 3.18 in.

An aged woman, with eyes uplifted and hands clasped, kneels between two angels, one of whom is writing the record of her life, while the other points to the empty hour-glass.

Rome, 1828. Ordered by an Englishman, Mr. Thompson. The two little angels suggested the two figures which were added to the mausoleum of Pius VII. Plaster model in the Museum.

Sepulchral Monument of a Wife.

Bas-relief; plaster. *Thorvaldsen Museum.* Height, 2 ft. 0.80 in.; width, 1 ft. 10.14 in.

An afflicted husband grasps the hand of his wife, who is taking leave of him.

Destination unknown.

Sepulchral Monument of a Young Woman.

Bas-relief; plaster. *Thorvaldsen Museum.* Height, 4 ft. 1.99 in; width, 3 ft. 3.37 in.

A young woman, with the right arm raised and holding a cross in the left hand, is ascending to heaven. The Genius of Death, with closed eyes, leans upon his extinguished torch.

Destination unknown.

Sepulchral Monument of —— Goethe.

Medallion; marble. *Upon the tomb at Rome.* Diameter, 1 ft. 6.89 in.

Portrait of the son of the celebrated German author.

Plaster model in the Museum.

Sepulchral Monument of the Painter Bassi.

Medallion; marble. *Upon the tomb in Italy.* Diameter, 1 ft. 6.89 in.

Portrait.

Plaster model in Museum.

Sepulchral Monument of Count Arthur Potocki.

Bas-relief; marble. *Cathedral of Cracow.* Height, 1 ft. 0.99 in.; length, 1 ft. 6.89 in.

Three children praying upon their father's tomb.

Rome, 1834. Ordered by the widow, and placed as an altar-piece in the chapel over the count's tomb. Plaster model in Museum.

Sepulchral Monument of M. Mylius.

Bas-relief; marble. *Milan.* Height, 3 ft. 2.97 in.; length, 6 ft. 3.19 in.

The car of Nemesis is represented drawn by two horses, one of which is rearing and is struck by the goddess. A dog runs beside the horses to point out the way. Upon the wheel are depicted the different phases through which Destiny may compel mankind to pass. Behind the car march two genii; one armed with a sword to punish the guilty, the other loaded with wreaths to reward the deserving. Upon the background of the bas-relief are figured the signs of the zodiac, the Balance being above the head of Nemesis.

Rome, 1834. Plaster model in Museum.

The Genius of Life and the Genius of Death.

Group; sketch. *Thorvaldsen Museum.* Height, 2 ft. 8.67 in.

The Genius of Life, winged, holds a lighted torch, and rests his right arm on the shoulder of the Genius of Death, whose torch is inverted. These two figures stand before a *meta*, upon which are a cinerary urn and a shroud.

Destination unknown.

PAN AND A YOUNG SATYR.

PUBLIC AND COMMEMORATIVE MONUMENTS.

MONUMENT TO THE MEMORY OF THE SWISS MASSACRED ON THE 10TH AUGUST, 1792. (See wood-cut, p. 73.)

Colossal figure carved in the rock. *Lucerne.* Height, 19 ft. 8.22 in.; length, 29 ft. 6.33 in.

Sufficiently described in the text. (See p. 73.)

Modelled at Rome, 1819; cut in the rock by Lucas Ahorn, of Constance. The plaster model is in the Thorvaldsen Museum. Height, 2 ft. 9.46 in.; length, 5 ft. 1.02 in.

EQUESTRIAN STATUE OF PRINCE PONIATOWSKI.

Bronze; colossal statue.

The prince, mounted upon a horse standing at rest, makes a gesture of command with his right hand, which holds a sword. He is clad in the Roman garb, and the Polish eagle is engraved on his cuirass.

Rome, 1827. The statue has disappeared. (See p. 79 *et seq.*) The Thorvaldsen Museum has two plaster models of this figure (height, 8 ft. 5.57 in., and 15 ft. 3.07 in.), the sketch of a previous model in a different attitude (height, 2 ft. 3.95 in.), and a separate plaster of the horse (height, 6 ft. 11.46 in.), as the artist first proposed to represent him, namely, at the moment when the animal hesitates to take the leap into the Elster. This horse was cast in bronze after Thorvaldsen's death, to serve as one of the four coursers attached to the car of Victory placed above the pediment of the

Museum. There is a plaster model of the equestrian statue of Poniatowski, at Leipsic, in the Gerhard Garden, near the spot where the prince expired.

Monument to King Frederick VI of Denmark.

Bust; four bas-reliefs; marble. *Near Skanderberg, in Jutland.* Height of the whole, 21 ft. 3.90 in.

The monument consists of a colossal bust of the king placed upon an enormous block of granite upon each of whose four sides a bas-relief is let in. These bas-reliefs represent: *The Emancipation of the Peasantry.* A Genius, wearing a tunic unfastened at the shoulder, is breaking the chains and the yoke. *The Institution of the Provincial Estates.* A Genius, a nude figure, with a mantle thrown over the left shoulder, is unrolling the parchment upon which is inscribed the royal decree. *The Administration of Justice.* A Genius with the left hand resting upon a sword holds a balance in the right: in one of the scales lies the royal crown, in the other a sickle. The owl is at his feet. The Genius is clothed in a tunic open on the right side. *The Protection of the Sciences and Arts.* A Genius entirely nude holds a crown in his hand and a lyre upon his arm. On the ground is a cist containing rolls of parchment.

The bust was modelled at Rome, in 1819; the bas-reliefs, at Copenhagen, in 1842 and '43. There are in the Museum plaster models of the bust and of the bas-reliefs measuring 2 ft. 0.40 in. by 1 ft. 4.53 in., but the marbles of the monument are much larger The *Emancipation of the Peasants*, the *Administration of Justice*, and the *Protection of the Arts* were also treated at the same time by the artist in still other models which were never executed. The dimensions are nearly the same. These plasters are also in the Museum, as well as a sketch for a statue of Frederick VI (height, 1 ft. 6.50 in.), modelled at Copenhagen in 1840, which was to have been executed of colossal dimensions for the Skanderberg monument. The monarch is represented seated upon the throne of Denmark, his right hand extended and his left holding a roll of paper. He wears his coronation robes.

Equestrian Statue of the Elector Maximilian I of Bavaria.

Bronze. *Wittelsbachplatz, Munich.* Colossal. Height, 18 ft. 0.53 in.; and with the marble pedestal, 35 ft. 5.19 in.

The elector wears the armor of the period of the Thirty Years' War. His head is uncovered. His right hand is extended in the act of giving an order; with the left he checks his horse.

Rome, 1833-36. (See p. 128.) There are in the Museum a plaster model of the statue (height, 2 ft. 7.49 in.), and two separate models of the horse (height, 13 ft. 3.44 in., and 6 ft. 7.52 in.).

MONUMENT TO LORD BYRON.

Marble. *Library of Trinity College, Cambridge.* Height of statue, 5 ft. 9.29 in. Bas-relief: height, 2 ft. 8.28 in.; width, 1 ft. 11.62 in.

The poet, in modern costume, is seated upon fragments of Greek columns. The head is uncovered; in his left hand is his poem of "Childe Harold"; and his right, holding a pen, is raised toward his chin. On the broken column are sculptured on one side ΑΘΗΝΗ, with the owl; on the other, the griffin and the lyre of Apollo. A death's head lies beside the column. The bas-relief represents the Genius of Poetry tuning his lyre, with one foot resting upon the bow of a boat.

Rome, 1831. (See p. 125.) The Museum has a small sketch of the statue, from which it differs slightly (height, 1 ft. 8.86 in.), and two plaster models (height, 5 ft. 8.89 in.). Also a plaster of the bas-relief, together with a repetition in marble.

MONUMENT TO SCHILLER.

Bronze. *Stuttgart.* Colossal.

The poet stands draped in an ample cloak, his head encircled with laurel, his right hand holding a pen, the left a book. Upon the pedestal are three bas-reliefs. *Apotheosis of Schiller.* The eagle of Jupiter, holding a scroll in his talons, supports a globe surmounted by a star, and having inscribed upon it the name of the poet. The Scorpion and the Bull, the signs of the zodiac which presided over the birth and the death of Schiller, also figure in the composition. On either side hover the Muses of Tragedy and History. *The Genius of Poetry* is represented flying, holding the plectrum in his right hand, and the lyre upon his left arm. Above his head is a star. *Victory.* This figure is soaring upward holding a palm-branch and a wreath. Her tunic, unfastened, leaves the right breast uncovered. Upon the fourth side of the pedestal is a lyre, supported by the griffins of Apollo, and the date 1839.

Rome, 1835; erected 1839. (See p. 129.) The Thorvaldsen Museum has a colossal plaster of the statue and a small sketch (height, 2 ft. 9.46 in.), in which the poet holds a scroll instead of a book. The plasters of the three bas-reliefs are also in the Museum (height, 2 ft. 0.80 in.; length, 4 ft. 3.18 in.; height, 2 ft. 11.03 in.; width, same; height, 2 ft. 10.25 in.; width, 2 ft. 9.46 in.).

MONUMENT TO GUTENBERG.

Bronze. *At Mayence.* Height of statue, 11 ft. 8.55 in. Bas-reliefs: height, 3 ft. 0.22 in.; length, 4 ft. 11.05 in. and 3 ft. 11.24 in.

The inventor of printing is represented standing, and in the costume of the Middle Ages; he holds in his right hand several movable types, and supported by his left arm the first printed Bible. In one of the bas-reliefs, Gutenberg is seated before a case and showing the types to his collaborator, Faust; the latter is leaning upon one of the engraved blocks in use before the invention of movable types. The other bas-relief represents Gutenberg examining a printed sheet, taken from the new press, upon which a printer is at work.

Modelled at Rome, from 1833 to 1835, by Herr Bissen from Thorvaldsen's sketches; erected at Mayence in 1837. (See p. 129.) The Museum has the plaster models, the sketch of the statue (height, 1 ft. 10.04 in.), and that of one of the bas-reliefs, *The Invention of the Printing Press* (height, 1 ft. 3.74 in.; width, 1 ft. 7.68 in.). There is also a plaster cast of the statue in the Library at Mayence.

MONUMENT TO COPERNICUS.

Statue; bronze. *Square of the University, Warsaw.* Height, 9 ft. 3.41 in.

The astronomer sits watching the heavens, at the same time measuring with a compass upon an armillary sphere which he holds in his left hand.

Rome, 1823. (See p. 79.) Plaster model in the Museum.

MONUMENT TO APPIANI.

Medallion and bas-relief; marble. *Academy of Fine Arts, Milan.* Diameter of medallion, 1 ft. 6.89 in. Bas-relief: height, 4 ft. 1.60 in.; width, 3 ft. 4.15 in.

In the medallion is sculptured the head of Appiani: the bas-relief represents Love singing the fame of the painter and the Three Graces sadly listening.

Rome, 1821. (See pp. 90 and 103.) The Museum has the plaster models, besides a repetition of the marble bas-relief.

MONUMENT TO LORD MAITLAND.

Bust and bas-relief; bronze. *Island of Zante.* Bust, colossal. Height of bas-relief, 2 ft. 7.10 in.; width, 2 ft. 1.98 in.

This monument was erected in memory of Lord Maitland's administration as commissioner of the Ionian Islands. The bas-relief, set into the pedestal, represents Minerva unveiling Vice, a woman richly clothed, and throwing her protecting arm around Virtue, who is distinguished by the simplicity of her attire.

Rome, 1818. Plaster models in the Museum.

MONUMENT TO HANS MADSEN.

Bas-relief; bronze. *Church of Svanninge, Denmark.* Height, 4 ft. 7.11 in.; width, 3 ft. 3.37 in.

This bas-relief commemorates an incident of the war of 1435. Hans Madsen, taken prisoner by the forces of Lubeck, escapes to the Danish army. He is represented bare-footed, holding a hop-pole by the aid of which he crossed the river, and is explaining to the Danish general the plans of the enemy. The general, wearing the iron armor of the fifteenth century, is accompanied by his secretary and his squire.

Nysöe, 1841. Ordered by the Count von Bille-Brahe. Hans Madsen had been curate of Svanninge. Plaster model in Museum, inscribed: NYSÖE, 5 MARCH, 1841.

MONUMENT TO PRINCE VON SCHWARZENBERG.

Sketch. *Thorvaldsen Museum.* Height, 3 ft. 3.37 in.

The general stands, holding in his hand the baton of command. Upon one of the sides of the pedestal Nemesis records the warrior's exploits; on the other, Victory offers him a palm-branch; while upon the front is represented the prince's entry into Leipzig in 1813. Under this last bas-relief is a lion couchant.

Rome, 1821. Ordered by Prince Metternich, but never executed; the lion alone has been cut in marble. (See DIVERS SUBJECTS.)

MONUMENT TO GOETHE.

Sketch. *Thorvaldsen Museum.* Height, 2 ft. 3.55 in.

The poet stands reading in a book which he holds in the left hand; the right, hanging by his side, holds a pen. At his feet a lyre rests against a cist.

Copenhagen, 1839. Ordered by a committee from Frankfort, but never executed. Thorvaldsen made at the same time another sketch (height, 1 ft. 6.50 in.), also in the Museum. It represents the poet seated and with his head raised.

CUPID AND BACCHUS.

MYTHOLOGICAL AND HEROIC SUBJECTS.

I.

GROUPS AND STATUES.

Mercury Argiphontes.

Statue; marble. *Thorvaldsen Museum.* Height, 5 ft. 8.11 in.

Mercury, having just put Argus to sleep by playing upon the syrinx, gently removes the instrument from his lips, and with his right hand draws his sword; fearing to wake his adversary, he holds the scabbard with his heel. The god is seated, but on the point of rising.

Rome, 1818. (See pp. 60 and 196.) This statue has been several times cut in marble: among others, for Mr. Alexander Baring, afterwards Lord Ashburton, in 1822; and for Count Potocki, in 1829. Another copy was cut in 1824, in which a defect in the marble made it necessary to suppress the petasus (winged cap), and which after the artist's death was purchased by the Spanish Government. The plaster model is in the Thorvaldsen Museum, and another in the Louvre. This statue is also in the Marble Palace at Potsdam.

Mars and Cupid.

Colossal group; marble. *Thorvaldsen Museum.* Height, 7 ft. 11.27 in.

Mars has laid aside his sword and helmet. He leans with his left hand upon his inverted lance; in the right he holds one of Cupid's arrows. The son of Venus has taken up the sword of the god of war, and smiles as he looks at ft.

Rome, 1810. Subject taken from the forty-fifth ode of Anacreon. (See p. 197.) The plaster model is in the Museum. The artist had previously, in 1808, composed a statue, *Mars Pacificator*, ordered by the Prince of Bavaria. (See p. 45.) The god was standing, holding in his right hand an olive-branch, and in his left his inverted lance. His sword and helmet rested against the trunk of a palm-tree, beside which were the doves of Venus. Some German journals would have us believe that this work was cut in marble for Russia and for England, but Thorvaldsen assured Herr Thiele that it was not so. Even the clay model has disappeared.

APOLLO. (See cut, p. 229.)

Statue; marble. *Purchased by Herr von Ropp, at Mitau.* Height, 4 ft. 9.08 in.

Apollo is standing, crowned with laurel, holding the plectrum in his right hand, the lyre upon his left arm. Beside him is the Delphic tripod.

Rome, 1805. Ordered by the Countess Woronzoff, who, however, obtained only a repetition. In the latter a tree-trunk took the place of the tripod. It is the model of this second statue which is in the Museum. (See p. 200.)

BACCHUS. (See cut, p. 85.)

Statue; marble. *Purchased by the Countess Woronzoff.* Height, 4 ft. 7.51 in.

The god standing, languid with the fumes of wine, holds a thyrsus in the left hand, and a goblet in the right.

Rome, 1805. Ordered by the Countess Woronzoff. (See pp. 33 and 198.) Repeated in marble for the Prince Malte Putbus, in the Island of Rügen. This statue is also in the Marble Palace at Potsdam.

ADONIS. (See cut, p. 193.)

Statue; Carrara marble. *Glyptothek, Munich.* Height, 6 ft. 2.01 in.

The young shepherd is returning from the chase; he has thrown his cloak upon the trunk of a tree, against which he leans, and upon which he has suspended a hare.

Rome, 1808. Ordered by the Prince of Bavaria. The plaster model in the Museum is not precisely like the marble, which was much retouched by the artist. (See pp. 45 and 200.)

JASON. (See cut, p. 23.)

Colossal statue; marble. *Purchased by Mr. Thomas Hope, in England.* Height, 7 ft. 11.66 in.

The hero is coming forward, armed with a lance and carrying upon his left arm the golden fleece, of which he has just gained possession after slaying the dragon which guarded it. He turns his head and seems to cast a parting glance of disdain upon his vanquished foe.

Rome, 1802. The Museum has a copy in marble, and the plaster model upon which may be distinguished the marks made by the artist for the guidance of the workman in cutting the marble, indicating changes to be made. Greater fulness was given to some of the muscles of the thighs and legs. (See pp. 29, 35, and 195.)

Pollux.

Copy, — statue; plaster. *Thorvaldsen Museum.* Height, 4 ft. 7.11 in.

Reduction of an antique colossal statue, one of the Dioscuri of Monte Cavallo.

Rome, 1797. (See pp. 25 and 194.)

Vulcan.

Colossal statue; marble. *Thorvaldsen Museum.* Height, 7 ft 10.48 in.

The god stands holding in his right hand his hammer, which he rests upon the anvil; in his left hand are his tongs. The sword and helmet of Mars and the arrows and quiver of Cupid, forged by Vulcan, lie at his feet.

Rome, 1838. (See p. 197.) The plaster model is in the Museum, and also a sketch (height, 1 ft. 11.62 in.).

Hercules.

Colossal statue; bronze. *Façade of the Palace of Christiansborg, Copenhagen.* Height, 12 ft. 10.33 in.

Hercules stands holding in his right hand his club, the end of which rests upon the ground. The lion's skin is thrown over his left shoulder.

Copenhagen, 1843. (See p. 197.) Cast in bronze by Dalhoff. The Museum has the plaster model, a sketch in plaster made in 1839 (height, 2 ft. 3.16 in.), and a first design (height, 1 ft. 11.62 in.), very different from the finished work. This last represents the god with his head covered by the lion's skin, holding in one hand the apples from the garden of the Hesperides, in the other his club, which rests upon his shoulder. In this figure Hercules wears a thick beard.

Æsculapius.

Colossal statue; bronze. *Façade of the Palace of Christiansborg.* Height, 12 ft. 9.93 in.

Æsculapius holds in his left hand the staff entwined with a serpent, and in the other medicinal herbs.

Two sketches, modelled in 1839, are in the Museum (height, 2 ft. 2.77 in. and 1 ft. 11.72 in.). The execution of the colossal statue was superintended, after the artist's death, by Herr Bissen.

Nemesis.

Colossal statue; bronze. *Façade of the Palace of Christiansborg.* Height, 12 ft. 9.54 in.

Nemesis stands holding the end of her mantle in her left hand, and the helm in her right. Her attributes, the reins and the wheel, are by her side.

Enlarged to colossal dimensions, after the artist's death, by Herr Bissen. Thorvaldsen had only modelled, in 1839, two sketches (height, 2 ft. 1.98 in. and 1 ft. 11.62 in.), which are in the Museum.

Minerva.

Colossal statue; bronze. *Façade of the Palace of Christiansborg.* Height, 12 ft. 10.33 in.

The goddess stands with her right hand resting upon her spear and holding in her left an olive-branch. The owl is at her feet.

Two sketches, modelled in 1839, are in the Museum (height, 2 ft. 3.95 in. and 2 ft. 0.40 in.). After Thorvaldsen's death, Herr Bissen had charge of the completion of the colossal statue.

Cupid and Psyche. (See cut, p. 41.)

Group; marble. *Purchased by the Countess Woronzoff.* Height, 4 ft. 5.13 in.

Cupid passes his left arm around the young girl, who holds the cup of immortality. He gently urges her to drink. Psyche hesitates.

Modelled at Montenero in 1804, and finished in 1805. A second copy in marble was bought by Prince Malte Putbus, of Rügen. A third marble and the plaster model are in the Museum. (See pp. 33 and 200.)

Love.

Statue; marble. *In Courland.* Height, 4 ft. 5.93 in.

Love crowned with roses leans against the trunk of a tree. He holds in his right hand a butterfly, symbolizing the soul, and in his left an arrow, with which he is about to torment the insect. The lion's skin of Hercules lies near the tree-trunk. Love, victorious over strength and the soul, has laid aside his bow and quiver.

Rome, 1811. The model of this statue, with which the artist was doubtless dissatisfied, has disappeared.

Love Victorious. (See cut, p. 63.)

Statue; marble. *Gallery of Prince Esterhazy, Vienna.* Height, 4 ft. 9.87 in.

The god is examining the point of an arrow, holding it in his right hand; his left hand holds the bow. He leans against a tree-trunk, over which is thrown the lion's skin of Hercules; and around him are other trophies of his victories over the gods, — the thunderbolt of Jupiter, the helmet of Mars, and the lyre of Apollo.

Rome, 1814. A plaster cast from the marble is in the Museum. (See p. 199.)

Love Victorious.

Statue; marble (variation of the preceding figure). *Thorvaldsen Museum.* Height, 4 ft. 9.08 in.

The head of Love is bent down, and the hand holding the arrow brought up against the breast. Among the attributes of vanquished gods, there are, in addition, those of Neptune and Pluto and the broken thyrsus of Bacchus; while in the very helmet of Mars the doves of Venus have built their nest out of bits of the plume.

Rome, 1823. Plaster model in the Museum. (See p. 199.)

Bacchus and Ariadne.

Group; plaster. *Thorvaldsen Museum.* Height, 1 ft. 5.71 in.

Bacchus and Ariadne are seated. The god holds a wine-cup in his left hand, while his right arm encircles the daughter of Minos. Ariadne bends forward to pour the wine into the cup, while her left arm is thrown over the shoulder of Bacchus.

Rome, 1798. (See p. 26.)

Achilles and Penthesilea.

Group; sketch. *Cabinet of Herr Thiele, Copenhagen.* Height, 1 ft. 9.65 in.

Achilles supports in his arms the wounded queen of the Amazons.

Rome, 1798.

Psyche. (See cut, p. 183.)

Stutue; marble. *Thorvaldsen Museum.* Height, 4 ft. 5.14 in.

A young girl with the upper part of the body uncovered, the drapery falling around the hips, and concealing the legs. Psyche is returning from the infernal regions, bearing the box which contains the perfume of beauty. She pauses with her hand on the cover, hesitating between fear and curiosity.

Rome, 1811. Plaster model in the Museum. A copy, half size, was made for the brother of Mr. Hope. (See p. 203.)

The Infant Cupid.

Statue; marble. *Thorvaldsen Museum.* Height, 3 ft 4.15 in.

The god is standing, his head raised, his left hand resting upon his bow.

Rome, 1814. The plaster model is also in the Museum.

Ganymede.

Statue; marble. *Purchased by the Countess Woronzoff.* Height, 4 ft. 5.54 in.

The youth wears the Phrygian cap, but is otherwise nude, except that his chlamys hangs from his left arm, which he extends in presenting the filled goblet. The right hand hangs down, holding the vase.

Rome, 1805, to the order of the Countess Woronzoff. The plaster model and a repetition in marble are in the Museum. (See p. 199.)

Ganymede.

Statue; marble. *Purchased by Herr von Krause, Austrian Consul at St. Petersburg.* Height, 4 ft. 4.36 in.

The attitude differs from that of the preceding. Ganymede is pouring the nectar into the bowl.

Rome, 1816. The Museum has a repetition in marble, and a plaster cast taken from the model. (See p. 199.)

Ganymede and the Eagle. (See cut, p. 103.)

Group; marble. *Purchased by the Duke of Sutherland, in England.* Height, 2 ft. 10.25 in.; length, 3 ft. 6.91 in.

Ganymede, kneeling upon one knee, offers drink to Jupiter metamorphosed into an eagle; he holds the amphora in his left hand, and with the left presents the bowl.

Rome, 1817. The Museum has the plaster model and a repetition in marble. There was in the artist's atelier, in 1824, another repetition, reduced, in marble (height, 1 ft. 0.59 in.). Herr Thiele did not know what had become of it. We think we have found it in Paris, in the possession of M. Hottinguer. (See p. 199.)

Two Caryatides.

Marble. *On each side of the throne in the Palace of Christiansborg, at Copenhagen.* Height, 6 ft. 11.85 in.

These two figures recall the caryatides of the Erectheum. One, holding her hand against her breast, is clothed in a Doric tunic, over which is a goat's skin: she personifies the people. The other wears, over an Ionic tunic, a peplum fastened at the shoulders by means of straps, and holds in her right hand a tress of her own hair: she represents the upper class of society.

Rome, 1813. Ordered by a committee of Poles, in accordance with a vote of the Polish Chambers, June 26, 1812; afterward purchased by the Danish Government. (See p. 51.) The plaster models are in the Museum.

HOPE. (See cut, p. 3.)

Statue; marble. *Thorvaldsen Museum.* Height, 5 ft. 4.17 in.

This figure, an imitation of Æginetic art, is made to conform to the semi-hieratic type adopted at that epoch to represent Hope. The goddess is moving slowly forward, with perfectly placid countenance, holding in her left hand the skirt of her long tunic, which reaches to the ground, and in her right a flower stripped of its corolla, and whose seeds are ready to fall. A broad diadem encircles her head, and her hair is arranged in heavy curls.

Rome, 1817 and 1818. (See p. 204.) The plaster model is in the Museum. Two reproductions in marble, slightly reduced, were purchased by Count William von Humboldt. One was placed in his *château* near Tegel, the other on the tomb of the Baroness, in the garden of the *château*. There is a plaster cast in the Museum at Berlin, and a copy in the palace of Sans Souci.

HEBE.

Statue; plaster. *Thorvaldsen Museum.* Height, 5 ft. 2.59 in.

The young girl is in the act of offering with her left hand a bowl filled from the amphora which she holds in her right. Her double Doric tunic is unfastened at the right shoulder, leaving the right breast exposed.

Rome, 1806. (See pp. 42 and 204.)

HEBE. (See cut, p. 207.)

Statue; marble. *Purchased by Mr. Alexander Baring, in England.* Height, 5 ft. 0.23 in.

This figure, a variation from the preceding, better expresses the mingled grace and modesty proper to the young goddess. The tunic is fastened at the shoulders, and covers the whole bosom. The attitude is the same.

Rome, 1816. (See pp. 56 and 204.) The Museum has a repetition in marble and the plaster model retouched by the artist. It was also copied in bronze, gilt (height, 1 ft. 0.59 in.), for Prince Christian Frederick, afterward King of Denmark.

The Three Graces. (See cut, p. 139.)

Group; marble. *At the country-seat of Herr Donner, near Altona.* Height, 5 ft. 8.89 in.

The figure in the middle stands facing to the front, the two others are seen in profile. The first places her arms around her two sisters, who in their turn lean upon and embrace her. The one on the spectator's right carries her hand with an affectionate gesture to the face of the first. Cupid, seated on the ground, is playing upon the lyre. Behind the group is a vase, over which are thrown the garments of the three sisters.

Rome, 1817–19. The marble is unfortunately veined. (See pp. 60 and 202.) The plaster model is in the Museum, together with a sketch (height, 1 ft. 11.22 in.) in which the attitudes are slightly different. The Cupid is omitted in this sketch, and in his place is a basket of flowers.

The Three Graces.

Group; marble. *Thorvaldsen Museum.* Height, 5 ft. 8.50 in.

This composition is a variation of the preceding. The attitudes are different, especially in the two figures on the right and left. One holds up an arrow which the other touches with her finger. The latter turns more to the front. The three heads are also differently inclined, and the positions of the legs are not the same as in the first model.

Rome, 1842. The plaster model is also in the Museum. (See pp. 60 and 202.)

Cupid.

Statue; marble. *Thorvaldsen Museum.* Height, 1 ft. 11.22 in.

A separate repetition of the Cupid in the preceding groups.

Rome, 1819. This statue has been many times cut in marble. The Museum has a plaster cast taken from the original model. (See p. 61.)

Venus Victrix.

Statue; marble. *Purchased by the Countess Woronzoff.* Height, 2 ft. 7.49 in.

Venus, nude, holding in her right hand the apple, the prize of beauty.

Rome, 1805. Also cut in marble for Herr von Ropp, at Mietau, Courland, in whose possession this copy still was in 1821. The plaster model has disappeared.

Venus Victrix.

Statue; marble. *Purchased by Lord Lucan, in England.* Height, 4 ft. 5.77 in.

The goddess, unclothed, takes up her garments with her left hand, and in her right holds the apple, at which she is looking.

Rome, 1813 to 1816. Marble copies were purchased by the Duchess of Devonshire (at Chatsworth), and Mr. P. C. Labouchère (at his villa near Windsor). (See pp. 56 and 201.) Another in marble is in the Pitti Palace, Florence. An excellent marble copy and the plaster model are in the Thorvaldsen Museum. Another plaster is in the Louvre. The statue may also be seen in the Museum at Berlin.

TERPSICHORE AND EUTERPE.

Statues; stucco. *Interior of the Palace of Amalienborg.* Height, 6 ft. 2.80 in.

Terpsichore is playing upon the tambourine; Euterpe holds a flute in each hand.

Copenhagen, 1794.

TWO MUSES.

Statues; stucco. *Great staircase of the Palace of Amalienborg (in niches).* Height, 6 ft. 0.44 in.

These two figures have so little that is characteristic that it is difficult to say which of the Muses they represent. The attitudes and draperies are wanting in style.

Copenhagen, 1794.

PEACE.

Group; plaster.

The goddess, represented as winged, stands upon a globe, holding a caduceus in her right hand, and embracing with her left arm the Genius of Plenty and Riches. She tramples under her feet the weapons of War.

1798 to 1800. This group, described by Herr Thiele, has doubtless been destroyed.

MELPOMENE.

Statue; sketch. *In possession of Madame Frederika Brun.* Height, 2 ft. 5.92 in.

The Muse, clothed in tunic and mantle, holds a mace in her right hand. The tragic mask lies at her feet.

Rome, 1800.

VENUS CROWNING THE VICTORIOUS MARS.

Group. *Disappeared.*

Rome, 1798.

VENUS AND CUPID.

Sketch. *Thorvaldsen Museum.* Height, 1 ft. 10.04 in.

The goddess is seated, and seems to be gently reproving her son who stands leaning against her. The left forearm of Cupid is missing: it probably held an arrow. In the right hand is a bow.

A MUSE TRIUMPHANT.

Group; sketch. *Thorvaldsen Museum.* Height, 2 ft. 2.37 in.

The Muse, crowned with laurel, is standing in a chariot. Her left hand rests upon a sceptre, her right holds a scroll. Seated on the edge of the car, Cupid holds the reins and guides the horses.

Rome, about 1827.

A MUSE TRIUMPHANT.

Group; sketch. *Thorvaldsen Museum.* Height, 2 ft. 4.34 in.

A variation of the preceding. The left hand of the Muse holds the scroll, the right is raised. Cupid, guiding the horses, stands upon the pole of the chariot.

Rome, about 1827.

VICTORY.

Statue; sketch. *Thorvaldsen Museum.* Height, 1 ft. 8.47 in.

The goddess is standing in a chariot, and firmly holding the reins of her horses.

This sketch served as a model for the colossal *Victory* which now surmounts the façade of the Thorvaldsen Museum. The statue was modelled and cast in bronze after the artist's death.

A SIBYL.

Statue; sketch. *Thorvaldsen Museum.* Height, 1 ft. 7.29 in.

The Erythræan Sibyl (the letters *ryth* are traced on the pedestal) leans upon a tripod, and holds in her left hand a scroll half opened. In her other hand is a stylus. Her drapery is ample, and her head is covered.

It had been the intention to place two figures of Sibyls, this and the one following, together with two Old Testament prophets, in the niches of the portico of the *Frue Kirke*, in Copenhagen, as showing that the coming of Christ was predicted by pagans as well as by Jews. (Müller.) The project was abandoned.

A SIBYL.

Statue; sketch. *Thorvaldsen Museum.* Height, 1 ft. 7.68 in.

The figure is standing: judging by the position of the upper part of the arms, the forearms, which are missing, were to have been raised. The head is covered, and an ample cloak envelops the shoulders. On the remains of the pedestal are found the letters *ma*, from which it is supposed that the artist intended to represent the Sibyl of Cumæ.

II.

BAS-RELIEFS.

§ 1. — *Mythological Subjects.*

VULCAN FORGING ARROWS FOR CUPID. (See cut, p. 84.)

Bas-relief; marble. *Purchased by Mr. Baillie for Mr. P. C. Labouchère; now in the possession of Mr. Henry Labouchère (Lord Taunton), Quantock Castle, near Bridgewater, England.* Height, 2 ft. 5.92 in.; length, 4 ft. 3.57 in.

Vulcan is forging the arrows. Venus is sitting in front of him, dipping their points into honey with which her son has mingled gall. Cupid has got possession of the spear of Mars. The god of war has taken up one of the arrows, and examines it with disdain.

Rome, 1814–15. Subject taken from the forty-fifth ode of Anacreon. (See p. 213.) The Thorvaldsen Museum has two plasters; the model and a repetition, varied, in which Mars holds with his left hand the drapery thrown over his right shoulder.

DANCE OF THE MUSES ON MOUNT HELICON.

Bas-relief; marble. *Purchased by the Baron von Schubart, for his villa at Montenero, near Leghorn.* Height, 2 ft. 5.13 in.; length, 5 ft. 4.17 in.

On the left is Apollo, seated upon a rock and playing upon the harp. The Nine Muses dance around the Three Graces, each Muse maintaining her distinctive character. In the background is a swan.

First modelled in 1804 at Montenero (see p. 34); cut in marble in 1807. In 1816, Thorvaldsen took up the subject again, and made several modifications: the heads of Apollo and Thalia are different, and the swan is swimming in the foreground. The Museum has a marble copy, and the plaster model of this variation.

THE PROCESSION TO PARNASSUS.

Bas-relief; plaster. *Thorvaldsen Museum.* Height, 2 ft. 1.98 in.; length, 16 ft. 4.85 in.

Apollo is in a chariot drawn by Pegasus, and driven by a Genius bearing a torch. The Graces advance dancing, guided by Love by means of wreaths of roses. Another Cupid hovers above the three sisters, strewing flowers in their path. Next come the Muses: first Clio, Euterpe, Thalia, and Melpomene; then Terpsichore and Erato, dancing to the music of a lyre played by a Cupid; then Polymnia with pensive step, Urania turning round to watch the stars, and Calliope writing. Mnemosyne brings up the rear of the Muses, accompanied by Harpocrates; behind them the Genius of Poetry, bearing a wreath of laurel and a palm-branch, guides the steps of Homer. The blind poet is singing, and accompanying himself upon the harp.

Rome, 1832. It was Thorvaldsen's intention to represent the procession of all the poets in an extended frieze, of which this was only the first section. (Müller.)

NIGHT. (See cut, p. 40.)

Bas-relief; marble. *Purchased by Lord Lucan.* Diameter of medallion, 2 ft. 7.10 in.

The goddess, her head bound round with poppies, wings her way through space bearing in her arms her two children, Death and Sleep. The owl accompanies her.

Rome, 1815. Often repeated in marble. The Museum has a copy in marble and the plaster model. (See p. 54.)

MORNING. (See cut, p. 22.)

Bas-relief; marble. *Purchased by Lord Lucan.* Diameter of medallion, 2 ft. 7.10 in.

The young Aurora flies through the air scattering flowers from both hands. A Genius rests upon her shoulder, holding an uplifted torch.

Copenhagen, 1815. Often repeated as a companion to the *Night.* The Museum has a copy as well as the plaster model. There are also many half-size repetitions in marble of *Night* and *Morning*. (See p. 54.)

THE AGES OF LOVE.

Bas-relief; marble. *Purchased by Mr. P. C. Labouchère, now in possession of his son.* Height, 1 ft. 8.07 in.; length, 4 ft. 11.05 in.

Psyche, seated beside a cage containing little Loves, deals them out to all who apply. A child innocently approaches to play with them, a little girl is half afraid to caress them; another, older, kneels in adoration before the Love Psyche is giving her; behind her, a young woman is passionately kissing the one she has received. Another woman, bearing in her bosom the fruit of love, holds by the wings the little god, who seems to be fast asleep. Love alights triumphant on the shoulders of a man who seems unable to bear so heavy a burden; and farther on he flies away laughing from an old man, who stretches toward him his trembling hands.

Rome, 1824. The plaster model and a repetition in marble are in the Museum. Herr Donner has at his villa, near Altona, a marble vase upon which the artist has sculptured this composition. (See pp. 100 and 216.)

THE SHEPHERDESS WITH A NEST OF LOVES. (See cut, p. 62.)

Bas-relief; marble. *Thorvaldsen Museum.* Height, 2 ft. 0.01 in.; width, 1 ft. 11.22 in.

In this graceful composition the different kinds of love are represented. The shepherdess is seated, holding the nest in her lap: one of the Loves is not yet awake; faithful Love caresses the dog; hopeful Love reclines his head upon the arm of the shepherdess; two others are passionately kissing each other; fickle Love is flying away, and the young girl in vain stretches her arm toward him.

Rome, 1831. Suggested by a painting found at Pompeii, representing, probably, Leda with Castor, Pollux, and Helen. (See p. 216.) The plaster model is also in the Museum. A copy in marble was purchased by the king of Würtemberg.

CUPID AND ANACREON.

Bas-relief; marble. *Purchased by the Count von Schönborn.* Height, 1 ft. 8.07 in.; length, 2 ft. 3.95 in.

Anacreon seated upon his couch is wiping the moisture from the little god, who stands before him, while Cupid thrusts an arrow into the poet's heart.

Rome, 1823. The subject is taken from the third ode of Anacreon. (See p. 214.) A copy in marble was purchased by Mr. Thomas Hope. The Museum has the plaster model, and a repetition in marble of Paros.

CUPID AND ANACREON. (See cut, p. 138.)

Bas-relief; marble. *Thorvaldsen Museum.* Height, 1 ft. 9.25 in.; length, 3 ft. 0.22 in.

A repetition, varied, of the above. The left leg of the poet is stretched out upon his couch.

Placed in a sort of arched recess as a companion to the *Cupid and Bacchus.*

CUPID AND BACCHUS.

Bas-relief; marble. *Purchased by Herr Knudzon, of Trondhjem.* Height, 1 ft. 8.86 in.; length, 2 ft. 3.95 in.

Bacchus reclining upon a goat's skin offers a cup to Cupid, who drinks. On the left lie Cupid's arrows; on the right, a panther is licking the vase which holds the wine.

Rome, 1810. The plaster model is in the Museum.

CUPID AND BACCHUS. (See cut, p. 267.)

Bas-relief; marble. *Thorvaldsen Museum.* Height, 1 ft. 9.65 in.; length, 2 ft. 11.43 in.

A variation of the preceding composition. The panther is reclining on the right, while on the left the cist of Bacchus stands beside Cupid's bow.

Rome, sometime after the foregoing. The upper part is arched like the second model of *Cupid and Anacreon*. The plaster model is also in the Museum.

Cupid, Bacchus, and Bathyllus.

Bas-relief; marble. *Purchased by Count von Schönborn*. Height, 1 ft. 8.07 in.; length, 2 ft. 2.37 in.

Bacchus and Cupid have climbed upon a wine-vat, and are dancing and pressing the grapes with their feet. Bathyllus is bringing fresh clusters, and pouring them into the vat.

Rome, 1811. The subject is taken from the seventeenth ode of Anacreon. The Museum has a repetition in marble and the plaster model.

Cupid leaving Psyche asleep.

Bas-relief; plaster. *Thorvaldsen Museum*. Height, 1 ft. 8.47 in.; length, 2 ft. 0.40 in.

Whilst Psyche is sleeping, Cupid silently departs.

Nysöe, 1841.

Psyche contemplating Cupid.

Bas-relief; plaster. *Thorvaldsen Museum*. Height, 1 ft. 8.47 in.; length, 2 ft. 1.19 in.

The young girl approaches the couch where Cupid is reposing: she holds the lamp raised above the head of the god and pauses in an attitude of surprise.

Nysöe, 1841.

Cupid reviving the Fainting Psyche. (See cut, p. 116.)

Bas-relief; marble. *Purchased by M. Dalmar*. Height, 1 ft. 10.83 in.; length, 3 ft. 0.22 in.

Psyche, having opened the vase which she brought back from the infernal regions and said to contain the perfume of beauty, has fallen fainting. Cupid hastens to remove the noxious odor, at the same time seizing an arrow with which to touch Psyche and thus bring her back to life.

Rome, 1810. The Museum has a copy in marble, and the plaster model (height, 1 ft. 7.29 in.; length, 2 ft. 7.49 in.).

The Four Elements.

Four bas-reliefs; marble. *Thorvaldsen Museum*. Height of each, 1 ft. 7.29 in.; length, 1 ft. 11.62 in.

1. *Love, ruler of heaven.* Armed with the thunderbolt of Jupiter, he is borne aloft by the eagle.

2. *Love, ruler of earth.* Armed with the club of Hercules, he leads by the mane a lion which licks his feet.

3. *Love, ruler of the seas.* Borne on the back of a dolphin, the god holds in his hand the trident of Neptune.

4. *Love, ruler of the under-world.* He is driving Cerberus with his bow, and has seized the bident of Pluto.

Rome, 1828. Often repeated in marble. The Museum has also the plaster models: two variations of *Love, ruler of heaven* (height, 1 ft. 9.65 in ; length, 2 ft. 1.98 in.), in which the god bestrides the eagle, and a sketch of *Love, ruler of earth*, in which he carries the club and brandishes an arrow (height, 1 ft. 5.32 in.; length, 2 ft. 1.19 in.).

Cupid taming the Lion.

Bas-relief; marble. *Purchased by Prince Malte Putbus, of Rügen.* Height, 1 ft. 4.14 in.; length, 1 ft. 6.50 in.

Cupid mounted on the lion seizes him by the mane and goads him with an arrow.

Rome, 1809. The sketch in plaster is in the Museum.

Cupid taming the Lion.

Bas-relief; marble. *Thorvaldsen Museum.* Height, 1 ft. 11.22 in.: length, 2 ft. 1.98 in.

A variation of the preceding subject. Cupid mounted on the lion is letting fly an arrow.

Rome, 1831. The plaster model is also in the Museum.

Cupid and Hymen spinning the Thread of Life.

Bas-relief; marble. *Thorvaldsen Museum.* Height, 1 ft. 7.29 in.; length, 1 ft. 11.22 in.

Cupid holds the distaff and spins, while Hymen, kneeling, twirls the spindle.

Rome, 1831. Subject taken from Theocritus. The Museum has also the plaster model.

Cupid and Hymen.

Bas-relief; marble. *Thorvaldsen Museum.* Height, 2 ft. 6.31 in.; width, 2 ft. 0.40 in.

Cupid and Hymen are represented flying: the former is shooting an arrow, the latter lighting his torches.

Nysöe, 1840. Composed to serve as a model for the medal struck on the occasion of the marriage of Prince Frederick Charles Christian and Princess Caroline of Mecklenburg-Strelitz.

Cupid and Ganymede.

Bas-relief; marble. *Thorvaldsen Museum.* Height, 1 ft. 4.92 in.; length, 2 ft. 1.19 in.

Cupid and Ganymede are seated facing each other, playing at dice to decide which is the handsomer. Ganymede has made the best throw; but Cupid, pointing to himself, declares that in spite of that he will always come off conqueror.

Rome, 1831. From a passage in Simonides indicated by the poet Ricci.

Cupid making a Net.

Bas-relief; marble. *Thorvaldsen Museum.* Height, 1 ft. 3.74 in.; length, 2 ft. 0.01 in.

The soul, represented under the form of a butterfly, has just been caught in the net.

Rome, 1831. Subject furnished by Ricci. The plaster model is in the Museum.

Cupid and the Dog.

Bas-relief; marble. *Thorvaldsen Museum.* Height, 1 ft. 3.74 in.; length, 2 ft. 0.01 in.

Cupid caressing the faithful dog.

Rome, 1831. Suggested by Ricci. The plaster model is also in the Museum.

Cupid gathering Shells.

Bas-relief; plaster. *Thorvaldsen Museum.* Height, 1 ft. 3.35 in.; length, 1 ft. 8.86 in.

Cupid hovers above the shore.

Rome, 1831. A sketch, suggested by the poet Ricci.

Cupid making Flowers grow.

Bas-relief; plaster. *Thorvaldsen Museum.* Height, 1 ft. 2.96 in.; length, 1 ft. 8.86 in.

Cupid, touching the earth with his arrow, makes flowers spring from a stony soil.

Rome, 1831. A sketch; subject given by Ricci.

Cupid writing the Laws of Jupiter.

Bas-relief; marble. *Thorvaldsen Museum.* Height, 1 ft. 6.50 in.; length, 2 ft. 3.16 in.

The king of gods is seated upon his throne; while the god of love, standing, writes with the point of his arrow.

Rome, 1831. Suggested by Ricci. The plaster model is in the Museum.

Cupid and the Rose.

Bas-relief; marble. *Thorvaldsen Museum.* Height, 1 ft. 1.77 in.; length, 1 ft. 11.22 in.

Cupid presents the rose to Jupiter and Juno, and begs them to make her queen of the flowers.

Rome, 1831. Suggested by Ricci. Plaster model in Museum.

Cupid setting Fire to a Rock.

Bas-relief; plaster. *Thorvaldsen Museum.* Height, 2 ft. 3.95 in.; width, 1 ft. 8.47 in.

The god, armed with a torch, sets fire to the walls of a cavern.

Rome, 1831. Suggested by Ricci.

Cupid with Roses and Thistles.

Bas-relief; plaster. *Thorvaldsen Museum.* Height, 2 ft. 3.16 in.; width, 2 ft. 1.19 in.

Love, seated, offers roses with the right hand, and conceals behind him the thistles which he holds in his left.

Rome, 1837. The Museum has a repetition (varied) in plaster (height, 1 ft. 11.22 in.; width, 1 ft. 5.71 in.), in which Cupid is standing.

Cupid sailing.

Bas-relief; plaster. *Thorvaldsen Museum.* Height, 11.02 in.; length, 1 ft. 6.89 in.

Love holds the sail in one hand; in the other, his bow which serves him as a rudder. The mast of the boat is entwined with a wreath of roses.

Rome, 1831. The Museum has a variation in plaster (height, 1 ft. 5.71 in.; length, 2 ft. 1.19 in.), in which Cupid is standing, resting upon the right knee, and the garland of roses is omitted.

Cupid caressing a Swan.

Bas-relief; marble. *Purchased by Count von Schönborn.* Height, 1 ft. 9.25 in.; length, 2 ft. 1.98 in.

Cupid holds the swan by the neck, while two young boys are gathering fruit which they place in a basket.

Rome, 1811. It has sometimes been repeated under the title *Summer*, to serve as a companion to *Cupid, Bacchus, and Bathyllus*, representing Autumn. To continue the series, *Cupid and Anacreon* might represent Winter; but there is no analogous composition emblematic of Spring. The Museum has a copy in marble and the plaster model.

Cupid upon a Swan.

Bas-relief; plaster. *Thorvaldsen Museum.* Medallion: diameter, 2 ft. 3.28 in.

Jupiter, metamorphosed into a swan in order to seduce Leda, alights in the water bearing Cupid upon his back.

Nysöe, 1840.

Cupid upon a Swan.

Bas-relief; plaster. *Thorvaldsen Museum.* Height, 1 ft. 11.62 in.; length, 2 ft. 3.16 in.

Jupiter, as the swan, swims toward Leda; Cupid, kneeling on his back, lets fly an arrow.

Nysöe, 1840.

Jupiter, Cupid, and Leda.

Bas-relief; plaster. *Thorvaldsen Museum.* Height, 2 ft. 3.16 in.; length, 3 ft. 3.37 in.

Leda, kneeling, caresses the swan; Cupid flies away, taking with him Jupiter's thunderbolt.

Bears the inscription: Nysöe, 3 Feb. 1841.

Cupid stung by a Bee.

Bas-relief; marble. *Purchased by Prince Malte Putbus.* Height, 1 ft. 7.29 in.; length, 1 ft. 9.65 in.

The child Cupid has been stung by a bee while plucking a rose; he complains, weeping, to his mother.

Rome, 1809. Subject taken from the fortieth ode of Anacreon. (See p. 213.) The Museum has a copy in marble and the plaster model of a variation (height, 2 ft. 2.77 in.; length, 2 ft. 0.40 in.), the upper part arched.

Cupid chained by the Graces.

Bas-relief; marble. *Thorvaldsen Museum.* Height, 1 ft. 3.74 in.; length, 2 ft. 4.74 in.

Cupid is bound to two trees by chains of roses. The Graces are reclining near him. One of them has taken one of his arrows, and another is feeling its point, while the third holds the end of the chain.

Rome, 1831. Subject taken from the thirtieth ode of Anacreon. (See p. 215.) The plaster model is in the Museum.

Jupiter, Minerva, and Nemesis.

Bas-relief; terra cotta. *Pediment of the Palace of Christiansborg, Copenhagen.* Colossal.

The sovereign of the gods, sceptre in hand, is seated upon his throne. The two goddesses, surrounded by their attributes, stand on his right and left. At the two extremities of the pediment are Tellus with a goat and Oceanus with dolphins. The signs of the zodiac are represented on the step of the throne.

Rome, 1808. The plaster model (height, 3 ft. 9.66 in.; length, 14 ft. 9.16 in.) is in the Museum. The terra cotta was not executed until after the artist's death by M. G. Borup, and was placed in the pediment in 1847.

Hercules and Hebe (*Strength*).

Bas-relief; marble. *Façade of the Palace of Christiansborg.* Medallion: diameter, 4 ft. 11.05 in.

The goddess of youth, standing, pours nectar into the bowl held by Hercules, who is seated upon a lion's skin, his right hand resting upon his club.

Rome, 1808–1810; placed on the façade of the palace, together with the three following medallions, in 1825. The plaster model is in the Museum. At the country-seat of Count von Schönborn, near Geibach, Bavaria, are marble copies of the four medallions originally ordered by the Duke of Leuchtenberg, who died before they were finished. The Museum has also reduced copies in marble; diameter, 2 ft. 8.67 in.

Hygeia and Æsculapius (*Health*).

Bas-relief; marble. *Façade of Palace of Christiansborg.* Medallion: diameter, 4 ft. 11.05 in.

Æsculapius is seated. Hygeia is feeding a serpent which twines around his staff.

Rome, 1808–1810. The plaster model and a reduced copy in marble are in the Museum.

Minerva and Prometheus (*Wisdom*).

Bas-relief; marble. *Façade, Palace of Christiansborg.* Medallion: diameter, 4 ft. 11.05 in.

Prometheus having formed a man out of clay, Minerva gives him a soul, represented by a butterfly which she places upon his head.

Rome, 1808–1810. (*Vide supra.*)

Nemesis and Jupiter (*Justice*).

Bas-relief; marble. *Façade, Palace of Christiansborg.* Medallion: diameter, 4 ft. 11.05 in.

The goddess, standing, one foot on the wheel of Fortune, reads to the sovereign of the world the actions of men. Jupiter, seated upon his throne, holds his avenging thunderbolt. Beside him is the eagle.

Rome, 1808-1810. (*Vide supra.*)

Hygeia and Cupid.

Bas-relief; marble. *Thorvaldsen Museum.* Height, 2 ft. 8.28 in.; width, 1 ft. 11.22 in.

Cupid offers food in a bowl to the serpent twined around the arm of the goddess, who is standing.

Rome, 1837. The plaster model is in the Museum.

Hygeia and Cupid.

Bas-relief; plaster. *Thorvaldsen Museum.* Height, 2 ft. 0.01 in.; length, 2 ft. 1.19 in.

Variation of the above. Cupid is crowning the goddess of health, who is seated and feeding the serpent.

Executed in honor of the twenty-fifth anniversary of the marriage of King Christian VIII and of Queen Caroline Amelia. Signed: Nysöe, 24 April, 1840.

Minerva.

Bas-relief; plaster. *Thorvaldsen Museum.* Medallion: diameter, 2 ft. 1.59 in.

The goddess is flying, having the owl beside her, and bearing her lance and shield.

Rome, about 1836.

Apollo.

Bas-relief; plaster. *Thorvaldsen Museum.* Medallion: diameter, 2 ft. 1.98 in.

The god is flying, bearing the lyre and plectrum.

Rome, about 1836.

Pegasus.

Bas-relief; plaster. *Thorvaldsen Museum.* Diameter of medallion, 2 ft. 2.77 in.

A genius bearing a torch and garlands is leading the winged steed.

Rome, about 1836.

The Muses.

Nine bas-reliefs; plaster. *Thorvaldsen Museum.* Diameter of medallions, 2 ft. 1.59 in.

The nine sisters hover in the air, each bearing her attributes.

Rome, about 1836.

Mnemosyne and Harpocrates.

Bas-relief; plaster. *Thorvaldsen Museum.* Diameter of medallion, 2 ft. 1.59 in.

The mother of the Muses, in a pensive attitude, raises her hand to her face. Harpocrates places his finger upon his lips.

Rome, about 1836.

The Graces.

Bas-relief; plaster. *Thorvaldsen Museum.* Diameter of medallion, 2 ft. 1.59 in.

The three sisters, hovering in air, tenderly embrace each other.

Rome, about 1836.

The Graces.

Bas-relief; plaster. *Thorvaldsen Museum.* Height, 2 ft. 1.19 in.; width, 1 ft. 10.44 in.

The three sisters are dancing, with arms intertwined.

Thalia and Melpomene.

Bas-relief; plaster. *Thorvaldsen Museum.* Diameter of medallion, 2 ft. 6.31 in.

Melpomene holds the tragic mask and the mace; Thalia, the comic mask and shepherd's crook.

Nysöe, 1843.

Erato and Cupid.

Bas-relief; marble. *Thorvaldsen Museum.* Diameter of medallion, 1 ft. 11.22 in.

Cupid leans on the shoulder of the Muse, who is seated and turns toward him, singing and playing upon the lyre.

Rome, 1830. Originally intended for the pedestal of the statue of Byron. Often repeated in marble.

Mercury bearing the Infant Bacchus to Ino.

Bas-relief; marble. *Purchased by Prince Malte Putbus, of Rügen.* Height, 1 ft. 7.68 in.; length, same.

Bacchus stretches out his arms to his mother's sister, who is to be his nurse.

Rome, 1809. Plaster model in the Museum. Was repeated, of larger size (height, 2 ft. 4.74 in.; length. 2 ft. 5.13 in.), in marble, for Lord Lucan. The plaster model of this repetition is also in the Museum.

Jupiter and Diana.

Bas-relief; plaster. *Thorvaldsen Museum.* Height, 2 ft. 4.74 in.; length, 2 ft. 8.28 in.

The artist has represented the goddess at the moment when she entreats Jupiter to allow her to remain a virgin.

Modelled for the birthday of the Baroness von Stampe. Signed: Nysöe, 20 April, 1840.

The Birth of Aphrodite.

Bas-relief; marble. *Purchased by Prince Malte Putbus, of Rügen.* Height, 1 ft. 4.92 in.; width, 1 ft. 3.35 in.

The daughter of the salt sea is borne to the shore in an open shell, supported by two dolphins.

Rome, 1809. Plaster model in Museum.

Apollo among the Shepherds.

Bas-relief; sketch. *Thorvaldsen Museum.* Height, 1 ft. 0.59 in.; length, 5 ft. 10.86 in.

Apollo is playing upon the harp, surrounded by Thessalian shepherds. Pan appears on the left, half hidden by a rock. On each side are sheep feeding.

Rome, 1837. Executed in marble by Galli for the villa of Signor Torlonia at Castel-Gondolfo.

A Young Bacchante with a Bird.

Bas-relief; sketch. *Thorvaldsen Museum.* Height, 1 ft. 7.29 in.; length, 1 ft. 6.11 in.

The young girl, nude, is seated upon a couch covered with the skin of a panther. The amphora, the thyrsus, and the tambourine are beside her. She raises her hand to play with a bird perched upon her finger.

Rome, 1838.

Hebe and Ganymede.

Bas-relief; plaster. *Thorvaldsen Museum.* Height, 1 ft. 6.89 in.; width, same.

The young girl delivers to the new cup-bearer to the gods the vase and the cup. The eagle is placed between Hebe and Ganymede.

Rome, 1833.

The Rape of Ganymede.

Bas-relief; sketch. *Thorvaldsen Museum.* Height, 9.05 in.; width, 7.08 in.

The young man passes his right arm around the neck of the eagle, and with his left seizes the bird's wing.

Rome, 1833.

The Rape of Ganymede.

Bas-relief; sketch. *Thorvaldsen Museum.* Height, 1 ft. 1.77 in.; length, 1 ft. 6.89 in.

In this variation the eagle soars perpendicularly. Ganymede's position is nearly the same.

Rome, 1833 probably.

VICTORY.

Bas-relief; marble. *Thorvaldsen Museum.* Height, 2 ft. 8.28 in.; width, 2 ft. 1.19 in.

This goddess, seated upon a suit of armor, with one foot resting on a helmet, is inscribing upon a shield the exploits of a warrior.

Rome, about 1830. Originally intended to ornament the pedestal of the statue of Prince Potocki, but replaced, at the request of the family, by the bas-relief of *The Angel of Death.* This victory seems to have been cut in marble for the pedestal of the bust of Napoleon I purchased by Mr. Murray. The plaster model is in the Museum.

VICTORY.

Bas-relief; plaster. *Thorvaldsen Museum.* Height, 3 ft. 2.97 in.; width, 2 ft. 3.95 in.

This figure is seated; beside her are a helmet and sword.

Rome, about 1830.

VICTORY.

Bas-relief; plaster. *Thorvaldsen Museum.* Height, 2 ft. 11.43 in.; width, 2 ft. 1.19 in.

The goddess is standing; the right hand, which holds a palm-branch, rests upon the shield; the left hand holds a lance; a wreath hangs from her arm.

Rome, about 1830.

VICTORY.

Bas-relief; plaster. *Thorvaldsen Museum.* Height, 3 ft. 1.79 in.; width, 2 ft. 1.98 in.

A variation of the above. The figure, which faces to the front, stands in a niche.

Rome, about 1830.

THE FATES.

Bas-relief; marble. *Thorvaldsen Museum.* Height, 4 ft. 5 14 in.; length, 6 ft. 1.62 in.

Clotho, on the left, holds the distaff; on the right Lachesis winds the thread upon the spindle. Atropos, in the middle, is armed with the shears and holds the hour-glass; beside her the Genius of Life holds a lighted torch. The owl hovers above the shears.

Rome, 1833. The plaster model, of smaller dimensions, is also in the Museum.

Mercury bearing away Psyche.

Bas-relief; plaster. *Thorvaldsen Museum.* Diameter of medallion, 1 ft. 11.62 in.

The messenger of the gods bears away the young girl toward Olympus.

The Myth of Cupid and Psyche.

Series of sixteen bas-reliefs; marble. *Villa Torlonia.* Oval medallions: height, 11.02 in.; width, 9.05 in.

1. Venus, jealous of the beauty of Psyche, begs her son to inspire her with an ardent passion for the vilest of mankind.
2. Cupid approaches to wound the sleeping Psyche with his arrows, but pauses, struck with the young girl's beauty.
3. The father of Psyche consults the oracle.
4. Zephyr goes to look for Psyche upon the mountain, where she had been exposed, and brings her back in his arms.
5. Cupid extinguishes the lamp, and softly approaches the couch where Psyche is reposing.
6. Cupid leaves the couch and steals softly away, while Psyche is still sleeping.
7. The sisters of Psyche persuade her that her unknown lover can be none other than the monster predicted by the oracle, and that she ought to kill him.
8. Cupid, awakened by a drop of oil falling from the lamp, starts up indignant; Psyche clings, supplicating, to the knees of the god.
9. Pan gives Psyche advice.
10. Venus orders Psyche to bring her water from the Styx.
11. The eagle brings the water of the Styx to Psyche.
12. Psyche presents herself to enter the bark of Charon.
13. Psyche offers a cake of honey to Cerberus.
14. Psyche, having opened the vase given her by Proserpine, falls fainting. Cupid comes to her aid.
15. Mercury bears Psyche to Olympus.
16. Cupid embraces Psyche, who holds the cup of immortality.

All these bas-reliefs, the subjects of which are taken from the Metamorphoses of Apuleius, IV to VI, were modelled at Rome by V. Galli, from Thorvaldsen's designs. The plaster models are in the Museum.

Cupid and Psyche.

Bas-relief; plaster. *Thorvaldsen Museum.* Height, 2 ft. 5.13 in.; width, 2 ft. 1.59 in.

Psyche, as a young girl, is caught in her flight by the boy Cupid, who throws his arm around her neck. Psyche turns around and her lips meet those of Cupid.

Nysöe, 1840.

Cupid and Psyche.

Bas-relief; marble. *At the Chateau of Nysöe.* Height, 8.26 in.; length, 9.44 in.

The children, Cupid and Psyche, embrace each other as they fly.

Thorvaldsen modelled this bas-relief as a parting gift to his friends on leaving them to return to Rome. It has been called the "Farewell to Nysöe." The plaster model in the Museum bears the inscription: Nysöe, 24 May, 1841. The marble was cut in Rome.

Cupid playing on the Lyre.

Bas-relief; plaster. *Thorvaldsen Museum.* Medallion: diameter, 3 ft. 1.79 in.

Cupid is flying: he sings, and accompanies himself on the lyre. Beneath him a swan is swimming.

Nysöe, 1843. Thorvaldsen named this composition "The Swan-song of Cupid." It was, in fact, his last work relating to the story of Cupid.

Hymen.

Bas-relief; plaster. *Thorvaldsen Museum.* Medallion: diameter, 2 ft. 9.46 in.

Hymen is flying, bearing a lighted torch in each hand. Below him are two doves.

Nysöe, 1843.

Figures from Antique Fable.

Twenty-two oval medallions. *Villa Torlonia at Castel-Gondolfo.* Height, 1 ft. 1.38 in.; width, 9.84 in.

1. Latona, flying from the serpent Python, and bearing in her arms Apollo and Diana.
2. Diana with her hind.
3. Diana, bathing, surprised by Actæon.
4. Actæon, changed into a stag, is devoured by his dogs.
5. Diana letting fly an arrow.
6. Orion falls, struck by Diana's arrow.
7. Dædalion, changed into a falcon, flies toward his daughter Chione, slain by Diana with an arrow.
8. Cupid conducts Diana to Endymion.
9. Endymion asleep on Mount Latmos.
10. One of Diana's nymphs polishing the bow of the goddess.
11. Another nymph examines the points of Diana's arrows.
12. A nymph is cleaning the quiver of Diana, while another young girl by her side holds the arrows.

13. A huntress nymph, bearing a torch and a spear, and accompanied by a dog.

14. Another huntress, bearing a hare and birds which she has killed.

15. Callisto, the nymph beloved by Jupiter, leans her head sadly upon her hand.

16. Atalanta, running, and holding in her left hand the golden apple thrown by Hippomenes.

17. Meleager slaying the Calydonian boar.

18. A young hunter places his foot on the lion he has just killed.

19. Adonis holding his hunting-spear; beside him is the anemone, the plant which sprang from his blood; and upon a neighboring hillock are the doves of Venus.

20. Narcissus, looking at himself in the water of a spring, while Cupid watches him with a mocking air.

21. Daphne changed into a laurel-tree. Apollo accompanied by Cupid wreathes around his lyre a garland of leaves gathered from the tree. The river Peneus, father of Daphne, reclines beside the laurel.

22. Pan is playing upon his flute made of reeds, into which the nymph Syrinx has been changed. Cupid makes sounds issue from the reeds themselves. The river Ladon, father of Syrinx, reclines on the right.

All these bas-reliefs, modelled in Rome in 1838, were executed after designs by Thorvaldsen, by V. Galli.

Pan and a Young Satyr. (See cut, p. 262.)

Bas-relief; marble. *Thorvaldsen Museum.* Height, 1 ft. 6.89 in.; length, 2 ft. 7.10 in.

The god is reclining with one arm resting upon a wine-skin. Upon his knees is seated the little satyr, whom he is teaching to play upon the syrinx.

Rome, 1831. The Museum has also the plaster model.

A Bacchante and a Young Satyr.

Bas-relief; marble. *Thorvaldsen Museum.* Height, 1 ft. 6.89 in.; length, 2 ft. 7.10 in.

The bacchante lies stretched upon a panther's skin, her left arm resting upon a basket. The little satyr is climbing upon the legs of the young woman, and biting eagerly at the bunch of grapes which she holds raised in her right hand.

Rome, 1833. Intended as a companion to the above. The plaster model is also in the Museum.

A Satyr and a Huntress Nymph.

Bas-relief; plaster. *Thorvaldsen Museum.* Height, 2 ft. 2.77 in.; width, 1 ft. 11.22 in.

The satyr is endeavoring to embrace the nymph, who resists his attempts.

Nysöe, 1841.

A Satyr and a Bacchante dancing.

Bas-relief; plaster. *Thorvaldsen Museum.* Height, 2 ft. 3.55 in.; width, 2 ft. 1.19 in.

The satyr crowned with fir-cones, the bacchante with ivy, are dancing with arms intertwined: one is playing upon cymbals, the other holds a thyrsus.

Nysöe, 1841.

A Satyr and a Bacchante dancing.

Bas-relief; plaster. *Thorvaldsen Museum.* Height, 2 ft. 5.13 in.; width, 2 ft. 1.98 in.

A companion to the above. In this new composition the satyr and the bacchante embrace each other with their left arms, and join their right hands above their heads.

Nysöe, 1841.

Hylas carried away by the Nymphs.

Bas-relief; marble. *Thorvaldsen Museum.* Height, 1 ft. 3.74 in.; length, 2 ft. 6.31 in.

Hylas kneels beside the river Ascanius to draw water, and is dragged into the waves by a nymph who has thrown her arm around his neck, while two other nymphs approach to lay hold of him.

Rome, 1831. The plaster model is also in the Museum.

Hylas carried away by the Nymphs.

Bas-relief; marble. *Thorvaldsen Museum.* Height, 2 ft. 3.16 in.; length, 3 ft. 7.30 in.

In this composition, a variation of the above, Hylas is standing. Two nymphs push him from behind; while another, seizing him by the leg, drags him into the waves.

Rome, 1833. The plaster model is also in the Museum.

Nessus and Dejanira.

Bas-relief; marble. *Purchased by Count Marulli, of Naples.* Height, 3 ft. 4.55 in.; length, 4 ft. 1.99 in.

The centaur, after having borne her across the river Evenus, attempts to carry off Dejanira: she resists, and calls upon Hercules for aid.

Rome, 1814. The Museum has the plaster model, and a repetition in marble.

Perseus and Andromeda.

Bas-relief; plaster. *Thorvaldsen Museum.* Medallion: diameter, 2 ft. 2.37 in.

Perseus flies through space upon the wings given him by Mercury, leading Pégasus, upon whose back is seated Andromeda, leaning her arm on the shoulder of her liberator. The hero holds in his hand the head of Medusa, while Cupid bears his sword. The vanquished monster lies at the foot of the rock, beside the broken fetters.

Nysöe, 1840. An overcharged composition, different from the usual style of the artist.

Love in Repose.

Bas-relief; plaster. *Thorvaldsen Museum* (underground gallery). Form, oval. Height, 2 ft. 5.13 in.; width, 1 ft. 10.04 in.

Love rests his right hand upon his bow, and holds an arrow in his left.

Copenhagen, 1789. Large silver medal at the Academy of Fine Arts. (See p. 8.)

Hercules and Omphale.

Bas-relief; plaster. *At Copenhagen.* Form, oval. Height, 1 ft. 7.68 in.; length, 2 ft. 1.19 in.

Stretched upon the lion's skin, Hercules with his right hand holds the distaff, and clasps the waist of Omphale. The Lydian queen rests her left hand upon the club, and passing her right arm over the hero's shoulder breaks off the thread from the distaff.

Copenhagen. Signed: B. Thorvaldsen fec. 1792. (See p. 12.)

The Seasons and the Hours.

Decorative work.

Executed in 1794, from the designs of the painter Abildgaard, and placed in the dining-room of the palace of Amalienborg.

§ 2. — *Heroic Subjects.*

Achilles and Thetis.

Bas-relief; marble. *Purchased by Signor Torlonia for the Palazzo Bracciano.* Height, 3 ft. 2.58 in.; length, 4 ft. 6.33 in.

Thetis, kneeling beside the Styx, holds the young Achilles by the foot and plunges him in the river to render him invulnerable; Minerva stretches her protecting lance above the child; while the river god, crowned with reeds, leans against an urn.

Rome, 1837. Plaster model in Museum. In a subsequent repetition the nymph Styx, daughter of Ocean, is substituted in place of the river.

Achilles and the Centaur Chiron.

Bas-relief; plaster. *Thorvaldsen Museum.* Height, 3 ft. 4.55 in.; length, 4 ft. 1.99 in.

The infant Achilles is seated upon the back of the centaur, who is teaching him to throw the javelin.

Rome, 1837.

Achilles and Briseis.

Bas-relief; marble. *Purchased by Herr von Ropp, at Mitau, Courland.* Height, 3 ft. 9.27 in.; length, 7 ft. 9.70 in.

The heralds of Agamemnon lead away Briseis, whom Patroclus has just delivered to them. The young captive departs sadly; while Achilles turns away his head in violent anger, clenching his hand and uttering imprecations.

Rome, 1803 to 1805. The plaster model is in the Museum, which has also a copy in marble. A repetition, ordered in 1815, was executed in 1820, somewhat smaller than the original, for the Duke of Bedford, who has placed it in his summer residence at Woburn Abbey, as a companion to the Achilles and Priam.

Achilles and Briseis.

Bas-relief; marble. *Purchased by Signor Torlonia for the Palazzo Bracciano.* Height, 2 ft. 3.95 in.; length, 4 ft. 5.54 in.

Variation of the above. The action of Achilles is less violent: the hero's hand rests upon his knee.

Rome, 1837. Plaster model in Museum.

Achilles and Patroclus.

Bas-relief; marble. *Thorvaldsen Museum.* Medallion: diameter, 3 ft. 3.16 in.

Achilles is dressing the wound of Patroclus, hit by an arrow.

Rome, 1837. Plaster model in Museum. Imitated from a similar scene on an antique vase, reproduced in the Monumenti dell' Inst. Arch. di Roma.

HECTOR CONFRONTING PARIS AND HELEN.

Bas-relief; marble. *Purchased by Herr J. Knudzon, merchant of Trondhjem, Norway.* Height, 2 ft. 3.95 in.; length, 3 ft. 0.61 in.

Hector stands holding his long lance, and reproaches Paris with shunning the combat and remaining in shameful inaction. The faithless spouse of Menelaus, occupied in some woman's work, raises her eyes toward Hector; while Paris, seated in a careless attitude, is furbishing his arms.

Rome, 1809. Executed to the order of a Russian general named Balk. Plaster model in Museum. A repetition belongs to Mr. P. A. Labouchère, Paris. (See p. 210.)

HECTOR CONFRONTING PARIS AND HELEN.

Bas-relief; marble. *Purchased by Signor Torlonia for the Palazzo Bracciano.* Height, 2 ft. 9.46 in.; width, 2 ft. 2.77 in.

A variation of the above. Paris has risen, Helen reproaches him with his inaction, and two women offer him a distaff.

Rome, 1837. Plaster model in Museum. (See p. 211.)

THE PARTING OF HECTOR AND ANDROMACHE.

Bas-relief; marble. *Purchased by Signor Torlonia for the Palazzo Bracciano.* Height, 3 ft. 0.61 in.; length, 6 ft. 0.83 in.

Hector has taken his son from the hands of the nurse; he has laid aside his helmet, whose crest terrified the child, and raises Astyanax in his arms. Whilst the hero invokes the gods, Andromache leans sadly on her husband's shoulder. Paris comes to rejoin Hector.

Rome, 1837. Plaster model in Museum. (See p. 212.)

PRIAM BESEECHING ACHILLES FOR THE BODY OF HECTOR.

Bas-relief; plaster. *Palace of Charlottenborg.* Height, 2 ft. 1.98 in.; length, 2 ft. 6.31 in.

Priam throws himself at the feet of Achilles; the Greek hero rises from his seat and hastens to raise the aged man. Behind the table, on the right, two companions of Achilles receive the gifts of Priam.

Copenhagen, 1791. (See p. 11.)

PRIAM BEGGING ACHILLES FOR THE BODY OF HECTOR.
(See cut, p. 192.)

Bas-relief; marble. *Purchased by the Duke of Bedford, and placed in Woburn Abbey, England.* Height, 3 ft. 1.40 in.; length, 6 ft. 5.16 in.

Achilles seated, and leaning upon a table, turns his face toward the old man, who kneels in supplication. Automedon and Alcinous stand behind Achilles. Priam is followed by two Trojans bearing gifts.

Rome, 1815. Plaster model in Museum. (See p. 11.)

Achilles and Penthesilea.

Bas-relief; marble. *Thorvaldsen Museum.* Medallion: diameter, 2 ft. 3.16 in.

The Greek hero has just wounded the queen of the Amazons. Surprised at her beauty, he raises her from the ground and places his hand upon her heart to ascertain if it still beats.

Rome, 1837. Plaster model also in Museum.

The Arms of Achilles. (See cut, p. 228.)

Bas-relief; marble. *Thorvaldsen Museum.* Height, 2 ft. 1.98 in.; length, 4 ft. 0.81 in.

Minerva gives to Ulysses the arms of the son of Peleus. Ajax, who hoped to have them, turns away full of anger and uttering imprecations. In the background the nereid Thetis, mother of Achilles, sits weeping beside the tomb of her son.

Rome, 1831. Subject taken from the Metamorphoses of Ovid. Plaster model also in Museum.

Homer.

Bas-relief; plaster. *Thorvaldsen Museum.* Height, 3 ft. 2.58 in.; length, 6 ft. 6.34 in.

The poet seated upon the steps of a temple, having laid aside his travelling staff, his bag and hat, sings, to his own accompaniment upon the lyre, before the assembled people. Beside him a young man writes down the poem upon a tablet, and another Greek listens with rapt attention. In front of Homer are grouped two young boys, one of whom is armed with a quoit; a man in the prime of life, a woman holding a child, a warrior brandishing his sword, and an old man leaning upon a stick. After these come two figures in antique drapery, one of whom is Mr. Henry Labouchère, and the other Thorvaldsen. (See p. 56, note.)

Rome, 1836. Mr. Henry Labouchère had ordered from Thorvaldsen a statue of Achilles, which, by the way, was never executed, the pedestal of which was to have been ornamented with several bas-reliefs, representing scenes from Greek Antiquity. The *Homer*, *Achilles and Thetis*, *Achilles and the Centaur Chiron*, *The Parting of Hector and Andromache*, were designed for this purpose; and the variations of *Achilles and Briseis*, and of *Hector confronting Paris and Helen*, were remodelled in order to be added to them.

Entry of Alexander into Babylon.

(See cuts, pp. 102, 182, and 206.)

Bas-relief; plaster. *At the Quirinal Palace, Rome.* Height, 3 ft. 10.06 in.; length, 115 ft. 5.82 in.

In the centre of the frieze, Alexander in a triumphal chariot stands erect, his head raised, his sceptre in his right hand and his left hand on his hip. Victory, holding with one hand the front of the chariot, supports herself by her wings and guides the horses.

Behind Alexander march two equerries and two men leading Bucephalus. Then Hephæstion on horseback, followed by Parmenio and Amyntas at the head of the Macedonian cavalry; after whom come the foot-soldiers. Then an aged warrior leading an elephant loaded with booty, and next a Persian general, with head bowed down, under the guard of a young soldier. Next a horseman spurring his steed to regain his place in the ranks. At the right extremity of the bas-relief a warrior points out the procession to a man in antique drapery, who is Thorvaldsen himself.

On the left, in the other half of the composition, the vanquished advance to meet Alexander. At their head the Goddess of Peace, bearing the horn of plenty, offers an olive-branch to the conqueror. Behind her, in a suppliant attitude, appears the Persian general Mazæus, accompanied by his five sons and two warriors. Then come women scattering flowers in the way; men are seen erecting an altar for burning perfumes in accordance with the orders of Bagophanes; then two heralds blowing trumpets. Next come presents for the Macedonian king, horses and a lion and tiger, chained. Chaldean astrologers issue from the city gate where are posted two Persian sentinels. Near the gate are a herdsman and his family, and a young shepherd driving home his flock. Vases of perfumes are placed along the top of the city walls, above which are seen the tree-tops of the hanging gardens. The god of the river Tigris, leaning upon an urn and holding a rudder and stalks of wheat, reclines beside the walls of Babylon; near him are a tiger, suggestive of his name, and the tower of Belus (or Babel). Two merchants take to flight in a boat; and farther on, in the shade of the palm-trees that grow beside the river, a young man is tranquilly fishing, while his dog is barking.

Rome, 1812. (See pp. 49 and 207.) In the Museum is a plaster cast taken from the model.

This frieze has been twice cut in marble. 1. The first, purchased by the Count of Sommariva, was in 1828 placed in that gentleman's villa, near the Lake of Como.

The proportions are the same as in the plaster of the Quirinal, but changes have been made in several of the figures. Alexander, his right hand resting on his sceptre, the left on the front of the chariot, turns his head and raises his eyes. Victory holds the reins in both hands. Peace is without wings, and the infant Plutus accompanies her. Three other musicians precede the two Babylonian trumpeters. The Macedonians count five new horsemen, and a warrior on foot follows the elephant in place of the belated cavalier. Finally, Sommariva himself appears in this frieze beside the artist who points out to him the procession. The plaster model of this variation is in the Thorvaldsen Museum (height, 3 ft. 10.06 in.; length, 134 ft. 3.80 in.). 2. The second marble, executed at the same time with the above, but finished later, has been placed in the palace of Christiansborg, Copenhagen. It differs in several points from the two models above described. Alexander and the Victory are nearly the same as in the Count of Sommariva's copy, but at the right hand extremity Thorvaldsen appears alone under a palm-tree. On the left, in place of the fisherman's dog, are several figures: a young man and a child watching the procession; another child climbing upon a camel, held by a camel-driver. The river Euphrates takes the place of the Tigris and his attributes The musicians and horsemen added to the first marble appear also in this, and there are in addition a group of Babylonians leading horses, a mother placing her little boy on the back of one of the sheep, and a little girl by her side. The Museum has a marble copy, half-size (height, 1 ft. 10.04 in.; length, 75 ft. 11.80 in.), of the frieze of the Christiansborg Palace, as well as full-size models of the added portions.'

Several plaster copies have also been made. One for the Duke of Leuchtenberg was placed in his palace at Munich. Another was purchased by an Englishman. These were taken from the frieze in the Quirinal. In France, the Louvre has a half-size model. There is also a copy at Potsdam.

In the Thorvaldsen Museum is the last model of the centre-piece, in which the head of Alexander, as in the antique medal, is shown in profile. Also a marble copy of the Alexander (a variation slightly differing from that of the Christiansborg frieze), and plaster models of two pieces which were not used: a young man leading a horse, and a warrior holding another horse, frightened, and rearing at the barking of a dog.

Copies of the Sommariva frieze, by an Italian named Pistrini, were for sale at Scagliola. They were very small, only 1.57 inches in height. The half-size model, like that in the Museum, was sold in Rome, in terra cotta, for a thousand scudi.

Alexander and Thais.

Bas-relief; marble. *Thorvaldsen Museum.* Height, 3 ft. 1.79 in.; length, 6 ft. 5.95 in.

Seduced by Thais and heated with wine, Alexander, turning a deaf ear to Parmenio who endeavors to persuade him, takes a torch from the hands of the courtesan to set fire to Persepolis. On the right are two Macedonian warriors, on the left two other courtesans are lighting their torches. A Persian turns away in anger and despair.

Rome, 1832. Plaster model in Museum.

Alexander and Thais.

Bas-relief; marble. *Purchased by Prince Maximilian, of Bavaria.* Height, 2 ft. 9.46 in.; length, 6 ft. 6.74 in.

Alexander orders the warriors who stand behind him to light their torches. A Macedonian whispers in the ear of one of the courtesans; an old man turns away overwhelmed with grief and leading a child, while a young man who accompanies them seems to meditate resistance.

Rome, 1837. Variation of the above. Plaster model in Museum.

NUMA CONSULTING THE NYMPH EGERIA.

Bas-relief; plaster. *Thorvaldsen Museum* (underground galleries). Height, 1 ft. 3.74 in.; length, 2 ft. 1.19 in.

The nymph, seated beside an urn whence escapes the water of a spring, bends toward Numa and places her hand on the tablet upon which the king is writing.

Copenhagen. Signed: B. THORVALDSEN FEC. 1794.

ALLEGORICAL COMPOSITIONS.

THE FOUR SEASONS AND THE FOUR AGES OF LIFE.

Four medallions; marble. *Purchased by King William, of Würtemberg.* Diameter, 2 ft. 3.55 in.

I. *Spring and Childhood.*— A young girl, nude, half seated upon a bank, takes flowers from a boy and weaves them into a garland. On her left, a tambourine leans against a basket covered with wreaths. A little child, entirely naked, stretches out his hand to offer a bouquet.

II. *Summer and Youth.*— A young woman, on her knees, is binding wheat-sheaves; another, still holding her sickle, is embraced by a young man who offers her fruit.

III. *Autumn and Maturity.*— A man is returning from the chase, accompanied by his dog and carrying his game upon his shoulder. He has a bunch of grapes in his hand and pauses before his wife, who is seated and nursing her child.

IV. *Winter and Old Age* (see cut, p. 150).— An old man wrapped in his cloak sits bending, with hands outspread, over a chafing-dish. His aged wife has risen to light a candle at the lamp which stands on the table. The cat is warming herself by the fire, and wet clothing is hung up to dry.

ART AND THE GENIUS OF LIGHT. (*A Genio Lumen.*)

Bas-relief; marble. . . . ? Height, 1 ft. 8.07 in.; length, 2 ft. 3.16 in.

Art is symbolized by a young woman seated, and resting her head pensively upon her hand; she holds a stylus and tablet. The Genius approaches to pour oil into the lamp, and thus brings light.

Rome, 1808. Plaster model in Museum. We know not what has become of the first marble. A half-size copy, also in marble, was presented to Mr. Hope. (See p. 37, note.) This composition was used by the engraver Fr. Brandt, for the reverse of a medal struck in honor of Thorvaldsen, which bore on its face the portrait of the artist. The legend, A Genio Lumen, engraved upon this medal, has often served to designate the bas-relief.

The artist made a variation of this subject, of which the plaster model is also in the Museum (height, 3 ft. 4.15 in.; length, 4 ft. 6.33 in.). The sitting figure has one foot upon a tabouret, a cist and a scroll are under her seat, and the Genius has a piece of drapery over his arm. The column bears the inscription, A GENIO LUMEN. (See cut, p. 2.)

THE GENIUS OF LIGHT.

Bas-relief; sketch. *Thorvaldsen Museum.* Medallion: diameter, 1 ft. 0.59 in.

The Genius advances with a torch in his hand and crowned with laurel. Beside him are a lyre, and a cist containing scrolls.

Nysöe, 1841. Made as a model for the reverse of a medal struck in the reign of Christian VIII as a recompense to be awarded to artists and writers.

THE GENIUS OF PAINTING.

Bas-relief; plaster. *Thorvaldsen Museum.* Medallion: diameter, 3 ft. 2.58 in.

The Genius is seated; his features recall those of Raphael; in his left hand he holds a vase for colors, in his right a paint-brush. He is painting the Annunciation of the Virgin.

Nysöe, 1843.

THE GENIUS OF ARCHITECTURE.

Bas-relief; plaster. *Thorvaldsen Museum.* Medallion: diameter, 3 ft. 2.58 in.

This Genius is leaning upon a column before which lie a tablet and a square. He holds in his hand a plumb-line and a compass; beside him is the owl, perched upon an Ionic capital.

Signed: Nysöe, 3 December, 1843.

THE GENIUS OF SCULPTURE.

Bas-relief; plaster. *Thorvaldsen Museum.* Medallion: diameter, 3 ft. 2.58 in.

The Genius, seated, holds in his hand the chisel and mallet. Beside him is a bas-relief representing Minerva issuing from the forehead of Jupiter.

Nysöe, 1843.

THE GENIUS OF SCULPTURE.

Bas-relief; plaster. *Thorvaldsen Museum.* Medallion: diameter, 3 ft. 1.79 in.

Variation of the preceding composition. The Genius is seated upon the eagle of Jupiter, at the foot of a colossal statue of the god.

Copenhagen, 1844.

The Genius of Sculpture.

Sketch in outline, drawn upon a slate. *Thorvaldsen Museum.* Medallion: diameter, 3 ft. 2.58 in.

A new rendering of the same subject. The Genius of Sculpture, having finished his work, reposes on the shoulder of the statue of Jupiter. The head of the statue is seen, a part of the breast and the thunderbolt.

Thorvaldsen made this drawing a few days before his death. (See p. 178.)

The Genii of Architecture, Sculpture, and Painting.

Bas-relief; plaster. *Thorvaldsen Museum.* Medallion: diameter. 2 ft. 7.10 in.

The three Genii embrace each other as they fly, each bearing the implements of his art.

Nysöe, 1843 This composition has been engraved for the gold medal given as a prize by the Copenhagen Academy of Fine Arts.

The Genius of Poetry.

Bas-relief; plaster. *Thorvaldsen Museum.* Height, 2 ft. 6.31 in.; length, 3 ft. 10.06 in.

The Genius, seated, is singing and playing upon the lyre: before him lie the stylus of Clio and a torch leaning against a cist containing scrolls; on the other side, a shepherd's crook and the tragic and comic masks, attributes of Melpomene and Thalia.

Rome, about 1836. The symbols of the Muses, as well as the zodiacal signs, Scorpio and Taurus, corresponding to the birth (November) and the death (May) of Schiller, lead to the supposition that this composition was intended for the monument of that poet. The upper part is arched.

The Genius of Poetry.

Bas-relief; plaster. *Thorvaldsen Museum.* Medallion: diameter, 3 ft. 3.37 in.

The Genius stands with head raised, the plectrum in his right hand, and the lyre in his left. At his feet are a cist and a laurel crown.

Copenhagen, 1844.

The Genii of Harmony and of Poetry.

Bas-relief; plaster. *Thorvaldsen Museum.* Medallion: diameter, 2 ft. 7.10 in.

The two Genii fly side by side; one plays upon the lyre, the other rests his arm upon the shoulder of the first, and holds the stylus and a scroll partly unrolled. The soul also appears, under the form of a butterfly.

The scroll bears the inscription: Nysöe, 30 July, 1843.

The Genius of Peace and of Liberty.

Bas-relief; plaster. *Thorvaldsen Museum.* Height, 2 ft. 6.31 in.; length, 6 ft. 3.19 in.

The Genius wears the cap of liberty surrounded by a wreath of laurel. A lion and an eagle are feeding from a large dish which he offers them kneeling. Behind the Genius is a dog, emblem of fidelity. The sword, helmet, shield, and banner, instruments of oppression, now become useless, lie against the trunk of a tree which is catching fire from a torch.

Copenhagen, 1844. (See p. 177.)

The Genii of Government.

Two bas-reliefs; marble. *Thorvaldsen Museum.* Height, 3 ft. 3.37 in.; length, 5 ft. 0.62 in.

One is seated, crowned with laurel, upon a lion; his right hand rests upon the tables of the law, his left upon a rudder.

The other, with head raised, holds a balance and a mace.

Rome, 1837. Intended for the pedestal of the statue of Maximilian of Bavaria, but not used. (See p. 129.)

Genii.

Twenty bas-reliefs; marble. *Villa Torlonia.* Oval medallions. Height, 11.02 in.; width, 7.87 in.

Genius of Poetry, with lyre and plectrum.

Genius of Tragedy, with mace and tragic mask.

Genius of Comedy, with crook and comic mask.

Genius of Music, playing upon the double flute.

Genius of the Dance, playing upon the tambourine.

Genius of Administration, bearing a rudder upon his shoulder.

Genius of War, unsheathing a sword.

Genius of Navigation, holding in his arms the prow of a skiff.

Genius of Commerce, armed with the caduceus of Mercury, and holding a purse.

Genius of Medicine, holding a cup and the staff of Æsculapius.

Genius of Astronomy, holding a compass and a celestial globe.

Genius of Religion, raising his hands to heaven, in prayer.

Genius of Painting, holding a brush and a vase for colors.

Genius of Sculpture, holding the mallet and chisel.

Genius of Architecture, with compass and square.

Genius of Hunting, armed with a spear and carrying game.

Genius of Fishing, with a line and a fish.

Genius of Horticulture, a flower in his hand and a basket of flowers on his head.

Genius of Agriculture, with wheat-sheaves and a sickle.

Genius of Justice, holding a balance.

Rome, 1836, modelled by V. Galli, after designs by Thorvaldsen. The plaster sketches are in the Museum. Some of them are oval, others square, and others repeated in both forms.

The Genius of the New Year.

Bas-relief; plaster. *Thorvaldsen Museum.* Medallion: diameter, 1 ft. 10.44 in.

The Genius, mounted upon skates, is traversing the zodiacal sign, Capricon. He holds upon his arm a garland of flowers (Spring), in his hands a sickle and wheat-sheaves (Summer), and a bunch of grapes (Autumn).

Nysöe, 1840, for 1st January, 1841.

Justice.

Bas-relief; plaster. *Thorvaldsen Museum.* Height, 2 ft. 9.46 in.; width, 2 ft. 0.01 in.

Justice, seated in the shadow of two palm-trees whose branches meet above her head, holds upon her knees an open code; her left hand is placed upon a sword; her right holds a balance, having in one scale a royal crown, in the other a peasant's sickle.

Signed: Nysöe, 22 May, 1841.

Denmark.

Bas-relief; sketch. *Thorvaldsen Museum.* Medallion: diameter, 1 ft. 6.50 in.

Denmark is represented under the form of a woman on her knees, praying. A Danish inscription records her prayer: God save the king (*Gud velsigne Kongen*).

Copenhagen, 1839. For the medal struck on the accession of Christian VIII to the throne.

THE PRINCESS BARYATINSKA.

PORTRAITS.

I.

STATUES.

The Princess Caroline-Amelia.

Plaster. *Thorvaldsen Museum.* Height, 5 ft. 9.68 in.

The princess, since Queen of Denmark, is dressed in a long robe fastened at the waist, leaving the shoulders and arms uncovered. The hands, one raised, the other lowered, hold a cloak which she is in the act of putting on.

Rome, 1827. There is also in the Museum a sketch (height, 1 ft. 6.50 in.).

The Princess Baryatinska.

Marble. *Thorvaldsen Museum.* Height, 6 ft. 0.44 in.

The princess stands in a pensive attitude, with her right hand under her chin, and holding in her left the drapery which falls from her shoulder.

Rome, 1818. Plaster model also in Museum. (See p. 60.)

The Countess d'Ostermann.

Marble. *Purchased by Count d'Ostermann.* Height, 4 ft. 6.33 in.

The countess is seated, her head in a pensive attitude, her hands resting in her lap. An ample drapery is thrown over her dress, which is confined by a belt at the waist.

Rome, 1815. The Museum has the plaster model, a copy in marble, and a sketch, in which the attitude is different (height, 1 ft. 5.71 in.). Two other *maquettes*, of nearly the same size, were probably made for this figure.

Thorvaldsen. (See cut, p. 151.)

Plaster. *At Nysöe.* Height, 6 ft. 7.13 in.

The sculptor, in his working dress, stands with a chisel in his left hand, and a hammer in his right. He leans upon the model of his statue of Hope.

Nysöe, 1839. (See p. 152.) The Museum has a plaster cast taken from the model, and a sketch (height, 2 ft. 2.77 in.).

Georgina-Elisabeth Russell.

Marble. *Duke of Bedford's collection, Woburn Abbey, England.* Height, 3 ft. 4.15 in.

The daughter of the Duke of Bedford, aged three years, is represented standing, and nude; her little hand alone holding her drapery upon the left hip.

Rome, 1814. The Museum has a plaster cast of the model.

Figure of a Child.

Plaster. *Thorvaldsen Museum.* Height, 3 ft. 5.73 in.

A young girl represented as Psyche, nude, with butterfly's wings: she carries her drapery suspended from her left arm, and holds one of Cupid's arrows, of which she is feeling the point.

Nysöe, 1839.

Luther.

Sketch. *Thorvaldsen Museum.* Height, 2 ft. 3.55 in.

The great reformer points to the Bible with his left hand, and, with his right hand raised, seems to be expounding the text.

Copenhagen, about 1840. Intended for the *Frue Kirke*, but not executed.

Melanchthon.

Sketch. *Thorvaldsen Museum.* Height, 2 ft. 3.95 in.

Melanchthon is standing, dressed in a long robe, holding the Bible, and having his cap in his right hand.

Copenhagen, about 1840. Intended as a companion to the above. Not executed.

Alberto Paulsen.

Sketch. *Thorvaldsen Museum.* Height, 1 ft. 5.32 in.

The young man, Thorvaldsen's grandson, is represented in a hunting dress, one foot resting upon the trunk of a tree. He is caressing his dog.

Nysöe, 1843.

II.

BUSTS.

[The greater part of the busts of contemporary persons enumerated in this Catalogue were probably cut in marble; but, in cases where we have no positive information to that effect, we have mentioned only the plaster models in possession of the Thorvaldsen Museum.]

Saint Apollinarius, Bishop of Ravenna.

Colossal bust; marble. *At Ravenna.*

Rome, about 1822. Plaster model in Museum.

Leonardo of Pisa.

Colossal hermes; marble. *Executed for the Museum of the Capitol.*

Rome, ——. Bears the inscription: *Leonardo Pisano detto Fibonacci principe de' matematici visse nel secolo* XII. On one side: *Monsignor Girolamo Galanti pose;* on the other: *Alberto Thorvaldsen scolpi.* Plaster model in Museum.

Maximilian, Elector of Bavaria.

Colossal hermes; plaster. *Thorvaldsen Museum.*

Rome, 1831. First model for the equestrian statue of the Elector.

Luther.

Hermes; unfinished sketch. *Thorvaldsen Museum.* Thorvaldsen's last work. (See p. 178.)

Louis Holberg, a Danish Writer.

Hermes; plaster. Nysöe, 1839.

NAPOLEON.

Colossal bust; marble. *Purchased by Mr. Alexander Murray.*

The artist has chosen to represent the apotheosis of Napoleon. Clothed as a Roman emperor, a laurel crown upon his head, the ægis on his shoulder, the hero rests upon the terrestrial globe, which in turn is upheld by an eagle. The back of the bust rests upon a palm.

Rome, 1830. Plaster model in Museum. A repetition in marble was placed in the *Salle du Trône*, in the palace of the Tuileries. (See p. 111.)

ALEXANDER I, EMPEROR OF RUSSIA.

Bust; marble. *Purchased by the Emperor.*
Warsaw, 1820. Often repeated in marble. (See p. 78.)

PIUS VII.

Bust; plaster. *Thorvaldsen Museum.* Model for the statue.

CARDINAL CONSALVI.

Bust; plaster. *Thorvaldsen Museum.*
Rome, 1824. Model for the monument.

LOUIS, PRINCE ROYAL OF BAVARIA.

Bust; Carrara marble. *Glyptothek, Munich.*
Rome, 1822. The Museum has the plaster model, and a repetition in marble.

FREDERICK VI, KING OF DENMARK.

Bust; plaster. *Thorvaldsen Museum.*
Copenhagen, 1819.

MARIA-SOPHIA-FREDERIKA, QUEEN OF DENMARK.

Bust; plaster. *Thorvaldsen Museum.*
Copenhagen, 1819.

CAROLINE OF DENMARK, PRINCESS ROYAL.

Bust; plaster. *Thorvaldsen Museum.*
Copenhagen, 1819.

WILHELMINA-MARIA OF DENMARK.

Bust; plaster. *Thorvaldsen Museum.*

Represented as a child.

Copenhagen, 1819.

Wilhelmina-Maria of Denmark.

Bust; marble. *Thorvaldsen Museum.*

The Princess is represented as a young girl.

The Museum also has the plaster model.

Christian-Frederick.

Bust; marble. *In Denmark.*

Hereditary Prince of Denmark, afterward King Christian VIII.

Rome, 1821. Often repeated in marble. Plaster model in Museum.

Caroline-Amelia.

Bust; marble. *In Denmark.*

Wife of Prince Christian Frederick.

Rome, 1821. Often repeated in marble. Plaster model in Museum.

Frederick-Charles-Christian.

Bust; plaster. *Thorvaldsen Museum.*

This prince, here represented at the age of eleven years, was afterward King of Denmark under the title of Frederick VII.

Copenhagen, 1819.

Frederick-Charles-Christian.

Bust; plaster. *Thorvaldsen Museum.*

The same at the age of nineteen.

Copenhagen, 1827.

Frederick-William.

Bust; plaster. *Thorvaldsen Museum.*

Prince of Hesse Philippsthal.

Rome, 1822.

Julia-Sophia.

Bust; plaster. *Thorvaldsen Museum.*

Princess of Denmark, wife of the above.

Rome, 1822.

Portrait of a Lady.

Bust; plaster. *Thorvaldsen Museum.*

Supposed to be that of the Grand Duchess Helena of Russia, modelled at Rome, 1829. (See p. 111.)

PRINCE C. DE METTERNICH.

Bust; marble. *Thorvaldsen Museum.*

Austrian Minister.

Plaster model also in Museum.

PRINCE PONIATOWSKI.

Bust; plaster. *Thorvaldsen Museum.*

Model for the head of the equestrian statue.

GENERAL PRINCE VON SCHWARZENBERG.

Bust; plaster. *Thorvaldsen Museum.*

WILLIAM VON HUMBOLDT.

Hermes; plaster. *Thorvaldsen Museum.*

Prussian Minister.

CHRISTIAN-CHARLES-FREDERICK-AUGUSTUS.

Bust; marble. *Thorvaldsen Museum.*

Duke of Augustenbourg.

Plaster model in Museum.

FREDERICK-AUGUSTUS-EMILIUS.

Bust; marble. *Thorvaldsen Museum.*

Prince of Augustenbourg.

Plaster model also in Museum.

BARON VON SCHUBART.

Colossal; marble. *Thorvaldsen Museum.*

Danish ambassador.

Rome, 1804-1805.

BARONESS VON SCHUBART.

Colossal; marble. *Thorvaldsen Museum.*

Wife of the above.

Rome, 1804-5.

COUNT VON RANTZAU VON BREITENBOURG.

Colossal; marble. *Thorvaldsen Museum.*

Danish Minister of State.

Rome, 1804-5.

Count von Bernstorff.

Bust; marble. *Thorvaldsen Museum.*

Danish Minister of State.

Modelled, Copenhagen, 1795. Cut in marble, Rome, 1802. (See p. 14.)

Count von Bernstorff.

Colossal; plaster. *Thorvaldsen Museum.*

Rome, 1804–5.

Count Adam von Moltke-Nutschau.

Colossal; plaster. *Thorvaldsen Museum.*

Rome, 1804–5.

Henry Hjelmstjerne.

Hermes; plaster. *Thorvaldsen Museum.*

Privy Counsellor to the King of Denmark.

Baron Hans Holsten.

Hermes; plaster. *Thorvaldsen Museum.*

Admiral.

Copenhagen. Inscription [illegible] 1840.

Count Christian von Danneskjold Samsöe.

Bust; plaster. *Thorvaldsen Museum.*

Countess Henrietta von Danneskjold.

Hermes; plaster. *Thorvaldsen Museum.*

Wife of the above.

Countess Louisa von Danneskjold.

Bust; plaster. *Thorvaldsen Museum.*

Afterward Duchess of Augustenbourg, daughter of the above.

Mademoiselle Ida Brun.

Hermes; plaster. *Thorvaldsen Museum.*

Afterward Countess de Bombelles.

Rome, 1810.

Baroness Christine von Stampe.

Hermes; marble. *At Nysöe.*

Plaster model in Museum.

Frederick-Siegfred Vogt.

Bust; marble. *Thorvaldsen Museum.*

Counsellor of State.

Plaster model also in Museum.

Bertel Thorvaldsen.

Colossal hermes; marble. *Academy of Fine Arts, Copenhagen.*

Rome, 1815. The Museum has a cast taken from the marble. A repetition in marble is in possession of Herr Donner, at Altona.

Horace Vernet.

Colossal hermes; marble. *Thorvaldsen Museum.*

Rome, 1833. The model, life-size, also in Museum. (See p. 130.)

Lord Byron.

Bust; marble. *Thorvaldsen Museum.*

Rome, 1817. Plaster model also in Museum. (See p. 58.)

Sir Walter Scott.

Bust; marble. *In England.*

Rome, 1831. Plaster model in Museum. (See p. 127.)

C. W. Eckersberg.

Hermes; plaster. *Thorvaldsen Museum.*

Danish painter.

Bears the inscription: Eckersberg, Roma, il 12 Maggio, 1816. Eckersberg painted a portrait of Thorvaldsen, which is in the Museum.

C. A. Tiedje.

Colossal bust; plaster. *Thorvaldsen Museum.*

A Danish poet.

Frederick Brandt.

Bust; plaster. *Thorvaldsen Museum.*

A Danish artist, engraver of medals.

J. C. Dahl.

Hermes; plaster. *Thorvaldsen Museum.*

A Norwegian landscape painter.

Oehlenschlaeger.

Hermes; plaster. *Thorvaldsen Museum.*

A Danish poet.

Nysöe, 1839.

Tycho Rothe.

Hermes; marble. *Thorvaldsen Museum.*

Philosopher.

Modelled, Copenhagen, 1795. Cut in marble, Rome, 1797. (See p. 15.)

Gaspard Bartholin-Eichel.

Bust; plaster. *Thorvaldsen Museum.*

J. Knudzon.

Bust; marble. *At Trondhjem.*

Merchant of Trondhjem.

Plaster model in Museum.

H. C. Knudzon.

Bust; marble. *At Trondhjem.*

Brother of the above.

Plaster model in Museum.

Madame Höyer.

Bust; plaster. *Thorvaldsen Museum.*

Mother of the Danish painter, C. F. Höyer.

C. H. Donner.

Bust; plaster. *Thorvaldsen Museum.*

Merchant of Altona.

Madame von Krause.

Bust; plaster. *Thorvaldsen Museum.*

Madame de Rehfuss.

Hermes; plaster. *Thorvaldsen Museum.*

Baron D'Eichthal.

Bust; plaster. *Thorvaldsen Museum.*

Banker in Munich.

Princess Baryatinska.

Bust; plaster. Model for the statue. *Thorvaldsen Museum.*

The Princess Narischkin.

Bust; plaster. *Thorvaldsen Museum.*

THE COUNTESS POTOCKA.

Bust; plaster. *Thorvaldsen Museum.*

SIR THOMAS MAITLAND.

Colossal bust; plaster. *Thorvaldsen Museum.*
Rome, 1818-19. For the monument.

LORD GOWER, DUKE OF SUTHERLAND.

Bust; plaster. *Thorvaldsen Museum.*

LORD W. BENTINK.

Hermes; plaster. *Thorvaldsen Museum.*

LORD EXMOUTH.

Hermes; plaster. *Thorvaldsen Museum.*

English admiral.

THE COUNTESS OF DIETRICHSTEIN.

Bust; plaster. *Thorvaldsen Museum.*

THE COUNTESS OF NUGENT.

Bust; plaster. *Thorvaldsen Museum.*

THE MISSES LUCAN.

Two busts; plaster. *Thorvaldsen Museum.*

Daughters of Lord Lucan.

LADY SANDWICH.

Bust; plaster. *Thorvaldsen Museum.*

MR. ALEXANDER BAILLIE.

Bust; marble. *In England.* Plaster model in Museum.

M. DIWET.

Bust; plaster. *Thorvaldsen Museum.*

MRS. HOPE.

Bust; marble. *In England.* Plaster model in Museum.

THE MESSRS. HOPE.

Two busts; marble. *In England.* Plaster models in Museum.

Sons of Sir Thomas Hope.

THE COUNT OF SOMMARIVA.

Hermes; marble. *Thorvaldsen Museum.* Plaster model also in Museum.

THE COUNT OF SOMMARIVA.

Bust; plaster. *Thorvaldsen Museum.* Executed several years later than the above.

THE MARCHIONESS DI FIRENZI.

Bust; plaster. *Thorvaldsen Museum.*

PRINCE BUTERA.

Bust; plaster. *Thorvaldsen Museum.*

THE PRINCESS BUTERA.

Bust; plaster. *Thorvaldsen Museum.*

GIOVANNI TORLONIA.

Bust; plaster. *Thorvaldsen Museum.*

Duke of Bracciano.

GAZI-EDDIN-HEYDER.

Bust; plaster. *Thorvaldsen Museum.*

King of Oude, author of a Persian Grammar and of the celebrated Persian dictionary, *Haft culzum*, "The Seven Seas." Modelled from a painted portrait. The king wears his national dress.

Rome, 1824.

VITTORIA CARDONI.

Bust; plaster. *Thorvaldsen Museum.*
Rome, 1821. (See p. 89.)

PORTRAIT OF A MAN.

Bust; marble. *Thorvaldsen Museum.*
The plaster model also in Museum.

PORTRAITS OF UNKNOWN MEN.

Twenty-one busts or hermes; plaster. *Thorvaldsen Museum.*

PORTRAITS OF UNKNOWN WOMEN.

Ten busts or hermes; plaster. *Thorvaldsen Museum.*

PORTRAITS OF UNKNOWN CHILDREN.

Two busts; plaster. *Thorvaldsen Museum.*

III.

MEDALLIONS.

THE PHILOSOPHER HENRI STEFFENS.

Bas-relief; plaster. *Thorvaldsen Museum.* Diameter, 1 ft. 6.89 in.
Nysöe, 1840.

PROFESSOR E. H. LÖFFLER.

Bas-relief; plaster. *Thorvaldsen Museum.* Diameter, 1 ft. 6.89 in.

Professor of drawing in the Academy of Fine Arts, Copenhagen.

FIGURE OF AN UNKNOWN WOMAN.

Bas-relief; plaster. *Thorvaldsen Museum.* Diameter, 1 ft. 6.89 in.

DIVERS SUBJECTS.

I.

STATUES.

A Young Shepherd.

Statue; marble. *Purchased by Herr von Krause, Wilsdruff, near Dresden.* Height, 4 ft. 10.26 in.

He is seated upon a rock, with his right leg raised and his left hand resting upon his crook. His dog is on his right side.

Rome, 1817. Has been repeated in marble a great number of times. Repetitions were purchased by Lord Grantley, Lord Altman, Count von Schönborn, Herr Donner, of Altona. In Count von Schönborn's copy a syrinx lies at the feet of the figure. The King of Prussia had this statue cast in bronze by Jollage and Hoffgarten. Another bronze copy was cast in Paris in 1828. Plaster model and a copy in marble in the Museum.

A Roman Soldier.

Statue; plaster. *Thorvaldsen Museum.* Height, 6 ft. 5.95 in.

The soldier, leaning against a róck, turns his head to listen.

Intended for the right side of the pediment in the *Preaching of St. John the Bap-tist*, but suppressed.

A Jew.

Statue; plaster. *Thorvaldsen Museum.* Height, 4 ft. 9.08 in.

This personage, seated in an attentive attitude, was also to have formed part of the group of St. John the Baptist, but the statue was not executed.

A Dancing-Girl.

Statue; marble. *Esterhazy Gallery, Vienna.* Height, 5 ft. 10.47 in.

The young girl wears a robe fastened at the waist by a belt, and has upon her head a wreath of flowers. The left hand is raised, the right lowered, and from one to the other flutters a light drapery.

Rome, 1817. (See p. 58.) The plaster model is in the Museum. Herr Thiele has the sketch.

A Dancing-Girl.

Statue; marble. *Purchased by Signor Torlonia, Rome.* Height, 5 ft. 10.47 in.

Variation of the above. The head is turned to the left, and both arms are lowered, to allow the statue to be placed in a niche.

Modelled soon after the above. Plaster model in Museum.

A Little Dancing-Girl. (See cut, p. 117.)

Statue; marble. *Purchased by Signor Torlonia, Rome.*

The little girl has set down her basket beside her. The upper part of her dress, having slipped down over the arm, leaves the bosom partly uncovered. Her hair is gathered back and knotted on the top of her head.

Rome, 1837. The Museum has a repetition in marble, the model in plaster, and a sketch, 2 ft. 0.40 inches in height. (See p. 204.)

A Dancing-Girl.

Statuette; sketch; plaster. *In possession of the Baroness von Stampe, Nysöe,* Height, 3 ft. 3.37 in.

The young girl holds a tambourine.

The Museum has a small sketch of this figure. Height, 2 ft. 0.40 in.

A Young Girl.

Statuette; sketch; plaster. *Thorvaldsen Museum.* Height, 2 ft. 3.16 in.

She is carrying a basket of flowers and offering a rose.

A Young Man.

Statuette; sketch; plaster. *Thorvaldsen Museum.* Height, 2 ft. 0.40 in.

The young man stands leaning against the trunk of a tree, with his dog beside him. The right hand is wanting.

A Recumbent Lion.

Statue; marble. *Thorvaldsen Museum.* Height, 2 ft. 10.25 in.; length, 5 ft. 2.99 in.

Rome, 1825. Probably intended to form part of the monument to Prince von Schwarzenberg. (See p. 105.) The Museum has also the plaster model.

II.

BAS-RELIEFS.

The Baroness von Stampe and her Children.

Bas-relief; sketch; plaster. *Thorvaldsen Museum.* Height, 2 ft. 0.15 in.; length, 3 ft. 3.37 in.

This composition represents an interior at Nysöe, in the *château* of the baron. Thorvaldsen is leaning upon an easel on which is the sketch of the Apostle Saint Andrew. Before him is the baroness, seated with her two daughters beside her. On the other side, her little son is playing with the artist's water-cup.

Nysöe, 1840.

The Baron von Stampe and his Sons.

Bas-relief; sketch; plaster. *Thorvaldsen Museum.* Height, 2 ft. 0.15 in.; length, 3 ft. 3.37 in.

The scene is laid by the shore of the sea, near which the barony of Stampe is situated. The baron has just been taking a bath, and is drying himself. The eldest son, also nude, is riding a horse toward the water; another son is returning from the chase, and is displaying his game.

Nysöe, 1840.

A Mounted Hunter.

Bas-relief; plaster. *Thorvaldsen Museum.* Height, 3 ft. 5.33 in.; length, 3 ft. 8.88 in.

Clothed in a lion's skin, the end of which is drawn over his head, he carries over his shoulder a spear to which is suspended a hare he has just killed. His horse is going at a brisk trot.

Rome, 1834.

A Mounted Huntress.

Bas-relief; plaster. *Thorvaldsen Museum.* Height, 3 ft. 4.15 in.; length, 4 ft. 1.21 in.

She is dressed in a short tunic, over which is the skin of a wild boar; in her right hand she holds a bow, and with her left is drawing an arrow from her quiver. A bird she has killed hangs from her belt, and a dog runs beside the horse.

Rome, 1834.

Victory crowning a Wounded Soldier.

Bas-relief; plaster.

An officer wearing a modern uniform is stretched upon the ground, his hand still grasping his sword. Victory holds a crown above the head of the dying man.

Destination unknown. This bas-relief has not been executed in marble. A drawing of it is given by Herr Thiele, vol. i, plate 77.

THE END.

(Note to page 243.) THE CHRIST.

A copy in marble of Thorvaldsen's statue of Christ stands upon the apex of the pediment of the Church of the Immaculate Conception, in Harrison Avenue, Boston.

(Note to page 272.) GANYMEDE AND THE EAGLE.

A repetition of this group, in marble (height, 1 ft. 4.75 in.; length, 2 ft. 1.13 in.), is now (1873) in possession of Mr. William Appleton, of Boston. The history of its acquisition is thus given by its owner.

"The Ganymede of Thorvaldsen (reduced size), now in possession of Mr. William Appleton, of Boston, was purchased in Rome, at the studio of the sculptor, in 1838. Mrs. Appleton (then Miss Warren, of Boston) was in Rome at the time, with her father and family, and visited the studio of Thorvaldsen with Mr. Henry Cabot, who purchased the Ganymede, and presented it to Mr. Appleton, the father of the present owner, for some friendly service rendered."

www.ingramcontent.com/pod-product-compliance
Lightning Source LLC
LaVergne TN
LVHW020213110826
845151LV00003B/703

9781425534080